P.E.P.

Providing Executive Protection

edited by

Dr. Richard W. Kobetz

Published by
EXECUTIVE PROTECTION INSTITUTE
Berryville, Virginia

Library of Congress Catalog Card Number: 90-85357

ISBN: 0-9628411-0-2

Kobetz, Richard W.
    Providing Executive Protection/Richard W. Kobetz
    Includes bibliographical references.
    1. Executive Protection   2. Bodyguards
    3. Dignitary Protection   4. Personal Protection
    5. Providing Protective Services   6. VIP Protection

Printed by
WINCHESTER PRINTERS, INC.
Winchester, Virginia

Printed on acid-free paper

Dedicated To:

*Eleanore, Kevin, Kim and Candi, all of whom have participated in
"The Family Business" from the very beginning and to those Personal
Protection Specialists who perform professionally everyday
throughout the world . . .*

Table of Contents

PART II: ADVANCE WORK, UNWANTED VISITORS, AND THE ROLE OF TECHNOLOGY.

PART III: FINE TUNING YOUR APPROACH

PART IV: DEFENSIVE MEASURES

PART V: ADDITIONAL CONCERNS

The Contributors

John J. Bakie

Mr. Bakie has served with the Baltimore County Police Department in a variety of assignments as a career officer. His present primary assignment is as a detective in the Intelligence Unit and he also works on the Dignitary Protection Team and the Hostage Negotiation Team. Detective Bakie has trained other police department and criminal justice agency personnel throughout the region on hostage negotiation techniques. He has attended the New Jersey State Police Training Academy at Sea Girt, New Jersey and the Northern Virginia Criminal Justice Academy in Fairfax, Virginia. He has had personal experience in providing personal protection to private families and on a variety of protective assignments.

Jetze Beers

Mr. Beers is the owner and manager of the Jordon Hollow Farm Inn and has been an international traveler for many years. He is a Nautical Engineer with five (5) years of military service in the Dutch Army. Born in Holland, he has been in the United States since 1980 and thoroughly enjoys Innkeeping. He speaks his native Dutch and can also converse in French and German. His chapter on proper dining, etiquette, table settings, wines and protocol encompass both traditional American as well as European traditional standards. He has instructed with and assisted the Executive Protection Institute for several years and is a member of the Nine Lives Associates.

Charles H. Blennerhassett

Mr. Blennerhasset is a most experienced professional in the field of personal protection. His background includes instruction in martial arts in Illinois and protective services work in Illinois, Texas, Virginia, and New York. He is presently responsible for advance work prior to any trips planned by several prominent individuals. Prior to accepting his present position, he was a protective team member for wealthy and recognized families involved in world travel and estate protection. His attention to detail and specific arrangements and concerns has brought him recognition for his creativity and specialization in the field of providing advance work.

Peter J. Brown

Mr. Brown has assisted the U.S. Secret Service when foreign heads of state have visited Maine and Mount Desert Island in particular by serving as an events coordinator, and principal's driver. He is a former volunteer emergency medical technician and member of the volunteer mounted patrol in Acadia National Park. Born in Turkey, he has done research in Japan as well as worked as a language instructor in Laos. He is a free-lance writer who deals primarily with the international satellite TV and soyfoods industries. He was one of several contributors to *Beyond the Iran-Contra Crisis: The Shape of U.S. Antiterrorism Policy in the Post-Reagan Era* which was published by Lexington Books. He graduated with distinction in Asian Studies from Connecticut College (B.A.).

Robert D. Chapman

Mr. Chapman has served in numerous operational, supervisory and managerial positions for twenty-seven years with the Central Intelligence Agency (CIA). He is most fluent in Spanish and Portugese and for over a decade devised defensive security tractics and taught law enforcement agencies throughout the world. In addition, he developed security strategies for U.S. personnel serving overseas and instructed military and foreign service officers and their families. He has been decorated on three occasions for hazardous duty and has been awarded over a dozen government commendations. During the past several years, he has performed security risk assessment for insurance companies, specializing in kidnap and ransom insurance for major corporation executives. He also serves as a consultant to the Armored Car Industry and several other corporations on security issues. His latest publication is entitled: *The Crimson Web of Terror.*

H.H.A. Cooper

Dr. Cooper is President of Nuevevidas International, Inc., a Texas corporation specializing in safety, survival techniques and conflict resolution. He was Staff Director of the National Advisory Committee Task Force on Disorders and Terrorism and is a prolific author whose writings on various aspects of extraordinary violence have been widely disseminated. His background includes chairman, United Nations Alliance for the Control and Prevention of Crime and Her Majesty's Civil Service. He currently lectures on terrorism and espionage at the University of Texas at Dallas and Southern Methodist University. His latest book entitled *Catching Spies* is available through Bantam Books.

Bruce L. Danto

Dr. Danto is a practicing psychiatrist and most active as a researcher, author and lecturer in security and law enforcement. He has the unique distinction of being the only man in his profession who has completed police recruit training school and was a sworn officer in the State of Michigan and an advisor to several law enforcement agencies. As a forensic and police psychiatrist he has specialized in characteristics of criminal behavior and aspects of dangerousness for those who deal with violent persons and who expose themselves to life threatening situations. His books include *Crisis Behind Bars: The Suicidal Inmate; So You Want To Be A Psychiatrist; Identification and Control of Dangerous and Mentally Disordered Offenders;* and *Prime Target, Security Measures for the Executive at Home and Abroad.*

Susan A. DiGiacomo

Ms. DiGiacomo earned a B.A. at the University of Toronto. She is a media consultant. Formerly Production Coordinator for Canada A.M., Canada's premier television, coast-to-coast morning news and current events program, she has been employed in various capacities in the investment community for the past ten years. She studied at the Royal Academy of Dramatic Art and worked for the United Nations in Geneva, Switzerland. In her spare time, she is a bilingual guide for the Royal Ontario Museum.

Eurgene R. Ferrara

Mr. Ferrara has been with the University of Cincinnati since 1978 and directs public safety for all medical center and campus security oeprations. His prior service includes twelve years with the Cincinnati Police Department as a cadet, patrolman, police specialist, sergeant of police and assistant director of the Cincinnati/Hamilton County Police Academy. His instructional expertise includes firearms, operational planning, officer survival techniques, executive and VIP protection. He organized, coordinated and trained the first Special Weapons and Tactics Unit for the police department and personally participated in training on programs throughout the nation on a wide variety of police and security issues. He holds a M.Ed. degree in training and personnel development from Xavier University and is a graduate of the FBI National Academy. He has also trained personal protective teams in Europe and South Africa.

Arthur B. Fulton

Dr. Fulton is a retired Inspector-Deputy Assistant Director of the Federal Bureau of Investigation with almost 25 years of service. He served as a Special Agent in Louisville and Covington, Kentucky and in New York City, and at the time of his retirement, was the Deputy Assistant Director of the FBI's Intelligence Division. Dr. Fulton holds a B.A. degree from Otterbein College, Westerville, Ohio; served as an investigator in the Counter Intelligence Corps of the U.S. Army; and earned a Juris Doctor Degree from the University of Pittsburgh School of Law. He is a member of the District of Columbia Bar, the American Bar Association, the American Business Law Association, and has been admitted to practice before the Supreme Court of the U.S. He is an adjunct assistant professor of business law and criminal justice at Lord Fairfax College near Winchester, Virginia.

Deborah M. Galvin

Dr. Galvin has an extensive academic background in criminology and security systems training. She has held a number of responsible positions in the electronic data processing and systems analysis fields and acted as a consultant on private security for more than a decade. An authority on female terrorism, she received her under-graduate and master's degrees from the University of Maryland (where she later taught) and

her doctorate from the University of Pennsylvania. She is an officer and a member of the Board of Officers of the Academy of Security Educators and Trainers (ASET) and has authored several of their publications and assists in conducting their Certified Security Trainer (C.S.T.) asessment center.

Jerome H. Glazebrook

Mr. Glazebrook is Executive Assistant and Special Advisor for Security to Dr. Henry A. Kissinger, the former Secretary of State and Chairman of Kissinger Associates, Inc. His career began with the U.S. military in the Republic of South Vietnam and as Principal Security Escort to the American Ambassador in Vietnam during the final years of the war. He was then promoted to the Chief of Detail for the Ambassador's personal security unit, assisting in the final evacuation of the Embassy personnel during the fall of Saigon. Subsequently, Mr. Glazebrook became senior security specialist and corporate officer for several prominent families, and their estates, and was later Chief of Security and Personal Assistant to the Chairman and CEO of a multinational Eurpean corporation. Mr. Glazebrook has handled all aspects of domestic and foreign advance work including liaison with domestic and foreign governments, police, military, and intelligence agencies.

Richard W. Kobetz

Dr. Kobetz is a recognized Consultant and Trainer for major corporations and government agencies on matters of security, counter-terrorism and executive protection. He is a former Assistant Director of the International Association of Chiefs of Police (IACP); has served as a member of the U.S. Task Force on Disorders and Terrorism; and as a Consultant to the Institute of Judicial Administration and the American Bar Association. He was a delegate to INTERPOL on issues of hostage rescue operations; and for over a decade, he directed the U.S. Attorney General's International Conference on Narcotics and Smuggling Intelligence. Dr. Kobetz retired as a Commanding Officer with the Chicago Police Department and has served in a variety of practical experience positions from patrolman to Chief of Police and special agent to Director of Security. His most recent publication is entitled *Target Terrorism: Providing Protective Services,* and he has contributed a chapter in the text, *Terrorism and Personal Protection,* by Brian M. Jenkins. Dr. Kobetz was awarded the first designation of Certified Security Trainer (C.S.T.), authorized by the prestigious Academy of Security Educators and Trainers, and is a Distinguished Fellow of the Academy.

John I. Kostanoski

Professor Kostanoski is an associate professor in the Department of Criminal Justice at the State University of New York, College of Technology at Farmingdale. Prof. Kostanoski is a past president and current vice president of the Academy of Security Educators and Trainers as well as a certified security trainer. He holds the highest honor the Academy awards to an individual, that of distinguished fellow. Prof. Kostanoski is a nationally recognized authority on the subject of portable protection systems and has designed numerous systems for agencies, corporations and institutions. He is the coauthor of *Security and Loss Control,* Macmillan Publishing Company and *Introduction To Security And Loss Control,* Prentice Hall Publishers. He is a consultant to the National Institute of Justice, U.S. Department of Justice.

W. Thomas Levering

Captain Levering has served with the Baltimore County Police Department for twelve years. He has been assigned to the Dignitary Protection Unit and the Hostage Negotiation Team as well as other department units. He has been actively involved in over twenty hostage scenes, where he personally acted as negotiator, supervisor or coach. Mr. Levering has also instructed and trained other police department and agencies throughout the East Coast on hostage negotiating. He is presently in the process of completing his master's degree at the University of Maryland and he has experience in providing personal protection for a private family and on other protective assignments.

Robert L. Oatman

Mr. Oatman is the former chief of detectives of the Baltimore County Police Department, a 1,500 officer police agency which adjoins and surrounds the city of Baltimore. He was a career officer with the department and served in a variety of positions through patrolman, detective, sergeant, lieutenant, captain, and major. He was the originator of the special operations response teams within his department and participated in team training exercises and served as the department's hostage advisor. He has personally negotiated approximately 100 hostage-taking incidents and his duties included providing protection to VIPs within his jurisdictional area. He is an accomplished instructor on protective missions and movements with experience in private family and celebrity protection. He holds a B.A. in Criminal Justice from the University of Baltimore and is a graduate of the FBI National Academy. He is the co-author of *You're The Target, Coping With Terror And Crime.*

Steve Rhodes

Mr. Rhodes is an accomplished practitioner of a variety of martial art styles and oriental (Chinese) exercise movements. He has designed some un-armed techniques to be utilized by protective personnel for disarming and blocking close-quarter attacks. He holds a black belt in Karate and has studied, under a special invitation, at the Sports Palace on mainland China, where he had a most unique opportunity to work with the world's leading experts in ancient martial arts. Mr. Rhodes is well versed in and instructs advance students in the martial arts forms of Kung-Fu, Wushu (Weaponry) and Tai Chi Chuan. He serves as Secretary-General, United States Wushu Federation; member U.S. Wushu Team, 1988-89; Bronze medal, Taijiquan, 1986 International Invitational Competition, Tianjian, China; First place, Men's Taijiquan and Men's Taiji Sword, 1987 U.S. National Kung Fu/Wushu Competitions, Houston, Texas; Certified Level 2 USWF Judge; Instructor, Shenandoah Taijiquan Society.

Pat Rice

Ms. Rice is a serious student of the various oriental (Chinese) exercise movements and marital arts styles. She has been co-director, since 1982, of the annual seminar entitled: A Taste of China; which brings together students and instructors from all over the world for study. She is the editor of the publication *WUSHU Today* and is an accomplished instructor, for protective programs and the Shenandoah TaiJi-Quan Society, member, U.S. Wushu Team, 1988-89; Honorable Mention, 1988 International Invitational Competition in Hangzhou, China; First place, Women's Taijiquan and Women's Push-Hands, 1986 and 1987 U.S. National Kung Fu/Wushu Competition, Houston, Texas; Certified USWF Judge; Certified Judge, China Wushu Association.

C. Steven Ruble

Lt. Charles S. Ruble is an instructor in emergency medical care and is certified as an Advance Life and Basic Life Support Instructor and Advance and Basic Trauma Life Instructor. He holds a certification in counter-terrorist driving skills and is trained in the accident avoidance courses. He holds the rank of lieutenant in the Fairfax County Fire and Rescue Service where he is qualified as a suppression, cave-in, structural collapse, and cardiac care officer. He has served as an instructor for the U.S. State Department where he created a training program for new agents which was titled "Emergency First Line Care." Lt. Ruble has also instructed for George Washington University and the Executive Protection Institute. He is the author of Training Key #375 "Emergency Care—Trauma" which was published by the International Association of Chiefs of Police.

Taylor R. Rudd, Jr.

Mr. Rudd retired as Assistant Special Agent in Charge of Training, U.S. Secret Service. He served as a career agent for twenty years in assignments that included: Special Agent, Intelligence Division; where he analyzed cases involving threats against the President and Vice-President and coordinated nationwide investigations concerning same. In addition, he was assigned to domestic and foreign security advances for the President, Vice-President, and other officials and worked actual protective details. Further, as Senior Course Instructor and Assistant Special Agent In Charge, Office of Training, he had experience in instruction, analysis of terrorist impact on Secret Service and supervised in-depth surveys of U.S. Capitol, Supreme Court and security precautions for fourteen governors. He holds a B.S. degree from Shepherd College.

Anthony J. Scotti

Tony Scotti is an internationally recognized authority on instruction in safe driving and protective techniques involving vehicles. His driving school started operations over a decade ago and he has been progressively improving defensive driving skills and instructional techniques. He has taught security personnel in 18 nations, police officers in 32 states and worked with numerous federal agencies. His students have been from 64 nations on 5 continents and he has trained personnel from over half of the U.S. Fortune 100 companies. He is the author of *Emergency Driving for Police Officers* and *Executive Safety and International Terrorism* both published by Prentice-Hall Company and he holds a B.A. degree in electrical engineering from Northeastern University.

John J. Strauchs

Mr. Strauchs is the president of Systech Group, Inc., located within the Washington, D.C. metropolitan region. He specializes in security engineering services for corporate headquarters. Prior to founding Systech, he was Principal for security engineering with Gage-Babcock & Associates and previously served with the U.S. Central Intelligence Agency. He is certified by the American Society for Industrial Security (ASIS), is presently a faculty member for ASIS, and is past chairman of a national ASIS standing committee. He has been an instructor in electronic security for Richard W. Kobetz and Associates, the U.S. Department of State, Bureau of Diplomatic Security Training Center, as well as for the University of Delaware. He was elected a distinguished fellow by the Academy of Security Educators and Trainers (ASET) and received the "President's Award" from ASIS.

EXECUTIVE PROTECTION INSTITUTE
Clarke County, Virginia

Preface

by Dr. Richard W. Kobetz

THIS **IS NOT** a fictional fantasy book on "bodyguarding, terrorism, tactical team tactics, shooting styles, hostage negotiations, martial arts, rappeling, exotic weapons or knife fighting." **It is** a book about the real world of providing personal protection. Personal protection that is prepared to deal with the possibility of deadly attacks and serious assaults along with the daily probabilities of accidents, fire, medical problems and embarrassments.

The art and science of personal protection relies for success upon proper advance work, pre-planning and avoidance of confrontation. The skill of being capable and competent enough to keep your principal out of harms way. The ability to provide a personal service, not in the capacity of a servant, but through performing specific services, which provide for comfort and convenience. These services allow for avoidance of delay and the unnecessary exposure of your principal while attempting to locate and obtain what is needed or anticipated.

What a waste of personnel resources for example, if "sweeping or searching" the hotel suite does not include checking the television set to see that it operates; making sure all the light bulbs work; assuring that nothing is missing which is normally supplied by the hotel; and, that objects left by a previous occupant are removed. To have repairs and replacements made on the hotel staff's timetable causes disturbances and the need to have someone standby. To control the environment contributes to the protection of your principal.

People who employ personal protection specialists are busy performers in many activities, they need convenience and avoidance of delays along with protection. Time saving activities and movements will overcome predictable delays while they also "harden the target," making it much more difficult for a principal to become a victim. The correct choreography of foot movements and pre-planning can serve to anticipate accidents, emergency medical problems, restaurant fires or encounters of a negative nature through proper control for avoidance of incidents. In fact, performance of personal services and being on the alert for potential problems along with counter-surveillance techniques and awareness of "stalkers"; far outweighs the over emphasis placed upon the need for weapons and martial arts skills.

In 1978, we created the title "Personal Protection Specialist" to more precisely define the role of a professional protector. We are very pleased that this terminology has been accepted and is now standard within the profession. For reader clarity, and variety, the terms executive protection, protective services and bodyguard are still employed throughout this book (with due respect to the negative connotation of the use of the "b" word). A comment is also in order here for those who will employ this work as a textbook for the study of this field. Several of the authors have repeated important ideas, concerns and philosophies which should serve to highlight to you the important points we wish to emphasize.

The world can be a dangerous place, domestically or internationally, through encounters with common criminals or trained terrorists. Those business leaders, entertainers, religious leaders, elected or appointed officials, who employ men and women to look after them are becoming aware that the days of the "gorilla in the suit" are over. They have given way to the new breed; whose appearance, behavior, manners, speech and demeanor blend them into their environment. They avoid problems and they can deal with *any* emergency—they are Personal Protection Specialists. And that is what this book is about.

A very special appreciation to all my colleagues who contributed their chapters and to those who have assisted in this total endeavor. Particularly to Peter Brown for his assistance in editing the contents; James W. Sterling for his work in indexing; Jane Ashby, Kelly Pelkey and Shirley Sunderlin for their secretarial and computer assistance and especially to Clare Hendrix of Winchester Printers, all of whom professionally kept this project on track.

DR. RICHARD W. KOBETZ
Arcadia Manor and Farms
Clarke County, Virginia

Introduction

by H.H.A. Cooper

" 'Well,' I say, 'we can stop here, or we can go ahead, or we can go back. Which do you want to do?' "[1]

Robert M. Pirsig

A GLANCE OVER THE LEFT SHOULDER

SOME TEN YEARS have passed since the publication of *Target Terrorism: Providing Protective Services.*[2] A great deal of water has flowed down many rivers around the world and passed beneath countless bridges since that slim text first saw the light of day. It shares, for all its age and blemishes, something in common with the present text. Both were written in response to an urgently felt need. When *Target Terrorism* was written, there was simply no text available for those who had begun seriously to systematize the teaching of those professionally engaged in the business of protecting the persons and other interests of those threatened by the growing menace of modern terrorism. Indeed, there was not much published at that time on the subject of terrorism worth reading at all. A few academics had made some interesting forays, mainly from an historic or theoretical perspective; but most of this writing was, as yet, tentative, and some plainly misleading.

In retrospect, what was written about terrorism in the early 1970's (supplemented by a burgeoning round of conferences designed to find out what, if anything, everybody else knew) has a distinctly quaint ring about it. There were some who predicted the rapid march towards some terrorist-inspired Armageddon, but most were inclined to feel that serious study of the subject was hardly worth the effort; that it simply would not be around that long. Thus, some whose names loomed large in that era and were cited as oracles and sages, have long since departed for other pastures and their workings now have about them the same flavor as the *Book of Enoch* and some of the apocryphal taint of that work. A great deal of influential rubbish was spoken and written about Muammar el Qathafi, but in truth some of the most notable and thought-provoking writings about terrorism flowed from authors of fiction.[3] But these, by themselves, were of little practical guidance through the thickets of the subject for busy professionals with an important job to do. They needed to know what terrorism was, how it manifested itself in its different forms, how serious and durable the problem was likely to be, and what measures they might, seriously, take to cope with it.

Target Terrorism was a modest attempt (undertaken within the financial and time constraints of its particular context) to address some of these concerns. It had to be something less than a treatise and a good deal more than a notebook. It did not advertise its limitations, and the reviews it received were too kind to point them out. But, in its day, it did the job it was intended to do and, certainly, no apologies are offered for it here. For all its real substance, one is still struck by the seeming leanness of its appearance. This was not unintentional. To those who judge these matters by the sheer number of pages between the covers, the authors who wrestled long and hard with the problem of what to include and what to leave out, would only retort with asperity after the style of Voltaire: if we had had more time, we would have written a shorter book!

These reminiscences are not offered here in honor of campaigns past. They have a practical, current purpose as we orient ourselves toward the task to be undertaken by the text now offered. For we had certain, fundamental choices before us as we considered what was to be accomplished. A new look at the instructional requirements for those providing protective services was needed. Once the needs had been properly identified, how might they best be addressed? Having anxiously observed the amazing success of Rambo I, II and III, etc., our first inclination was, simply, to do likewise and produce, to the best of our ability, a sort of *Target Terrorism II,* with all the trimmings. Our enthusiasm for the task (in the sole realization that the financial rewards would certainly be less than Hollywoodesque) was short-lived. *Target Terrorism* was a child of its age. Its utility outside a certain time frame was uncertain, and a mere update would deform what the original contained of enduring value. Neither its form nor its structure lent themselves, usefully, to the production of a sequel. Those lucky enough to have, or be able to lay hands on, a copy of the very limited edition of *Target Terrorism* will still find much of value in it and a good deal that has retained its relevance and freshness into our times.

But we were persuaded (with not too much difficulty) that we could not continue to dwell in the past. Nor could we, for long, tread water in the present. We had to find a vehicle which would carry us into the future, and let our experience guide us in the production of a completely new text that would meet, more adequately, the requirements of those who were going to train the new professionals, entering in increasing numbers, this exciting and challenging field of providing protective services. It is incidental, but assuredly something of a relief, that it is really much easier to write an entirely new text than it is to refurbish an old. We are not yet ready to inscribe RIP on the poignant covers of *Target Terrorism,* themselves a grim reminder of the dangers of providing protective services for public figures[4], but we must acknowledge the need for a fresh start, untrammeled by the burdens of our own past writings.

We have not shrugged off the past; indeed, we gratefully recognize, here, our indebtedness to it. *Target Terrorism* acquired a value and a place in the literature far beyond the modest role assigned to it when it was written. It can still be read with profit by some who, in our own age, seem to be intent not only on reinventing the wheel, but in claiming the resultant artifact as an original creation of their own. Those interested in such trivia might expend a pleasant few hours research in pursuit of the definitions of terrorism offered by these "new-wave" pundits since the publication of *Target*

Terrorism[5]. We would, respectfully, interject our own thoughts on the matter here. Before anyone writes anything about terrorism, a visit to the library is in order. A glance at some of the latest offerings would induce one to believe that those responsible for them had done little or no research and were wholly unaware of what had gone before. At least *Target Terrorism* was launched with no such arrogant pretensions.

Having determined that a new book and a fresh approach were needed, it remained to decide what form these should take. In a certain sense, *Target Terrorism* was, itself, a composite. It owed much (and duly acknowledged its indebtedness) to many who were not responsible for any of the words that eventually appeared in print. It was a synthesis of experience, a distillate drawn from life, or, more correctly, the lives of the shadow players who had so long acted out its script. It took, hammered out, and harmonized, the specialist contributions of a few who, thrown together in a particular crucible, produced the instructional amalgram that was converted by the alchemists into the book. The actual process was no less metaphysical than it sounds. There was no consultation or even discussion; there was neither the time nor the reason for either. Again, the context within which *Target Terrorism* was written lent itself to such arbitrariness.

The text was not a team effort, but it served the team that had inspired it and fairly represented what they required of it. When Rome was in danger, the two consuls had, perforce, to be replaced by a dictator, but only a fool would pretend that he alone saved the city. Who but the most naive would contend that Churchill won the Battle of Britain, or that Stalin alone, before the gates of Moscow, beat back the Nazi hordes? There remained, however, for the present work, the *Target Terrorism* option, the synthesizing of a single text, without specific attributions, and only an introductory acknowledgment of a formal nature. That has been eschewed in favor of a different approach here. It has seemed better, more efficient, more authentic to let the different voices speak for themselves; over the years, the chorus has been greatly enlarged.

This is a very different book, more practical, more focused on what for *Target Terrorism* was implied by its secondary title, namely providing protective services. Our major, personal criticism of *Target Terrorism* as a teaching text is that it was not enough of a "how-to" book in the treatment of the latter. This endeavor is intended to remedy the deficiency. The "how-to" aspects are those which receive prominence. This is a manual for those who aspire to do the job—and to do it right. Doing it right means, in this business, doing it right the first time. There may not be a second chance.

We are thoroughly persuaded that, even given all the time in the world, it would not have been possible, usefully, to have produced a shorter book. Though the focus is narrower, there is simply more to be said, and the space must be devoted to saying it. Those who believe that the principles of bodyguarding can be reduced to a hip-pocket text not only betray their ignorance of the dimensions of the task, but of the nature of the business of providing protective services. Those who undertake this exacting work need thorough training *before* they embark upon it. Of course, they receive constant, on-the-job training as they go about their daily business, often without comprehending that they are, in fact, subject to such a regimen of instruction. But in moments of crisis (even minor ones) they can hardly pull out a work of reference (however small, neat, and attractively packaged) so as to find the answers to their problems. Those who provide protective services for a living are men and women of action.

While some employees expect Superman and Wonderwoman for the salaries they are paying, there are few that we have trained who are inclined to read on the run;

only Clark Kent has time for a quick squint at the instruction manual while changing in the phone booth. It is not, then, the size, but rather the way it is used that is the ultimate determinant of satisfaction. We decided, therefore, that on this occasion we would produce an instructional text of more ample proportions than our original concept and, moreover, one that would give full and visible rein to the many and varied voices that would contribute. Yet, we have not sought to fatten the beast, but, rather, to put more flesh on its bones. It is a bigger production without, necessarily, being more lavish. Its essential purposes remain the same. It is a teaching text, a supplement to a practical, hands-on course of instruction. We know what we wanted to do. We must leave others, the consumers, to decide whether we have done it adequately or whether it might not have been better done in a different way. What we must say, here, is that you cannot become a bodyguard simply by reading a book. Or by attending a course of instruction or gaining a diploma.

Conversely, it is equally true that you can become a bodyguard without doing either. We, and not for selfish reasons, simply would not recommend it. We have been concerned, all these years, each after our distinctive fashion, to professionalize this highly specialized function; to give those who perform it standards by which they might be measured and against which they might measure themselves; and to promote and encourage a sense of responsibility which we had already come upon in so many practitioners in inchoate form. There is a process at work here, of which we are proud to have been a part. This text is offered in furtherance of that process.

BODYGUARDS: SO WHO NEEDS 'EM?

> "Uneasy lies the head that wears the crown."
> *William Shakespeare*[6]

The simple and, perhaps, to some, not very pleasing answer is: not many. Not nearly enough to cause mass resignations among those who, holding interesting, responsible, and lucrative positions have nevertheless always hankered after joining the ranks of this ancient but often misunderstood profession. The good bodyguard, today, does not come cheap[7]. And who, after all, wants a bad bodyguard? Or even an indifferent one? The economics of providing protective services dictate that the bodyguard, in our day and age, and in our society, is a luxury item. There is a kind of circularity in all this: the rich and famous (along with a few surrogates) need bodyguards—because they are rich and famous. There may be many others, in fact, in need of protective services. But they are, for such people, just too much of a luxury[8]. They simply cannot afford them, even though they are needed.

So, when we speak of these matters, we are really discussing quite a narrow market. The true irony in all this is that some of those who can afford such personal protection purchase it even though, on a disinterested evaluation of their situation, they do not really need it. But, then, that is the true meaning of a luxury. After all, who really *needs* a Lamborghini? A car is a car is a car. Living under threat is one thing. Being actually victimized is another. Comparatively few of the class at risk are ever actually victimized. Of those who live out their lives free of anticipated harm, it is very difficult to establish with any degree of certainty whether the provision of protective services was decisive in the result. On a few occasions, a very few, indeed, fortunately, the bodyguard proves his or her worth. On even fewer, as in the case of Prime Minister Olaf Palme of Sweden[9], for example, doing without the accustomed bodyguard has proven fatal.

All this is a little like allowing an insurance policy to lapse; there is a curious tendency for the harm insured against to occur shortly after the premiums are permitted to go unpaid. What this really points up is the need for objective risk assessment on behalf of those who, as a class, might feel the need to have special care to avoid the harm others might wish to cause them. The measurement of risk in these kinds of situations can never be an exact science, but nor is it something to be undertaken with divining arrows or by reading the entrails of poultry[10]. Nor, generally, is it a task for those whose primary business is the provision of the protective services themselves.

Those who work, professionally, as bodyguards, learn, in the course of their employment, a great deal about the evaluation of risk, for themselves and for others. They can hardly do their job efficiently without taking the appropriate risk factors into account. But risk assessment calls for a high degree of objectivity, for the detachment that comes from not being exposed to or sharing the risk. There is a necessary division of labor in this that is healthier for all concerned. Those who advise on whether there is a need for the provision of protective services and, if so, what kind, ought not to be the same persons as those who will, eventually, be engaged to provide them if they ever seem to be required[11].

Almost as important as the question posed above, and closely related to it is when are the services of a bodyguard, a personal protection specialist, needed? Again, this is not a question to which a useful, general answer can be offered. Each case is different and each renders up its own, particular answer. If you are born into a ruling dynasty, you may need such protection from the cradle to the grave. You may be given it whether you need it (or want it) or not. Nor, and this is of some importance, may you have very much choice in the matter of who provides those services for you. What you get, in such a case, is impersonal personal protection. To those who get the assignment, this is just another job. It is small wonder that a comparatively high number of such principals end up as just another statistic in the black notebook of history. This is always the dilemma of the public figure, who is deemed to be in need of personal protection and whose bodyguard has to be be paid for out of the public treasury.

Paying for your personal protection out of your own purse is no guarantee that you will fare any better, but it does provide the incentive to take a greater interest in the matter. Most people do not fall into the class that requires to be cosseted in this way all of their lives. The need for protective services of one kind or another usually arises as a result of some change in status or lifestyle; success has brought with it not only benefits but unanticipated problems. Those who live in obscurity, who are not noticed, are rarely envied and, consequently, less at risk than those who are constantly in the public eye. Many rich executives have, peaceably, lived out their lives in such obscurity without ever having to give any thought to hiring a bodyguard. Only those have true personal security whom none wishes to harm. Those whose power or riches bring them not only fame or notoriety, but the envy or hatred of others need all the protection they can get[12].

If your enemies know where to find you and have made a study of your vulnerability, you can do without protective services of any kind and trust to luck. For many, sooner or later, comes some unpleasant experience that persuades them that luck is too fickle to be trusted. Some take a long time before making up their minds to seek professional protection. It is not always parsimony that has prompted the delay. While in some circles, employing a bodyguard, like keeping a mistress, is regarded as chic, most right-minded people are concerned about the impact such a step will have upon their lives. For, if the provision of protective services is taken seriously (and, frankly, it is not much use if it is not) this step will radically alter the lifestyle of the person electing to adopt such a regimen. Having a bodyguard may or may not save your life. It will most certainly change it.

The need for personal protection is not always an either or matter. There are different levels of protective services to meet different needs. Thus, the need for protective services is not necessarily constant or pitched at the same level. For many European heads of state, the idea of having personal bodyguards was, but a short while ago, bordering on the ludicrous. Members of ruling dynasties, who were close enough to the top to be conspicuous, did not mingle with the common people and those who, like the King of Sweden, felt able to do so were so assured of the peaceful intentions of their subjects that they saw no need for such personal protection. When the need to interpose some sort of barrier was felt, a trusted retainer, often elderly and quite out of shape, was held to suffice. These attitudes linger, but the kidnaping of Freddie Heineken (and the cost of getting him back)[13] must surely have given pause to many and not on that continent alone.

We are living through some very trying times, with new values rapidly superseding old and wealth being generated on an unprecedented scale. We have yet to find a solution to its more equitable distribution and it is safe to predict that no solution would be acceptable to all or even a majority. We have, tragically, had to adjust ourselves to the violent resolution of so many of the world's problems. Violent death and destruction have become so commonplace in the waning years of the second millennium A.D. that they scarcely shock those who are not directly touched by their immediate misery. The terrorist has to work much harder for effect. The world has, unquestionably, become a more dangerous place for some who, but a few years ago, would have been virtually insulated from these ills. The opportunities for sharing misfortune with those upon whom good fortune ordinarily might be thought, as a matter of course, to smile have greatly increased. If you stay at home all your life and you have the means to do so, you can build for yourself an almost impregnable fortress.

You might, of course, still be poisoned by a disgruntled servant or close relative or associate anxious to fall into an anticipated inheritance and too impatient to let nature take its course. But you increase the risks of suffering harm every time you sally forth across the drawbridge. What kind of risks are out there, and how do you guard against them? Are some places more dangerous—for you—than others? Are the risks constant, or do they vary, substantially, from time to time? Most important of all, in the present context, can a well-trained, experienced personal protection specialist make a significant difference to the measure of risk[14]?

We believe that, in many instances, he or she can. We feel it advisable to point out, however trite the illusion, that even the finest of protective garments will not save your life if you fail to wear it or wear it incorrectly. Nor will it suffice to deflect the poisoned morsel prepared for your delectation by the assassin who has studied your habits and measured your protection to see where your vulnerabilities lie. A word to the wise: those who need a bodyguard badly enough to have gone to the trouble and expense of employing one, ought not to try to live their lives as though the need does not exist. That is a waste of time and money and, on occasion, of the very life it was all supposed to protect.

SO YOU STILL WANT TO HIRE A BODYGUARD?

> "He that delicately bringeth up his servant from a child shall have
> him become his son at the length."
> *Proverbs 29:21*

It is probably the case that some people pay a good deal more for more security than they will ever need. When the need arises; it is better to have too much of a good thing than too little. Measuring security needs is a little like trying to determine when the stock market has hit bottom. Despite all the charts, graphs, and newsletters, none of this is terribly scientific. Those in the market for a bodyguard want to make sure they have spent their money wisely and that, at the crucial moment, they do not find themselves stuck with a lemon. They may not then be around to complain. If you really do need a bodyguard, it certainly pays to get the best that money can buy. And to have your protection in place when it is required. But therein lies the rub. Money certainly buys services.

But it does not always, or even often, buy Service. Indeed, this latter commodity may not even be for sale. Certainly, money, of itself, can rarely, if ever, be guaranteed to purchase loyalty. Yet, in this business, loyalty is perhaps the most precious commodity of all. A bodyguard without loyalty is unlikely to risk his or her own skin to save that of his or her principal. A disloyal bodyguard is a time-bomb waiting for an opportunity to unleash its destructive potential[15]. Many an otherwise invulnerable principal owes his or her demise to the actions or inactions of a disloyal bodyguard. Mercenaries do not make reliable bodyguards; if your bodyguard can be bought by you, he or she can be bought by others. Some can be purchased for surprisingly little. Only a priceless few cannot be bought at all. Realistically, it must be appreciated that providing protective services is a business like any other in this respect. There are good, indifferent, and bad suppliers. There are a few, whose dedication and performance are superlative, and some who ought not to be in the business at all. Finding the "right" bodyguard is *never* an easy matter. It may take a good deal of trial and error, or result in a good deal of disappointment or grief for the seeker after these services.

The chances of "getting it right" the first time are greatly enhanced by going about the job in the right way, and, in particular, by pitching one's expectations at the appropriate level. Those who ordinarily make their purchases with some discernment generally have some idea of what they are seeking. There is no such thing as "a bodyguard", in this sense, any more than there is "a suit" or "an automobile". Taste, needs, availability and a host of other factors shape the search and the selection. The wise, whatever their personal ideas on these matters, will seek expert advice, as they would in any field with which they are personally unfamiliar[16]. This is a serious matter. If you really want to hire a bodyguard for more than cosmetic effect, remember you may be literally putting your life in his or her hands.

Responsible guidance begins with an admonition about its own limitations in the matter. The Golden Rule here is: deal only with those you can trust. Avoid shady markets and all who make exaggerated, unsubstantiated claims on behalf of themselves or others. There are many "fly-by-nights" in this field. If your supplier has been in this business for a reasonable length of time, ten years or so, you may presume that his endurance tells something of his value and probity. Beware of those who have scented a burgeoning market and have entered it importunately from some wholly inappropriate "elsewhere".

Next to an appropriate disposition for providing protective services, experience and training are the elements that ought most to command the attention of prospective employers of bodyguards. These latter more readily lend themselves to objective, verifiable appraisal. A cautionary note is worth sounding, here. A certificate doth not a bodyguard make. Like a law school or a medical school diploma, it attests only to the satisfactory completion of a specific program of training (in the case of the bodyguard, a relatively short one), no more nor less. It certainly confers no automatic entitlement to a job as a bodyguard or even certification of competence to do the job.

To the knowledgeable, however, it does tell much that is of value in appraising a candidate for a position. In recent years, there has been a proliferation of establishments offering training for those who would provide protective services. Their organization, training methods and materials, instructional facilities, equipment, and the qualifications and quality of their teaching staff display wide variations. Most offer some sort of certificate to those who have taken their courses of instruction, (which are often quite handsome and nearly always most impressive as wall adornments) so that the issuing establishment can be appraised by those having the capacity to undertake the task. Some of the questions which might usefully be asked are:

• How long has the establishment been in existence as a provider of training for bodyguards?

• Does it provide (or has it in the past provided) training of a different kind and, if so, how closely is this related to or compatible with the training required for the providing of protective services?

• Is it independent, associated with some other operation, or a franchise operation?

• Is it headed or directed, personally, by a nationally known and respected figure in the business of providing protective services, or is the name of such an individual merely associated in some way with the establishment and its programs?

• What are the qualifications and experience of the instructional staff *regularly* associated with each of the establishment's programs?

• Is the school run directly under federal, state, or local government auspices or under the official auspices of some foreign government?

• Is the school licensed, approved, or supervised by any governmental authority in connection with the provision of training for bodyguards?

• How long is the program and what is the course content? Are the course materials original and proprietary or derived?

• Do those who graduate from the establishment's programs remain in active association with it after receiving basic instruction, having opportunities of follow-up or advanced training, and operational involvement?

Training, properly conducted, is a very serious business. By this means, fundamental principles of conduct are systematically instilled in the prospective bodyguard, which will serve to orient his thinking and actions throughout his working life. If he has been poorly or inadequately trained, this will quickly show, and bad habits in this area of endeavor are difficult if not impossible to eradicate later. Training should never be seen as a once and for all exercise; in a very real sense, the bodyguard is in a constant process of training and re-training. He is continually honing old skills, and adding new ones to his repertoire. What is stressed, here, is the overriding importance of good, basic training. This is the sure foundation upon which all else is built.

Another aspect of the matter is worthy of some attention. Some will have received their basic training in the course of their service with some official body, the military, perhaps, or the United States Secret Service, this latter being, doubtless, the finest public provider of protective services in the world. Yet the limitations of this training must be clearly understood when the person who has undertaken it moves from a public to a private setting to exercise his functions. The training is predicated upon a variety of factors which will no longer obtain once the official status has been exchanged for a private one. The official bodyguard will have substantial support services upon which he can rely for much of that which the private bodyguard must provide for himself. While this necessity may, of itself, serve to enlarge the capacity and understanding of the private bodyguard, it, inevitably, leads him into territory for which his original training may not have prepared him adequately and in which he must learn to fend as best he can. This is especially true in the case of operational intelligence, which the private bodyguard must often learn to collect himself as best he can while serving, when the task is done, as his own analyst[17].

All this is onerous and time-consuming, for there is no division of labor, but the point made here is that there is rarely any preparation, much less training, for the transition. None of this negates the basic training the individual may have received, but it underlines the need for additional training of a wholly different kind to permit of its useful adaptation and supplementation. One more related point may be made in this connection. The official bodyguard can generally expect cooperation in varying degrees from other official entities anywhere in the world his duties might take him or her. The utility of this cannot be overestimated. It is often taken for granted, until such valuable facilities are seen to be no longer automatically available to the private individual. There is no necessary carry-over from these official positions; connections have to be re-worked and re-developed from a purely personal angle and the success of this effort depends upon the skill of those engaged in it, and whatever reciprocity they are able to muster.

Experience is another factor which must be subjected to searching examination by a prospective employer. Again, it is all too easy to take matters for granted to the detriment of the process. Having served with an elite military unit, for example, may invest the ex-serviceman or woman with a certain glamour of peculiar value on the cocktail party circuit, but, what did he or she actually do? Did they play a prominent part in actions for which the particular unit is renowned? Campaign medals are awarded by some countries in Peter Sellers-like fashion for simply being there, whereas awards for gallantry are not. Again, the real issue is the relevance of the experience to the business of providing protective services. The winning of a Congressional Medal of Honor for wiping out, single-handedly, half a dozen enemy machine gun nests obviously speaks to a high degree of personal courage, but the opportunities for displaying, as a bodyguard, the martial skills involved will, hopefully, be few and far between.

The point would seem to be overstressed, here, were it not for the numbers who apply to be bodyguards on the strength of experiences that would more properly fit them for doing search and rescue missions into the heartlands of the USSR rather than what is required of them as providers of protective services. Evidence of coolness under fire on, say, the Plain of Jars or the deserts of Oman is a useful indicator of personal bravery, but it must not be mistaken for relevant experience or technical competence in the field of bodyguarding; having served far from the front on the ambassador's personal detail is much more to the point. The sort of experience to be looked for is that gained by having done the job of bodyguarding elsewhere at some time materially close to the present; having looked after Churchill during World War II has, presently, little more than historical significance.

The "elsewhere" has, also, to be closely investigated. Did "they" do things in a way that would be acceptable in the country of prospective employment? One who has long served, faithfully and well, as a bodyguard for an Eastern potentate in far-off lands might feel understandably out of place where a scimitar-wielding onslaught upon a perceived assailant would be considered a bizarre happening. Daddy Warbucks might get away with this; others would prefer to settle for something more conventional. The key questions always are: *for whom did you previously work as a bodyguard, and why did you leave that employment?* Obviously, there are as many acceptable as there are unacceptable answers to these questions.

Understandably, good employers like to retain good bodyguards, those who have given, and continue to give, good service. The reasons for leaving ostensibly good employment must always be carefully examined, for they tell much about the suitability for future employment in some other situation. The provision of protective services constitutes a career for those who undertake this difficult and sometimes dangerous work. They can hardly be faulted for seeking advancement in their chosen field of employment. Sometimes, a bodyguard of proven worth will be sought out and made an offer he or she cannot refuse[18]. More usually it will be the bodyguard who takes the initiative in seeking to make an advantageous career move.

Some assignments are by nature of short duration. There are those who prefer the challenges offered by change and deliberately elect to practice their profession by undertaking such assignments on a regular basis. These changes are a conscious choice and pose few problems, where they are encountered, for those inquiring into these matters. Other kinds of "job-hopping" raise more serious questions as to why the bodyguard may have elected to move on elsewhere. These matters touch upon issues of integrity and competence. No principal would wish to place his or her life in the hands of one who can be lured away by promises or money and other fine things; the very notion raises disturbing thoughts for the future. An unhappy, or time-serving bodyguard is a security risk. One learns to be wary of those who are unhappy too frequently or who can scarcely await their contract's end so as to move to yet another "permanent" position.

Experience is a large and somewhat elastic concept. Some decide to enter the field of providing protective services from another which, while furnishing no direct experience of this business has, nevertheless, endowed them with a rich legacy of general experience that can be turned to good account. Here, sensitive, well-attuned training can compensate for lack of a "track record" in the particular field, provided the deficiency is faced in all honesty. Nor is the prestige of past positions necessarily to be equated with appropriate experience that might be converted to use by those who have effected this career shift. Twelve years with the Federal Bureau of Investigation spent largely in the sophisticated pursuit of various violators of federal law may be far less relevant than the experience of a patrolman who has consistently "moonlighted" so as to provide dignitary protection and other related services as the need for them in his own jurisdiction has arisen. Much law enforcement work and military service does provide a useful springboard from which to launch a useful, second career in providing protective services, but the true limitations of the prior experience must be recognized and compensated for appropriately.

Every career has its commencement, a moment at which the neophyte enters its ranks for the first time, fresh from some school or another, or by way of transition from some other area of occupational activity. Only the most arrogant, ignorant, or foolhardy aspire to move into the top job right away. The realistic appreciate that they build their own portfolio of experience on the job and make haste slowly while learning all they can about the way things are done. Such "rookies" are to be admired and encouraged rather than regarded with old-timer's scorn. In some not too distant future, the best among them will have their own disciples and will be valued on account of the experience and counsel they can bestow on others. The experience relevant to providing protective services is gained, in strictness, while *being* a bodyguard. That experience may be usefully supplemented by being told about it, or reading about it, or being taught about it in some simulated setting. But there is nothing quite like, or so effective as, on-the-job training. Here, the real life begins.

This is true of so many of life's important activities. It is equally true that few people welcome the role of guinea pig, of providing a useful learning experience for others— and paying for it into the bargain. Who would really relish entrusting his or her life and fortunes to an inexperienced bodyguard, however good he or she might one day turn out to be as a result of the experience gained? Surgeons have to gain practical experience somehow, but few would take pleasure in being the subject of a major operation undertaken by a scalpel-wielding novice fresh out of medical school. Ideally, experience should be acquired through something in the nature of an apprenticeship under or alongside a seasoned protective services specialist. This gives the necessary confidence to the consumer while providing the needed opportunities for on-the-job training and skills development. Those organizations that are large enough to permit of this should see, in the interests of ensuring that their own establishments are kept up to strength, that all these opportunities are productively utilized. Those who make a profession out of providing protective services, develop their own distinctive style that marks them out from the rest. They want to build a service in their own image; they want things done "Their Way". With the right raw material (and if it is really raw, so much the better) and a systematic program of instruction and placement, this goal can be efficiently accomplished, to the benefit of all concerned.

SO YOU HIRED A BODYGUARD? NOW WHAT?

> "He profits most who serves best."
> *A.F. Sheldon*
> *Motto for International Rotary*

A bodyguard's job is to provide a very special kind of personal service. His entire career and operational functioning revolve around that single concept, that notion of service. His work has no meaning save in that context. In Cartesian fashion, the bodyguard might well say "I serve, therefore I am". Whether as an employee or an independent contractor, the task of the bodyguard is to provide protective services; as a bodyguard, that is his or her whole and entire duty, nothing more nor less. He or she may, as a quite separate matter, undertake to provide other services of a compatible but distinct nature. The character and scope of such an arrangement must be clearly understood by both parties from the outset. Thus, one who is engaged to provide protective services may hold the dual position of chauffeur/bodyguard. There is, clearly, a duality of functions here, but also an observable congruity; the two jobs do fit together. A well-trained bodyguard will have learned the skills of defensive (and, where necessary, the employment of offensive) driving and in displaying his or her prowess at the wheel he or she may be assisting not only in the transportation of but also in the personal protection of his or her principal.

This is a very different arrangement from one which is predicated upon assigning someone who is regularly no more than a driver the additional task of protecting his or her passenger. This distinction must be clearly appreciated by those having responsibility for arranging and managing these matters, for upon it turns the question of whether there are any protective services at all provided as a result. There is a certain short-sightedness in trying to employ a well-trained, professional bodyguard about other tasks. It is a false economy. It betrays a lack of knowledge of what providing protective services is all about. On occasion, there is a disingenuous belief that when no danger appears to threaten, the bodyguard might as well be usefully employed about some other business. After all, it is reasoned, he or she costs enough to keep about the place so why not make sure the bodyguard is gainfully occupied? This is not an issue of dignity (I don't do windows) but, rather, a matter of function. A bodyguard is employed on the calculated assumption (be it correct or erroneous) that his or her services *as bodyguard* will at some time or another be needed. It is rarely, if ever, possible to predict with certainty when that moment may arrive. How unfortunate when it does, should the bodyguard be found walking the family dog instead of beside the person he or she has been engaged to protect[19].

This is not a book intended for the education of those who hire bodyguards, though the evidence shows that many are sorely in need of one addressed to them alone. If by some happy chance they read this one, so much the better, but they are not the audience aimed at here. Our words are directed, primarily, at those who serve rather than those who are served. It is the bodyguard who must define and delimit the ambit of his own functions, for rarely are those who engage his services capable of undertaking the task. Indeed, they may not even be aware there is work to be undertaken in this regard. The provision of protective services is not a self-defining employment. What is involved may be seen in different ways by different people. There is so much room for dissatisfaction on this account alone.

There is, perhaps, no greater cause of discontent on the part of those who seek to provide such services or among those who are the recipients of them, than the holding of contrary impressions about what is to be supplied. No-one likes to be imposed upon or required to do that which he or she has not implicitly consented to do in the ordinary course of the working relationship. Resentments breed, performance is affected, and service suffers as a result. *Before* the provision of protective services is undertaken, it is advisable that both parties to the arrangement reach a clear understanding of what is comprised in it. Anything less is certain to lead to trouble when the arrangements are given practical effect. The arrangements must sensibly take account of the fact that the provider of protective services is a human being, with all the physical limitations that this implies. He or she cannot be omnipresent; there must, at the very least, be time for food and rest. This, in itself, creates an area of exposure that must receive close attention. If round-the-clock protection on a regular basis is required, clearly, one person will not be sufficient to cover the assignment. If more than one bodyguard is employed, are they compatible? Do they have a clear idea of their respective responsibilities?

Obviously, anything less than full coverage raises problems concerning the best disposition of the available services. Any person who sometimes employs a bodyguard and at others dispenses with such services should be aware of the risks entailed in such a procedure. It raises the basic question as to whether such protection is necessary at all. If it is and, presumably, this is the rationale for the services of a bodyguard being retained in the first place, prudence would dictate that the most careful thought be given to those opportunities that might allow those services to be dispensed with or curtailed. Those wishing to do some kind of harm to a protected person will seek out his or her vulnerabilities[20].

Protective services ought never be dispensed with casually; in high-risk situations, they ought not to be dispensed with at all. It is part of the duty of the conscientious provider of protective services to spell these things out for those he or she protects. Learning how to do it gently, correctly, and efficiently is an important part of the bodyguard's business. Sometimes it is necessary to protect others against the consequences of ill-considered actions. The bodyguard must accustom himself or herself to thinking for the person protected in these matters. It must not be left to the good sense of those who have engaged the services of the bodyguard. Their appreciation of what is required may be flawed, colored by inappropriate considerations, or just plain defective. The conscientious bodyguard will not allow those he or she protects to stray into dangerous situations or dangerous procedures. There are important professional responsibilities to discharge, here, and failure to do so not only makes the job more difficult. It can, of itself, occasion harm.

Educating one's employer is always a delicate and difficult matter. In moments of obvious, present danger, those persons who are wise and truly understanding are content to surrender their authority and dignity to those professionals to whom they have confided their safety[21]. Thus we have seen even the president of the United States hustled without ceremony out of danger, or pushed, unceremoniously, to the floor of a speeding automobile to escape an assassin's bullet. This is hardly a pleasant experience for the chief executive involved, but it is far better than the alternative, and questions of dignity must give way before measures designed to ensure survival[22].

Those who would ordinarily consider themselves less exposed to acts of hostility that might call forth similar protective responses need to be carefully apprised of any such treatment well in advance of it occurring. There is a certain unpleasantness about the contemplation of these things not unlike that involved in the making of a last will and testament or advance funeral arrangements; they are only truly relished by the morbid or the warped. Few principals are likely to interrogate their bodyguards closely on these matters: "What will you do if someone comes at me with a gun, a knife?" Certain assumptions are made which are not always correct, although this may not come to light until after the event. The good bodyguard tries to spare his principal the embarrassment of surprise in any department. In matters touching so closely upon what to expect in a crisis, there is a positive obligation to inform and instruct. The provision of protective services is rarely a static activity. Mainly, it involves carefully choreographed, competently executed movements.

Learning these patterns and arrangements, their meaning and purpose, is a large part of the professional bodyguard's stock in trade. Communicating them, in practice, to those he or she protects is of equal importance. As in a well-performed dance routine, there should be an unspoken understanding between the partners as to their respective roles and actions. Great subtlety is called for on the part of those providing protective services so as to bring about this symbiosis. Ideally, there should be nothing obvious, nothing forced. The principal is paying for the kind of protection that will enable him or her to go about his or her ordinary, everyday business and social activities with as little inconvenience as possible[23]. He or she looks to his or her bodyguard to provide that kind of unobtrusive, personal security. The bodyguard is concerned with the intricacies of each protective movement; the principal should be only dimly aware, if at all, that he or she is a part, indeed the very center of it.

Good advance work, flexibility, and fast footwork on the part of those providing the protective services are essential to connect the principal with the rhythm of the movement. There is something about the way good bodyguards position themselves, their presence, demeanor and movement that is quietly reassuring to their principals. In the main, the good bodyguard educates his or her principal by example. The process varies from case to case, determined largely by the personality and style of the principal, but the need is universal. However good the chemistry between the parties, none of this comes together of its own accord. The bodyguard has to work at it for it is all part and parcel of his or her job.

Life, as President John F. Kennedy pointed out, is not fair. What has been written here clearly throws the burden of making the protective services arrangements work onto the shoulders of the bodyguard. However unfair this may appear at first blush, it will quickly become apparent with experience that this is the only way, in the great majority of instances, that these arrangements will work at all to the satisfaction of all parties. Moreover, and this, perhaps, is the crucial factor, principals expect it. It is part—a large part—of what they believe they are paying for.

It is incumbent upon the provider of the protective services to make the major adjustments as well as attending to the fine tuning. This is the true meaning of service in the present context, as in so many others. There are some principals for whom it is a joy to work. They are understanding, caring, and appreciative. It is simply in their nature to be so. Overall, a majority of human beings are far less considerate—and see no real reason why they should be otherwise. They view these matters in strictly commercial terms. Among those whose position, prosperity, or success in life demand that they make special arrangements for their own personal security and that of those who are close to them, the proportions of the caring to the indifferent are unlikely to differ significantly. There are always some among the general population as well as special segments of it for whom the rendering of services, at any price, is a kind of hell on earth for those serving, leaving them in a constant state of anxiety for the arrival of the moment when they can say, "Take this job and shove it"[24].

These latter truly buy a most precarious kind of protection; they tend to change "bodyguards" with a depressing regularity. Nothing that is said, in the present work, whether or not it might come to their attention, is likely to change matters. The bad employer generally receives the kind of service he or she deserves. This book is written in the interests of those who deserve, and are entitled to expect, better, and addresses some of the ways in which those improvements might be gained. It is our firm view that the major share of responsibility for creating the kind of atmosphere in which protective services can be rendered efficiently and to the satisfaction of all parties rests with those providing the services. It should be an important part of their career training to equip themselves to undertake this task. The bodyguard may be a crack shot and the fastest draw in the West, an advanced exponent of the martial arts, and an expert behind the wheel to boot, but if he or she lacks the proper people skills that enable him or her to relate, comfortably, to his or her charges, all that goes for nought.

All of which goes to underscore an important point: while brawn, undoubtedly, comes in very handy now and then, in this business, the providing of protective services as a career is very much a matter of mind over muscle. The training of the bodyguard must develop the mental equipment required for the job as well as the technical skills that will enable the person concerned to function correctly in his or her chosen profession. The bodyguard must work on his or her own attitude before trying to change those of others. The customer is not always right, but, simply because he or she *is* a customer, they are always entitled to be treated as though they were. It is simply good business to do so.

A service given grudgingly is no service at all; it is profitless for both parties. Arrogance, whatever its well-spring, inhibits service and renders it nugatory. Pride enhances service. It is arrogant in the extreme to believe yourself to be better than those you are paid to serve[25]. Your principal is paying you, not *vice versa*. You would do well never to let this stray far from your awareness. If you truly resent this state of affairs, you ought not to be doing this job, for it cannot be effectively done by those who harbor such attitudes. In the business of providing protective services, you cannot protect until you have learned how to serve. For some, this is the hardest lesson of all.

A FEW MORE WORDS BEFORE YOU READ ON.

> "Ideas are useless unless used."
> *Thomas J. Peters & Robert Waterman, Jr.*[26]

This is a practical book, written by practical people for practical people. It represents an unusual collection of a great deal of on-the-job experience. It has been produced, for the most part, by unusual techniques; working bodyguards do not go about their business with a notebook in one hand and a writing implement in the other. By the time some of them decide to set down their reminiscences in orderly fashion, much of the utility of these has been lost for those who might have learned from them. We have tried to capture some of the spontaneity and action of the process of providing protective services, something we felt, on mature reflection, to have been lacking in *Target Terrorism*. As we observed at the start, this, by way of contrast, is a "how-to" book, with all the charm and dangers such texts so often carry within themselves. It should never be overlooked that its primary purpose is as a basic, instructional tool, designed to supplement a particular, long-established training program. It is not possible to learn the business of providing protective services *simply* by reading a book.

This text is, then, an adjunct, a training aid which, it is hoped, properly used will contribute to the rounding and polishing of the aspiring bodyguard. We obviously believe in the usefulness of what we have produced; only time will tell if we are correct in our estimation. We also recognize that we live in a busy world and the lives of those who regularly provide protective services are busier than most. Only those who enjoy the bliss of worthwhile idleness, who must perforce do so for a living, or who are extremely dedicated really *read* textbooks. How many learned tomes lie unopened upon the bookshelves, while their owners wait for that day (which so rarely comes) when they might have an opportunity to read them[27]? We are flooded with information from all sides, to which we feel obliged to attend simply in order to keep up-do-date in some department or another. We are suffering from an information indigestion that no amount of *Rolaids* can relieve. Reading books becomes a chore, a burden so that we tend to accumulate not only books we have never read at all, but also a separate pile that we have, for some reason or another, read in part, put down or to one side, and never picked up again.

Modern life has so many other distractions, not least the electronic media that, for some, has wholly replaced reading as their major source of information. It has not been our intention, here, to add to the heap, or the quota of its ever-growing dimensions. We do believe that selected reading is important for those who take their profession seriously. It is possible to be a functional illiterate and still be a very good bodyguard. But we doubt that it is possible to be the very best of bodyguards while suffering under such a handicap. Our concerns are less with those who require remedial assistance in these matters than with those who, though well able to read and appreciate, simply let things slide through pressure of work or the lure of other pursuits. These, we earnestly urge to make the effort. We truly feel this book makes a worthwhile demand upon their limited time and energies.

There are those in every profession who sincerely strive toward excellence. To these we offer a special word of encouragement. This is a business in which, unlike some others, excellence is recognized and appropriately rewarded. The extra effort is worthwhile. It is possible to rise to the top, and to remain there. And there is room at the top. But it does take hard work and personal qualities that are given but to a few. This book would never have been written without the assistance and enthusiasm of some of those who have been recognized among this elite. Like such persons in other fields of endeavor, they have generously shared of their experiences that others might profit from them. One day, they will pass on the torch to others. We are convinced that none can afford to rest on their laurels. Every assignment, even for the most experienced, is a *learning* experience. Surprising new things come to light every day for those with inquiring minds. In this, as in so many other businesses, the ultimate accolade is customer satisfaction.

This is always very gratifying, when it is achieved, but it can lead to dangerous complacency: the boss is pleased with me so I must be doing all right. Such complacency can lead to stagnation, and, thence, to decline. The perfectionist is his or her own sternest critic. It is not enough to satisfy others, however pleasing that may be, if you are unable to meet your own established standards. We hold to the view that however good the performance, it is always possible to do better. It is generally those who subscribe to this thesis, and put their ideas into practice, who come to excel. When you are enjoying what you are doing, it is hard to believe it will not go on forever. Some manage a surprisingly lengthy career as bodyguards before going on to other things. But it is a profession that is notoriously susceptible to burn-out through a special variant of what has now come to be called executive stress.

Sometimes, there are physical symptoms, a general malaise, at others a sort of unexplained restlessness or irascibility. The warning signs should never be shrugged off or ignored; they are trying to tell you something important about yourself and your relationship to the job. Nothing is more demoralizing than having reached an acknowledged peak of excellence only to detect the inevitable signs of decline. This is an exacting profession. It takes its toll in physical and mental terms. There is a career after passing one's peak, but dissatisfaction and inevitable, invidious comparisons enter upon the scene. Prize fighters never seem to know when to quit and unscrupulous managers rarely advise them to do so. There is a sadness about their efforts.

In the protective services business, job-hopping can be a palliative but it is rarely a permanent solution. We would counsel early recognition that there is a life after bodyguarding, albeit a very different one, and the experience gained in providing protective services for others can often be turned to good account as the foundation of a rewarding, second career. There are always positions of trust for those who have learned and displayed the virtues of service and absolute confidentiality in the employment of another. This is a comforting thought that we hope may see many a provider of protective services through yet another 28 hour day.

We conclude this introduction with ten aphorisms or rules that we feel should guide those who would practice this demanding profession. They embody much of what has been written thus far and anticipate what is to follow:

- Expect the unexpected[28]
- Leave nothing to chance[29]
- Master the basics[30]
- Be open to change[31]
- Do what works best for you[32]
- Emulate but don't imitate[33]
- Keep in condition, mentally and physically[34]
- Guard your tongue[35]
- Never forget who is the Boss[36]
- Know when to quit[37]

NOTES

[1] *Zen and the Art of Motorcycle Maintenance,* New York: Bantam Books, (1975), page 209.

[2] Richard W. Kobetz and H.H.A. Cooper, Gaithersburg, MD: International Association of Chiefs of Police, (1978).

[3] See "Fiction May Become Fact", H.H.A. Cooper, IV TVI Journal, Nums. 1-3, Spring, 1983, pages 10-13.

[4] The jacket of *Target Terrorism* bears the legend: "A cover photograph depicts Italian children praying at the site of the slaying of Aldo Moro's five bodyguards, March 16, 1978 in Rome, Italy. Courtesy of World Wide Photos, Inc."

[5] An egregious example is *The Explosion of Terrorism,* Beau Grosscup, Far Hills, NJ: New Horizon Press, (1987). See, especially, pages 10 et seq.

[6] Henry IV Part II, Act 3:1.

[7] See, for example, "Business booms for Israeli-trained bodyguards", Focus, *Jewish Week,* Inc., March 27, 1987, page 27, "Each case is different, says Tal, but a bodyguard costs $200 a day plus expenses".

[8] See, on this, "The Hardest Question", Richard W. Kobetz and H.H.A. Cooper, in *Terrorism and Personal Protection,* Ed. Brian M. Jenkins, Boston: Butterworth, (1985), pages 388/394.

[9] Palme, who had his fair share of those who might have wished him dead, was killed by a lone gunman in Stockholm, Sweden on February 28, 1986 while walking home with his wife after a visit to the cinema. He had given his bodyguard the night off. See, *The Washington Post,* March 1, 1986, page A16.

[10] See, on this *Evaluating the Terrorist Threat: Principles of Applied Risk Assessment,* H.H.A. Cooper, Gaithersburg, MD: International Association of Chiefs of Police, CTT Series, (1979).

[11] This is a specialized extension of what was discussed in "Paying the Price for Good Advice", 12 *Security Systems Administration* No. 11, November, 1983, at page 10.

[12] Sometimes, all the money in the world is insufficient to buy what is required. See, for example, "U.S. Spent Millions for Sadat's Protection." *Dallas Times Herald,* October 8, 1981, page A-19.

[13] For an excellent account of this, see *Executive Safety and International Terrorism,* Anthony J. Scotti, Englewood Cliffs, NJ: Prentice-Hall, (1986), pages 63-65.

[14] On this point, see *On Assassination,* H.H.A. Cooper, Boulder, CO: Paladin Press, (1984), page 165. Careful analysis of the circumstances of the killing of John Lennon suggest that a bodyguard might have made the crucial difference between life and death in that case.

[15] As happened in the case of the late Indira Gandhi, Prime Minister of India, killed by her own bodyguards in November, 1984.

[16] On this, generally, see, "Buying Executive Protection", H.H.A. Cooper, 13 *Security Systems Administration,* No. 10, October, 1984 at page 26.

[17] For the importance of this, see Cooper, op. cit. supra note 14 at page 191.

[18] High officials leaving the service of the United States, for example, who have enjoyed, in office, some sort of federal protection, and who feel a need to continue that level of protection on their return to private life, sometimes seek to retain the services of those who served them in an official capacity.

[19] Using a professional bodyguard to walk the dog is rather like using a first-rate diamond as a glass cutter. Of course, if the bodyguard were employed specifically to provide protective services for some animal (Spuds McKenzie, perhaps?) the matter would be viewed, here, in a different light.

[20] Again, Scotti's book is strongly recommended to those who wish to study, in detail, how this is done. Op. cit. supra note 13.

[21] President Ford may not have looked very dignified when he was fired upon by Sara Jane Moore, but he survived, thanks at least in part to the protective measures taken by those guarding him.

[22] The speed with which President Reagan was conveyed from the scene of his shooting to the hospital where he was operated upon, undoubtedly saved his life.

[23] This is what, elsewhere, we have referred to as "the de Gaulle solution", or perhaps, more exactly, "the de Gaulle option". Op. cit. supra note 8 page 389.

[24] See, in this connection the comment on the treatment of his bodyguards by the late Anastsio Somoza Debayle in *Somoza.* Bernard Diederich, New York: E.P. Dutton, (1981), page 332.

[25] The words of Malcolm Forbes are worthy of attention on this, as on so many other matters: "Those who act as if they know more than their boss seldom do. Those who do, have sense enough not to make it obvious—to the boss."
The Sayings of Chairman Malcolm, Malcolm S. Forbes, New York: Harper & Row, (1978), page 33.

[26] *In Search of Excellence,* New York: Harper & Row, (1982), page 206.

[27] In an amusing, pertinent aside in a radio program discussing the sociological impact of the TV writers' strike it was said, "Reading books? They'll never catch on!" Robert Boyd, *Weekend Edition,* PBS, July 24, 1988.

[28] On this, see "Expecting the Unexpected", H.H.A. Cooper, XLIX *The Police Chief,* Num. 4, April, 1982, pages 54-55.

[29] It has been pertinently observed that "The essence of good security is to trust no one". *Spy in the U.S.,* Pawel Monat, with John Dille, New York: Harper & Row (1962), page 53. This has many dimensions, but in the present context, it is especially relevant in the sense incorporated into this injunction. There is no greater condemnation, after something has gone wrong, than the explanation, "I thought X was taking care of that".

[30] It is always a mistake to try to learn the fancy footwork before mastering the basic steps. It can lead to disaster. An old Arab proverb has it: "Whoever has not first dug a well, should not steal a minaret".

[31] "We have to change about in this world. You cannot keep going on in the same channel all the time." A.W. Mellon, cited in *The Mellons,* David E. Koskoff, New York: Thomas E. Crowell (1978), page 282.

[32] This is an application of the Peters & Waterman apothegm, "Stick to the Knitting". op. cit. supra note 26, pages 292-305.

[33] The sage Anwar-i-Suhaili reminds us that "no effort makes a black crow into a white hawk". Be All That You Can Be—as the Army commercial has it, but recognize your own limitations.

[34] Most salutary is a reading of the work of the great Japanese strategist, Miyamoto Musashi, whose *A Book of Five Rings,* Woodstock, New York: Overlook Press, (1974) acquired something of a cult following in business circles after its introduction to an American audience. The integration of the spiritual and the physical is especially marked in this work. Note, too, his insistence upon repeated practice of drills and exercises.

[35] Sa'adi reminds us, "A man's own tongue may cut his throat". But there is a further injunction, here. The bodyguard must protect not only the person of his or her principal, but also that individual's secrets. The bodyguard who has loose lips is a candidate for early retirement, or worse.

[36] Again, Malcolm Forbes:
> Once in a while
> There's wisdom in recognizing that
> The Boss is.

Op. cit. supra note 25 at page 31.

[37] This is not to be confused with the admirable quality of persistence or perseverance in the face of adversity or daunting odds. The matter turns upon questions of obligation and the ends to be served. Some have a nice sense of these things and can safely heed the inner voice. Others need to be firmly but gently told. For those who would appreciate the difference from a fine case study, see, *The Shattered Silence*, Zlwy Aldouby and Jerrold Ballinger, New York: Coward-McCann, (1971), the story of a brave, Israeli spy, Edi Cohen, who went about his business just a little too long.

Nine Lives Associates

WHAT IS N.L.A.? Nine Lives Associates (N.L.A.) is a select group of Law Enforcement, Correctional, Military and Security professionals who have shared a unique training experience through their attendance and participation in the program entitled PROVIDING PROTECTIVE SERVICES. These special programs, emphasizing personal survival and advanced techniques for the protection of others, are provided by Richard W. Kobetz & Associates, Ltd. The common understanding, skills and fellowships developed under conditions of stressful realism has been translated into a permanent and exclusive professsional association. Members recognize each other world-wide by a distinct Black Cat lapel pin, symbolizing the group's striving for a special kind of professional excellence.

Members of N.L.A.

- Are certified as Personal Protection Specialists (P.P.S.).
- Benefit from membership in an exclusive fraternity.
- Exchange and obtain information through a worldwide network.
- Have access to exclusive placement services.
- Maintain communications through a secretariat office.
- May purchase items of wearing apparel with membership logo.
- Obtain discounts on training programs and book purchases.
- Participate in annual training conferences and advance programs.
- Receive special newsletters and announcements.
- Secure opportunities for part-time assignments in providing protective services.

PART I

Organization, Threats, and Intelligence

ONE

Threat Assessment in Personal Protection

by Eugene R. Ferrara

THE BASIS OF PERSONAL PROTECTION is threat assessment. It is impossible to determine the correct type and amount of protection unless the type and amount of threat has been established. Attempting to protect everyone from everything all of the time is neither efficient nor effective. (It also is not possible!) Thankfully, we have not yet reached the point where everyone needs protection. And even the people who do need it, don't require the same level of protection all of the time. The development of an effective personal protection program demands that a determination be made of the level and type of threat that exists for an individual at a particular time, in a particular set of circumstances.

The best personal protection program is the one that affords the appropriate level of protection with the minimum intrusion on the normal life-style of the person being protected. The key to establishing this level of protection is to perform a threat assessment.

Once the potential for harm has been evaluated, a determination must be made as to what resources and actions are necessary to control the risks. Where possible, the avoidance of the risk is preferred. In cases where elimination of a risk is not possible, efforts should be made to minimize the consequences of that risk. Just as all situations do not produce the same level of threat, all threats do not have the same level of consequences. A good threat assessment will address both issues; thus allowing the appropriate response.

Perhaps this would be a good time to discuss the security continuum. This concept proposes that security and convenience are at opposite ends of a continuum. (For the purposes of this discussion assume *security* to be the absence of risk and *convenience* the absence of inhibiting factors on one's life-style) Movement toward one end of the continuum results in an equal movement away from the other end.

SECURITY ◄──────────────────────────────────► CONVENIENCE

The security continuum helps explain why no one is completely without risk. In order to achieve absolute security it would be necessary to totally restrict our ability to do the things we want to do.

As an example, assume the president of the United States was to be absolutely secure at all times. One method of achieving maximum security would be to place him in a protective shield; perhaps a concrete bunker in the basement of the White House with mine fields surrounding the building. While this would offer a great deal of protection, it would also greatly inhibit the President's ability to perform his duties. His effectiveness as a world leader would be greatly inhibited, if not eliminated. This could produce the very effect desired by those who would threaten him.

For most people it is not a question of which end of the continuum is correct for them. Rather, the determination to be made is where on the continuum will they exist? What amount of risk are they willing to assume in exchange for the measure of convenience? What is the cost-to-benefit ratio?

As a personal protection specialist, it is important to remember that the person being protected will make this determination for himself. The job of the protector is to assist by evaluating the threat and offering alternatives that provide adequate security while minimizing the inhibitions to the protected's life-style.

A story concerning Charles DeGaulle is a good example of this point. As the story goes, Charles DeGaulle was responding to suggestions from his security chief. The chief had outlined a response plan for threats that had been made against DeGaulle. The security chief suggested that DeGaulle not go to a public meeting for which he was scheduled, as the threat was too great. Mr. DeGaulle's response was something to the effect that—"It is my job to be DeGaulle. It is your job to protect DeGaulle." In other words, his job was to be the elected head of state for France. The job of the security was to protect the head of state while he conducted the business of state. If Charles DeGaulle had to cease doing what heads of state do, then the security chief had failed in his mission.

The purpose of a threat assessment is to determine what risks exist and to separate serious from non-serious risks. In this manner, we can develop plans that will avoid some of the risks, and we can determine how much of our resources to deploy against the threats that cannot be eliminated. Thus, we do not over-react or under-react. Over-reaction and under-reaction are almost invariably the result of knee-jerk responses. They come from a lack of planning; a failure to anticipate and prepare for an event. The inability to predict the future contributes to risk. Risk exists where the future is unknown.

Essentially, threat assessment is a form of planning, and as such it lends itself to systematic analysis. One of the easiest analysis formats to use for this purpose is the process of problem solving. The traditional steps in problem solving are as follows:

1. DEFINITION OF PROBLEM
2. IDENTIFICATION OF OPTIONS
3. EVALUATION OF OPTIONS
4. SELECTION OF BEST OPTION
5. IMPLEMENTATION OF SELECTED OPTION
6. EVALUATION OF RESULTS
7. NECESSARY ADJUSTMENTS, IF ANY (REDEFINING PROBLEM)

This chapter will examine each of these steps in more detail; with practical applications to the field of tactical planning.

But, before beginning the actual process of problem solving, it is necessary to determine what you are trying to accomplish. What is the mission? You cannot tell if you are making progress unless you know what you intended to do in the first place.

Most people would recognize that a protection specialist should keep the protected person safe from physical harm, such as assault or assassination. But, is that enough? What about harm from accidents? or illness? What about harassment? Shouldn't the protection specialist consider these as threats from which the principal is to be protected?

In brief terms, the protector should consider as his mission the safeguarding of the principal's *physical well-being, his peace of mind,* and *his privacy.* Anything that intrudes on these factors is worthy of being evaluated as a potential threat.

Now that we have established the mission of personal protection, let's look at problem solving as it relates to that mission.

PROBLEM DEFINITION

The first step in problem solving is problem identification. This is the most critical, and most difficult step in the process. The most frequent reason for poor problem solving is that rather than define the problem, we describe the mess caused by the problem. The real problem is the cause, not the effect. If one identifies what caused the mess, one has identified the problem.

If we determine that anything that intrudes on the principal's physical well-being, peace of mind, or privacy is a threat, it would be easy to conclude that the intrusion itself is the problem. Such is not the case. Actually, whatever causes the intrusion is the real problem, and efforts at elimination or reduction of that cause is the correct response.

For example, if you are protecting a person who must travel to Colombia, there exists a threat to that person's physical well-being and peace of mind. Faulty problem identification might conclude that person's presence in Colombia is the problem. In that case, the solution is not to go to Colombia. Based on the DeGaulle syndrome, your principal may tell you that is unacceptable. Now what? You have a real dilemma.

On the other hand, if you explore the cause of the problem you will find that your principal's presence in Colombia is the effect of the problem, not its cause. If you analyze the threat, and you determine that your principal is at risk because he may become the unwitting victim of the drug-related violence, you can develop plans that minimize the exposure. Perhaps by arranging travel routes that bypass the known areas of concern you can avoid the violence. However, if your analysis determines that your principal is at risk because he is the specific target of threatened violence, or that he fits the profile of past victims, the threat requires a different response. Your plans would be in greater detail, and probably include more resources such as armored vehicles, armed guards, etc.

As can be seen, the identification of the cause of the threat enhances the problem solving process. This type of threat assessment leads to a better probability that the best solution can be found.

IDENTIFICATION OF OPTIONS

Once the problem has been correctly defined, the next step is to identify the possible solutions. This requires that ALL options be included. The tendency in this step is to try to determine the value of each option as you think of it. This should be avoided. It is very difficult for the brain to be involved in two processes at the same time. The activities of creative thinking and evaluation are almost mutually exclusive. Therefore, resist the temptation to evaluate the options at this stage. Keep the creative juices flowing; list every option you can identify, regardless of how ridiculous it may seem. You can always eliminate it later.

An extension of the tendency to evaluate too early is to predetermine that options are unacceptable. In problem solving it is counterproductive to predetermine. You should never say never. This does not mean that all options will be acceptable. It just means that all options should be evaluated. Some options may be unacceptable on the surface, but could be modified and thereby become a valid solution. If you have eliminated this option prematurely you will never know.

A short review of the history of hostage negotiations might help illustrate this point. In the early days of development, many hostage response teams were of the opinion that a static situation should remain static. In other words, if a hostage taker was confined in a building, the response team should not consider meeting the hostage taker's demand for a vehicle. The reasoning was that it was more difficult to control a mobile situation than a static one.

However, further consideration has shown that the granting of a request for a vehicle does not necessarily mean the abdication of control. There are many opportunities to make alterations to the vehicle that would give control to the response team. The vehicle could be equipped with electronic tracking devices for surveillance; listening devices could be placed within the vehicle to allow the response team to overhear conversations; a remote control device could be placed on the ignition of the vehicle so the response team could stop the vehicle whenever desired.

With some thought on the issue it might become advantageous to the response team to grant the demand for a vehicle. They could conceivably improve their control of the situation with careful planning. However, none of these options would be developed if the granting of a vehicle was prematurely eliminated from consideration.

EVALUATION OF OPTIONS

Now that potential options have been identified, it is time to perform an analysis of each option based on a cost to benefit ratio. This means listing the pros and cons of each option. The two questions inherent in this analysis are: Is this option likely to help solve the problem? And what does it cost?

In terms of costs, we are not only talking of dollar costs. "Costs" may also include such things as the loss of technical or strategic advantage in the overall situation; loss of public image for the principal, or his company; legal liabilities for violating laws or regulations governing the particular situation. The list of potential costs depends upon the situation and the options being considered.

For example, assume you work for a multi-national company and one of your company's executives has been kidnapped. The group that is holding this executive makes a ransom demand for one million dollars. One obvious option is to pay the ransom. However, you find that the executive is being held captive in a South American country where the paying of ransom is illegal. Now, the costs of implementing this option not only includes the ransom money, but possible legal implications. In some cases, the government of the country may have the authority to seize the assets of the company for this violation.

Now that the "costs" of this option are known you may want to reconsider using it. That doesn't mean you quit trying to find a solution, it doesn't even mean you don't use this option. It simply means you now have a basis for making an intelligent, informed decision. Having identified potential costs, you now can evaluate this option in comparison to other possible actions.

SELECTION OF THE BEST OPTION

The evaluation of options on a cost-to-benefit ratio should make the selection of the best option easier. When each potential action is reviewed on this basis there is a net gain or loss established. If the costs outweigh the benefits, you have a net loss; if the benefits outweigh the costs, you have a net gain. When the net gain or loss of each option is known, a comparison of each option on this basis should greatly assist the selection process.

As an example, let's assume that the person you are protecting must travel to another city. Based on intelligence you have developed, you determine that it would be best if you could cover this detail with a weapon. However, you are not authorized to carry a weapon in the city of destination. There are several options available to you. You can ignore your intelligence data and go without the weapon. You can carry a weapon illegally. You can ask your principal to delay his trip until you can obtain a gun permit. You can find a local police officer from the city of destination who has personal protection skills and hire him for the detail.

If you ignore your intelligence and go without the weapon, you may risk serious harm to your principal as well as yourself! The only benefit is that the trip doesn't have to be delayed. On a cost-to-benefit ratio, this option has a net loss. Depending on the degree of threat your intelligence has developed, and how credible your source, the net loss may be high or low. It is, nonetheless, a net loss. The risk has not been addressed. If you choose this option you are making a decision to assume the risk.

The decision to carry a weapon without authorization produces the benefit of making the trip on time, and being able to respond to a life-threatening situation with firepower, if necessary. The costs are the risk that you may be arrested and your principal would be embarrassed. If there were an attempt on your principal's life, and you were able to repel the attempt because you were carrying a weapon, this risk may be significantly less than the benefit. There would be a net gain in that case. If you carry the weapon and no attempt is made, and no one discovers you have the weapon, there is no gain or loss. However, there is potential for a net loss if you are discovered and there is no attempt on your principal. Even worse, you may be discovered before the attempt and be unavailable to offer any protection for your principal because you are tied up in legal actions as a result of your violation of the local gun laws.

The choice of delaying the trip until you can obtain the necessary permits to allow you to carry the weapon is, in most instances, not your decision to make. Unless the threat is heavy, and the source of intelligence very credible, this is not a good decision. The significance of the loss is dependent on the reason for the trip. If it is a very important trip then the loss-to-benefit comparison produces a net loss. If the trip can be altered without much difficulty, then there may be a net gain.

In this example, the option to hire a local police officer with protection skills (assuming one is available) produces the best net gain. The trip can be made on time, as scheduled. The necessary weapons(s) can be on-site without risk of violating any laws.

The only costs will be the funds necessary to pay the officer for his time. In some cases the local government may consider your principal of enough importance that they would supply such an officer from their on-duty staff. That makes the net gain even greater.

In any event, this type of selection process is more likely to produce a positive result than selecting an option on face value.

IMPLEMENTATION OF THE SELECTED OPTION

Once an option has been selected, an implementation plan has to be developed. This step can be fairly involved. In some cases, there may be more than one method of implementation; in which case an evaluation of each method should be done. (This is basically the same process as that used to evaluate the option itself.)

Even in a case where there is only one method to implement the option, it usually requires more than a single step to get the job done.

In the case we used for "selection of option" phase it was determined that the hiring of a local police officer might be the best option. Using that example, let's look at some of the logistical issues that must be addressed.

How will you determine whether there is anyone in the city where you are going who can fill your requirements? Does anyone on you detail have professional contacts in this city? Can the local police chief offer any assistance in identifying a member of his department who would be able to fill the detail? There are a number of ways to locate the right individual, but looking in the telephone book under "gun for hire" is not recommended.

After you have selected an officer, there remains the issue of where and when he should meet the detail. Also, where within the detail will he be assigned? To whom will he report? What will his specific responsibilities be? Since he is familiar with the city, you might consider using him as the driver for the principal. Perhaps he can even conduct a basic advance for your detail.

These examples do not constitute a complete list of planning issues, but they represent a sample of the type of thought that must be given to the implementation of your selected option. The better the plans for implementation, the better the results will be. Remember "PROPER PLANNING PREVENTS POOR PERFORMANCE."

EVALUATION OF RESULTS

The evaluation of results not only occurs after the incident is over, but throughout the implementation of the chosen option. During the implementation there should be periodic review to determine if the expected results are occurring. These periodic checkpoints should be programmed into the plan and known to everyone involved in the implementation. This ongoing evaluation provides opportunities for adjustments to the plan, or abandonment of the option if necessary.

Circumstances can occasionally change a situation so that the chosen options does not work as originally planned. Sometimes this can be corrected by altering the plan for implementing the option, and sometimes the option itself must be scrapped. For this reason, it is wise to have a contingency plan.

NECESSARY ADJUSTMENTS, IF ANY

When the ongoing evaluation indicates things are not progressing as anticipated, changes may be necessary. This requires that the problem be redefined, based on the new information. Problem redefinition starts the process of problem solving over again. In this sense, threat assessment is never truly finished. Being involved in personal protection is much like being a dairy farmer: No matter how well you milk your cows today, tomorrow they will have to be milked again.

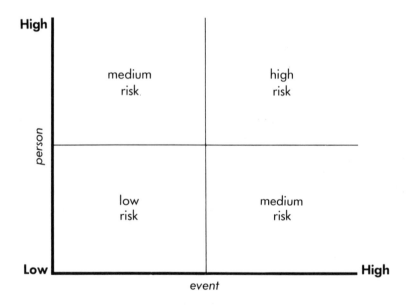

RISK CHART

The analysis of threat should include a combination of the risk attached to the person being protected and the event he or she is attending. An X/Y axis chart can be used to graphically display the threat level.

Example: A controversial, high profile person would rate high on the "X" line. If he/she were attending a low profile, non-controversial event that would rate low on the "Y" line. The juncture of these two lines would occur in the medium risk area of the chart.

TWO

Operational Intelligence: Profiling Your Principal

by H.H.A. Cooper

"Expect no help from your country if you're doing business overseas. You're on your own."

Ross Perot[1]

KNOWLEDGE, as Lord Verulam informed us, is power. All knowledge, even the most trivial, is in some way valuable, but it is pertinent information, in the right hands at the right time that helps to generate the power to appreciate and influence the course of events. One lost in the Sahara may know all about how to construct igloos, fly-cast for trout, or navigate white-water rapids, but the knowledge is of very little use to him unless he has the fortitude, capacity, and means to adapt it to his current predicament. The minds of many of us are cluttered with an extraordinary range of useful as well as useless trivia. There is rarely a shortage of knowledge as such; the trick lies in sorting it all out and putting it to good use.

What is required is a relatively uncomplicated process whereby we can determine quickly and efficiently what we want to know, what knowledge we require to cope with matters in hand, and a method for obtaining and organizing it so that it may be deployed to its best advantage. The methodical approach is not something that comes naturally to many people. More people tend toward the haphazard, the chaotic, even, than the reverse. In the realm of the creative arts, such an approach to life may be permissible and, sometimes, productive of the occasional masterpiece. For most others, a more regulated engagement is essential if what is required of them is to be successfully accomplished and, more-over, accomplished on time.

Becoming proficient in this area takes a lot of hard work. Those who undertake the business of providing personal protection for others need to attain a high degree of organization of their resources in order to be able to operate at peak efficiency. They cannot afford to work on hunches, guess work, or pure luck. They must, accordingly, adopt the right mind-set and train to that end. Here, we shall examine a methodology designed to assist them in their task.

Suppose you were given the job of providing physical security for a certain building. You would hardly gather up the tools of your trade, whatever they might be, or start calling equipment and other suppliers before making an inspection of the property. Common sense dictates such a survey before anything else is done. You might begin such an examination by noting the dimensions of the building; its physical characteristics; its shape and construction. You would remark upon its points of entry and exits. Then, perhaps, you would consider its location, where it is situated, and how that environment might affect your task. You would study the peculiarities of the building and identify those features that might make your job easier or more difficult.

Such an assessment necessarily takes place *before* you begin the installation of whatever you feel is called for by the case. Diagnosis always precedes treatment, even in the most urgent of instances. The importance of the diagnostic procedure, and what is learned from it, is stressed here. It is not something to be undertaken casually or unsystematically. It is all too easy for even the most experienced to omit something of importance in the course of their review; there are always so many distractions.[2] The wise, and the knowledgeable, allow for such contingencies and establish, beforehand, a comprehensive check-list. As each point is given the appropriate consideration, it is marked off, and the action taken, or to be taken with respect to it, noted. In that way, nothing of significance is missed, and the work proceeds smoothly and efficiently.

Does it not make sense, then, to carry out a similar procedure with respect to those human beings whose safety and security become the responsibility of those who have undertaken to protect them? The task of designing the survey—determining what ought to go into it—arranging it and its resultant materials in useful form, may be incomparably more complex than the illustration just given, but it is just as necessary and the methodical approach to what is essayed even more demanding. There are, obviously, many ways in which the assessment of the security needs of a human individual differ from a survey conducted to the same end with respect to a piece of real property.

There are, for example, human sensibilities to take into account as well as the mobility of the human protectee. But the process of evaluation is, essentially, the same in both cases, calling for informed study, the exercise of professional judgment, and the elaboration of some kind of instrument or check-list. It is this latter that will be called, herein, the *protected person profile*, or the *personal protection profile*.

Before turning our attention to the matter of this profile, itself, how to construct it and what ought to go into it, we must first deal with some ancillary issues of the highest importance. The gravity of what is being proposed, here, cannot be overemphasized and not only must the matter be undertaken very seriously, but the responsibilities that arise directly out of the undertaking must be clearly understood and the proper safeguards introduced. No one is, in theory, more capable of doing harm to the protected person, intentionally or otherwise, than the person who undertakes the provision of personal protection. Who, after all, gets closer to the person protected than the bodyguard?[3]

There are questions of extreme sensitivity in all this and we must canvass them forthrightly and with great care. Failure to do so opens up areas of weakness that are the very antithesis of what is comprehended in the provision of protective services. Were they given their druthers, most persons who employ others to protect them would like their bodyguards to know as little about them, their business and intimate affairs as possible. Most settle, prudently, to limiting such knowledge to what they deem necessary so that the job can be done. But, therein lies the rub. Every gap in the knowledge of the person providing protective services represents a potential hazard to the person being protected, a blind spot in the defenses through which an enemy might creep or rush. For how can you, sensibly, guard against a risk if the circumstances likely to give rise to it are deliberately withheld from you? How can you discharge your responsibilities, in the highest degree, if you are kept in the dark about matters pertinent to the exercise of your function.

Additionally, the risk to which you are yourself exposed may be greatly augmented as a result of your being sent "blind" into some dangerous situation because you were not favored with information that would have led you to appraise the hazards on a higher scale and prepare for them accordingly. If you suffer harm, as a consequence, in the performance of your duties, you may have a cause of action against your employer, but before jumping for joy at the prospect, consider the difficulties of bringing and sustaining such an action against one who, doubtless, can afford to hire the best legal talent. Consider, too, the effect this might have upon your career for, unquestionably, in such cases a central issue is likely to be the judgment and competence of the person providing protective services. What might be a useful shield might have a lesser value by way of offense. Do not be propelled into taking precipitate action however angered you might be at what has occurred. Remember: you may be faced with paying the price of having taken bad advice and this could be high.

What we are concerned with here is: What does the person providing protective services really need to know about the person he or she is protecting and that individual's business and personal affairs? The short answer is: everything that has a bearing upon his or her ability to discharge, effectively, the obligations undertaken in this regard. Where these have not been, precisely, spelled out in considerable detail, it may be a most arduous task, in any particular case, to establish exactly what is comprehended within this short answer.

We can readily see that there is, in these matters, a fundamental collision of interests, a contradiction of purpose, within the singular sphere of the protected individual as such. The protected person buys privacy at the expense of his or her own safety and security. There is, of course, no desire to achieve such a contradictory result, or, usually, even any acknowledgment that this is the logical consequence of what is done. Few, indeed, are the protected persons who realize that denial of the fullest information to those rendering protective services on their account can, in the best of cases, jeopardize their interest and, in the worst, have fatal results.

Were they forced to defend their positions, they would doubtless argue that what was concealed by them was simply not the business of the bodyguard to know, that he or she had no need of such intelligence in order to be able to perform the protective tasks they had been hired to undertake. The need to know, in any particular case, is an issue of fact. In some cases, knowing "everything" that can be known about a protected person's life, history, habits, associations, business and pleasure, amounts to nosiness or worse. Moreover, it is conceivable that such extensive, detailed knowledge might, in its own way, be as dangerous as the reverse, of knowing too little about what might be required to do the job. As in most other departments of life, a sensible balance has to be struck. Sometimes, this can be done, delicately, without any direct discussion of the matter at all; an unspoken understanding is arrived at in these matters between agent and principal.

The discretion of the English butler (at least in fiction) is legendary; service is accomplished urbanely, with sensitivity and without articulation of the potentially embarrassing. But, practically, we must recognize that we are living in the age of "Kiss and Tell" books, and few with secrets are desirous of entrusting more of them than necessary to others who, for whatever reasons, might later have occasion to tell—even at the cost of compromising their own security. This is a very human issue, a matter of interpersonal relations, and some people are just better at managing their affairs than others. There is, also, an important question of trust close to the heart of this. Those who truly object to anyone getting really close to them—however sound the reasoning for their reservations—had better not employ bodyguards at all. This is all a little like buying expensive protective clothing, and then not wearing it because you find the perspiration it produces offensive.

Those who provide protective services can expect no help, or even initiative, from others in these matters. They are strictly on their own in an operational sense. They must consider, prudently, what information they need to do the job and how best to set about obtaining and organizing it for their purposes. It is most important that they are cognizant of the associated obligations this imposes upon them. The highest of these, by far, is confidentiality. The information they gather and process could be highly damaging—lethal, even—if it were allowed to pass into the hands of those who might wish to do harm to those they have been engaged to protect. Not only is exceptional sensitivity required of those who collect information about their principals, but they must also exercise the highest degree of care in all aspects of its handling. In particular, such information, in whatever form it is to be found must be stored under the most rigorous of safeguards and access to it strictly controlled at all times.

These responsibilities cannot be overemphasized. The bodyguard's stock-in-trade is the confidence reposed in him or her by the principal or employer. Such persons are made privy to secrets of an extraordinary order because it is felt, wisely or otherwise, that they can be trusted. A breach of that trust is, short of an intentional, murderous assault upon the principal, perhaps the most heinous act that a bodyguard can commit. It destroys the entire basis upon which the protective relationship is built. Even an unintentional lapse might have devastating results. Trustworthiness is a state of mind, it is a reflection of how the individual views him or herself in relation to others and the responsibilities to which those relationships give rise. There is no place in the rational scheme of things for the untrustworthy bodyguard; it is, indeed, a contradiction in terms.

What follows, then, is based upon assumption of trustworthiness in the persons to whom this instruction is addressed and a proper awareness on their part of the obligations generated by the trust reposed in them. Without these elements and understandings, the advice given in these matters would be as irresponsible as allowing scientists unrestricted license in the creation of weapons of mass destruction. There is an underlying consideration of professional ethics that is a necessary preliminary to any discussion of these matters and no apology is made for raising and stressing it in this place. Information in the wrong hands can kill as surely as any firearm or edged weapon. How these arrangements for the secure custody of the information comprised in the protected person profile are developed and put into effect will vary according to the organization of the provision of protective services in each case.

Protective organizations range from a one man or woman operation on an occasional or as needed basis to a complicated, multi-person department with specialist assignments and a wide spectrum of personnel options. It is recommended, in every case, that the protected person profile be closely held by the person in overall charge of the protective services operation, whatever his or her designation or operational responsibilities. That person will then utilize the information and issue instructions on the basis of it, without revealing its existence, content, or physical whereabouts. In a very real sense, the information represents or stands for the person to whom it refers and it must, accordingly, be given the same degree of protection, however different the nature of those safeguards, as the human being in the case.

One more counsel of caution is extended here on these matters. Ideally, some secrets ought not to be committed to any form of permanent or quasi-permanent storage arrangements at all. This is widely recognized by those familiar with the problems of securing high-grade operational intelligence.[4] In theory, an exceptionally talented individual with eidetic capabilities of an extraordinary order, might construct, mentally, a perfectly fashioned profile of his or her principal, adding to its portfolio of information as required and abstracting from it whatever might be operationally necessary to handle the business of the moment. Such a remarkable individual would hardly stand in need of the modest counsels offered here. Nor would he or she be likely to be found for long among the ranks of those providing protective services; a more profitable engagement of such remarkable qualities would obviously suggest itself ere long.

Those of lesser ability can, nevertheless, take counsel from the example of such impossible paragons. There are some things which the wise bodyguard keeps in his or her head and does not confide to paper. He or she may even have to affect not to have knowledge of what is known. These delicate dissimulations call not only for superlative feats of memory, but also for a certain taciturnity of disposition that may be somewhat unnatural and hard to attain for some. Some information is so sensitive that it can only be safely retained in the human memory of those to whom it has been entrusted. And it is only safe so long as those persons remain tight-lipped about what they know. What follows is hard to counsel, but it is vital to the success of the process. It is the only basis upon which trust can be established. If once that trust is abused, it is doubtful if it can ever be restored. As a cornerstone, therefore, we must insist upon the following: THERE MUST BE NO LEAKS.

The professional life of the bodyguard depends upon the strictest adherence to this principle. The point should be made, here, that *all* information of the kind contemplated in connection with the construction of a protected person profile must be regarded as sensitive. It is just that some items are incomparably more sensitive than others. *All* the information compiled needs to be carefully guarded, but some of it needs to be more jealously guarded than the rest. The question is left, then, with respect to the bulk of the information we shall be discussing, as to the form to which it shall be reduced and the safeguards on its storage and handling having regard to the operational purposes for which it is required.

Traditionally, important information has been reduced to writing of some kind; for the sake of clarity and ease of reference, it is usually typed up and filed in some sort of respository from which it can be retrieved as required. In organizations that deal in large quantities of information to which many persons have access in different degrees, some sort of central registry is established to control the flow of items into and out of the system and to provide the necessary safeguards. In smaller organizations, less formal arrangements are set up to serve similar ends. There are always certain basic needs which have to be met. Information, important enough to be saved, needs to be organized into a convenient form for future reference and when these arrangements are decided upon, a means must be established whereby selected items can be retrieved for use as required.

Nothing is so useless as information that cannot be found when it is needed. The personal protection profile is a particular arrangement of sensitive information relating to a certain individual. It is designed for ease of reference and to facilitate operation. This is a utilitarian instrument having purely practical purposes. It is used to help get the job done more efficiently. In our times, more and more information systems of all kinds have been computerized. Information formerly held in files or dossiers is now stored on tape, disks, or diskettes and is accessed by persons working at stations or terminals often remote from the place where the information is physically stored. Although EDP operations have been provided with specialized security features of varying levels of sophistication and efficacy, they remain fundamentally susceptible to penetration and the loss of vital, highly secret information.[5]

No EDP system is completely secure, but some are manifestly less secure than others. The integrity of any system can be compromised. Every security measure reduces, in some way, the utility of the system to those who legitimately operate it. There is a clear parallel, here, with those measures with which those who provide personal protection are more familiar. There have, in recent years, been spectacular penetrations of even some of the most highly protected EDP systems so that it is not unreasonable to say that entrusting very sensitive secrets, indiscriminately, to a computer is an irresponsible exercise of the functions of the person to whom such information was confided. Secrets can even be stolen from a computer without it becoming apparent that there has been any unauthorized intrusion or loss.

It is most strongly recommended, therefore, that the personal protection profile not be confided in whole or in part, to a computer, even if the information it contains is encrypted, and that only a single copy be in existence and that under the personal custodianship at all times of the person entrusted with holding and managing it operationally. These are not responsibilities that can be safely delegated to others. In particular, there should be no secretarial or clerical intervention in these matters. Remember always: a secret shared is a secret lost.

Information, for the purposes of constructing the personal protection profile, is procured through observation or inquiry. The provider of protective services should ever be alert for information affecting his or her charges. People with mutual or interacting interests tend to gossip about matters of common concern.[6] The astute operator will assiduously collect all such information, evaluating it, discarding the trivial and unreliable, and storing the remainder. The trick of course, is to obtain it as cheaply—and pleasantly—as possible, that is, without giving away valuable information of one's own or acquiring the unsavory reputation of being an uncontrolled gossip oneself. Acquiring information in this way is an art in itself and some persons exhibit greater skills in these matters than others.[7] Information, of all kinds, may be raw or processed. Very little information coming the way of those who provide protective services is completely raw; at best, it will be part processed. Only that which comes from original, personal observation will be untainted by the efforts of others to shape it and give it form. Most information, then, whether from government or private sources, will be processed, altered by the subtle chemistry of opinion and commentary which molds it into a distinctive, meaningful product of someone's intellect and industry.

When, for example, we read a guide book to a foreign country, we may be rightly impressed with how much information it contains, how helpful its contents are in orienting the intending traveler and appraising him or her of what to expect. Yet, such a compilation is never free from bias. Someone has made selections as to what to include and what to leave out. Such decisions are important parts of the processing. Personal preferences abound, and sometimes deform the content. The wise user takes all this into account and utilizes the guide accordingly, supplementing its instruction with other information gleaned from sources that serve as counterweight or as a check upon its accuracy.

Before any information is incorporated into the personal protection profile its reliability should be rated. A simple system, on a scale, say, of one to five, is convenient and provides an accurate enough guide. Perhaps the most important element in such an evaluation is the source from which the information in question is derived.[8] Does this represent a proven record of reliability in these matters? Can it be expected, in the nature of things, to have direct knowledge of the matter in question? Most important of all, is it truly impartial or does it have some axe to grind in the matter? It must be suspected that all official information is in some way affected by considerations of policy; even to the point where it might be deliberately adulterated or concealed as to keep it out of reach of even friendly hands.

The information gatherer must be constantly on the alert against the possibility of being deliberately misinformed. Many possible scenarios suggest themselves in the context of the present subject. Someone anxious to prevent a certain protected person from traveling to some place or another might well broadcast alarming news of an extraordinary danger designed to alter that person's plans or otherwise diminish the quality of the trip in a significant fashion. False reports of a particular threat may be circulated so as to divert attention from another, real, hidden menace directed at the target from some other quarter. All information of this kind has to be taken, prudently, into consideration, but clearly, some items require more expert evaluation than others. Knowing when—and how—to seek such advice is an art in itself and one which is less common than might be supposed.

The true value of all information is determined by the uses to which it can be put. Information which is not usable, for whatever reason, has merely a curiosity value. Information of all kinds can be used positively or negatively; in other terms, for offensive purposes, to strike out or to shield. Examples of these different usages readily suggest themselves. If you have information that a particular person intends some definite harm to your principals, you can use that information to denounce that person to the authorities thus making a positive move to forestall the anticipated attack. On the other hand, the same information can be employed defensively so as to orient measures designed to avoid or frustrate the harm from the source from which it is apprehended.

The choices relative to the different uses to which information may be put are ruled by a number of factors. It may be that the information, while not sufficiently certain or strong to allow for positive action to be taken against the person or persons suggested by it, is yet of enough value to urge protective measures, which might usefully be undertaken. In other cases, the paramount need not to expose the source of the information limits or inhibits the use which can be made of it. Other kinds of information, which may be included in the personal protection profile have a more benign application, being of a character that simply allows the person providing protective services to acquire a better overall understanding of his or her principal so as to be able to anticipate and meet specific needs and contingencies.

An example will make clear not merely the utility but the necessity from a protective standpoint of knowing certain things. Suppose the protected person expresses a desire to dine at a certain restaurant, which to the prudent, informed professional seems to pose higher than ordinary security risks for the individual concerned. Knowing that individual's personal preferences and the grounds upon which the choice of restaurant was made may allow the person providing protective services to suggest an acceptable, less problematical alternative or, if such a course is not possible, to take whatever steps might be necessary to guard, adequately, against the apprehended hazards. The information critical to the protective function in this case is related to the principal and his or her style, peculiarities, likes and dislikes rather than knowledge, direct or indirect, of any presumptive harm directed at the principal from some quarter. Seen in isolation, information of this kind can border on the trivial and its relevance is rarely in immediate evidence, but in practice it is often of inestimable value in orienting or strengthening protective measures which need to be undertaken or introduced.

Most of those regularly employed in the provision of protective services engage, almost as a matter of course, in the acquisition and utilization of information of this sort. They could hardly function effectively without so doing. What the personal protection profile does is to formalize the process of organization, retention, and utilization of this kind of information. Those who provide personal protection may well have, during the course of their service, many frank, casual conversations with their charges in which much useful, revealing information may be unguardedly imparted, the value of which, operationally, may not be apparent at the time.[9] Such nuggets should be carefully appraised and, where advisable, stored for future reference. The personal protection profile is a useful framework within which such information may be retained until it might prove operationally advantageous to employ it.

During the United States' presidential election campaign of 1988, the voting public (and other interested parties) were treated to much talk about 'facts.' It was drawn to our attention, courtesy of Mark Twain, that facts are stubborn things. It did not take the astute and verbally sophisticated long to realize that what were being paraded as straight 'facts' by all the candidates were really interpretations of those 'facts,' interpretations that lent themselves, in some cases, to the grossest of distortions of the underlying factual material, the impact of which is, itself, a fact capable of being felt and appreciated, for many years to come.

In truth, raw intelligence, the 'facts' in their purest form, is rarely of much immediate use for operational purposes. Only after it has been evaluated and its significance appropriately measured, can it be usefully applied to the matter in hand. This process, obviously, lends itself to deliberate manipulation by interested parties, a 'spin' as we became accustomed to saying, is applied to the 'facts' so that their appearance and meaning are intentionally altered. There are clear implications for the provision of protective services. At worst, the manipulation of 'facts' can become outright disinformation. The applications to the matter in hand are manifold. Threats can be manufactured, threat levels invented. Situations requiring some sort of protective response or avoidance are suggested with the intent to divert attention or resources, or alter the course of prospective action; the possibilities are endless for such mischief. We must note, also, the phenomenon of self-deception at work here. People most often believe that which they earnestly desire to believe.[10]

Perception passes itself off as fact. The trick for those interested in inducing the condition is to learn the mechanisms by which such results can be obtained. Those who use information to orient their operational needs in the field of protective services must be ever on guard against drawing or being led to draw the wrong conclusions from what they learn. It is often said that if it has feathers and a bill, walks like a duck, swims like a duck, and quacks, it may well be a duck: (other commentators may be inclined to ascribe an even higher degree of certainty to the conclusion offered). On the other hand, it is always wise, where matters of life and death turn upon the answer, to provide against the possibility—however remote—that it might not, after all, be a duck. Among those whose training has not been in the discipline of formal logic (obviously, the vast majority of mankind) there is a tendency to reason over-generously from given premises.

People tend to draw firm conclusions unwarranted by the weight of the evidence. This is particularly the case where the information is of a general character or has become uncritically sanctified through repeated usage, especially by those regarded as "authorities" in the field. It is not difficult to find examples to demonstrate such tendencies. A personal protection specialist might reason: Libya has been known to support terrorism. Therefore, Libyans are terrorists and any dealings my principal might have with them are dangerous. Clearly, such a wide proscription approaches the absurd. Yet, in practice, such faulty reasoning is not uncommon. One can reach a conclusion, seen to be correct in the event, by a wholly erroneous process of reasoning or even by no reasoning at all.[11]

Being right in the result does not validate *ex post facto* the process used in arriving at the conclusion. The lesson of all this is that it is unhelpful and even dangerous in some cases to collect facts indiscriminately and without the capacity to make intelligent use of them. Misinterpreting facts, seeing them in the wrong light, can lead to their being acted upon operationally in ways harmful to the interest of those affected.

A profile is an outline composed of those elements by which a particular individual may be recognized and, to a greater or lesser extent, understood. It may be crudely drawn, in bold, slashing strokes so as to give prominence only to the most distinctive or obvious features; the imagination is left to do the rest after the criteria for recognition have been established. Some profiles are finely etched in great detail so that every facet of the individual so represented is laid out for inspection. A profile ought not to be an exhaustive character study. Brevity, economy of line, is always implicit in the exercise. The utility of the exercise is impaired as the profile becomes enlarged to resemble a dossier.

In its simplest form, the profile addresses the question: what is this person really like? The personal protection profile is more exactly oriented to answer the question: what problems are inherent in the task of protecting this person? In another sense, a profile may be seen as a framework in which relevant data is inserted so as to build up a composite. On such a view, the arrangement becomes all important. If things are assembled incongruously, the ultimate construct will not be recognizable for what it is supposed to be. A simple profile for an individual might be produced along the following lines: name; age; sex; race; religion; nationality; occupation; civil status. While these details are important, so important, indeed, that they comprise what is required by most passports and other identity documents, they do not even begin to address the concerns of those who would undertake the protection of the individual so described.

This basic framework needs to be extended, the data sets must be more generous, and more carefully arranged before the security needs of the individual in question, both of the moment and prospective, can be assessed. That person is part of a larger universe and any profile that fails to take account of the setting in which the person lives, moves, and acts is inadequate for the purposes of the personal security specialist. The profile is part of a bigger picture. [12] That picture must be carefully surveyed for facts suggestive of potential problems for the individual situated within it. The protected person is an integral part of a certain universe within which he or she resides and security needs are determined by the relationship of the individual to that universe and its elements.

It is convenient to have a mechanism for examining that universe so as to situate the individual recognizably within it. The following, shorthand arrangement is suggested for the purpose.

People
Organizations
Places
Property
Ideas
Time

People are related to other people in a wide variety of ways: by blood; by marriage; by friendship or enmity; by business; by leisure; casually or intimately. Each of these relationships can be, of itself or in conjunction with other factors, a particular security hazard. A dangerous, irregular, amorous liaison; a jealous spouse; an avaricious, unscrupulous business associate; problem children—the list of possibilities is endless.

It is enough to say, here, that what the provider of protective services does not know in this regard can adversely affect his or her professional performance and effectiveness at best while at worst it could lead to a loss of life and a wrecked career. How your protected party is related to the rest of humanity, near and far, is of the utmost professional interest to you. You cannot have too much data on the point.

Organizations are both collections of people and representative entities in their own right. Some organizations are loose and informal whereas others are distinguished by the cohesiveness of their structure. Some are permanent and enduring phenomena, while others are temporary and evanescent. The organizations to which people belong, voluntarily or obligatorily, tell a great deal about them, their characters, connections, aspirations, and problems.

Organizations are the building blocks of society. They carry important information of a political character, of power and hierarchy. Families, clans, tribes, nations, all give individuals a distinctive stamp, conferring benefits, and raising presumptive obligations. Belonging to an unpopular organization can bring predictable hazards. The point need not be labored here, but it is evident that simply being an "American" in the wrong place at the wrong time can, of itself, constitute a notable hazard that must be factored into any protective service program.

Places, again are an important link to the humans who frequent them or who are connected with them in some way. Where people are born, where they live, work, play are all of the highest importance, in assessing personal risk. Some places are dangerous for some persons and not for others. Locations that are comparatively safe at some times, and for some people, take on a dangerous aspect for others according to their relationship to them; it is always the relationship of the person to the place that must be uppermost in the minds of those providing protective services.

Attachment to place whether through abstractions such as nationality, or practicalities such as preference give rise to a host of security considerations. The interaction of place and political considerations is worth pondering. The danger to President Kennedy in traveling to Dallas in 1963 had been correctly assessed and made known to him and to his advisers. The danger suggested special security measures, which were not taken, with fatal results.

Property may be seen as the link binding the human individual to tangibles or intangibles over which he or she would exercise dominion. The notion of property has both legal and practical aspects, but the principal significance of property is economic, a concept which, in turn, generates its own political and sociological dimensions having important implications for the status and security of the individual concerned. Claims to property, its use, distribution, and enjoyment may give rise to competing claims, the resolution or non-resolution of which can have the effect of producing serious problems for the parties in conflict. Property may be of all kinds, slight or substantial, but, by reason of its economic significance, it may be safely assumed that most personal protection needs of the kind treated of in the present work are in some way or another related to problems connected with property.

It is axiomatic that it is the rich and famous who need bodyguards; the security of the unempowered and the less affluent is threatened by entirely different considerations. A lesser man may be taken hostage. He is unlikely, in the full knowledge of his circumstances, to be kidnapped for a money ransom.

Ideas are abstract entities which serve to situate an individual within the world in which he or she moves and dwells. Ideas are the fuel of human society. They help to shape the world as we know it. The ideas to which men and women subscribe have a profound influence upon their lives and activities. Religion and ideology are especially important, and both are important sources of conflict and security problems. The ideas of the influential expose them to personal risk in distinctive ways, especially when these ideas are propagated and promulgated in the political arena.

In an even more direct sense, in the present context, the ideas held by an individual about his or her personal security and what should be done to enhance it can be decisive in providing the framework within which protective services are allowed to operate. Clearly, this is an enormously complex area of engagement, but the personal protection specialist must try to acquire a sound understanding of where his or her charges reside in this great universe of ideas.

Time is the unfolding continuum within which all human and other activity takes place. It determines, for individuals and associations of all kinds, what can and cannot be accomplished within its parameters. Things that may be possible at one time may not at another. How often do we agonize over the imperatives of time! Time is a fierce enemy, especially so for the security professional. Security measures that might prove efficacious were there sufficient time for them, are useless if there is not. We are all, regardless of our station in life, creatures of our time. The good and evil that might befall us is inevitably to be seen against the remorseless backdrop of time against which all our doings are plotted and unfold.

The personal protection specialist is more a prisoner of time than most. In a very real sense he or she mortgages time to the person served. Giving your bodyguard the night off can cost you your life, as witness the tragic fate of Olaf Palme. A fatalist might take the view that when your time is up you are sure to go, as illustrated by the ancient story of death on the road to Damascus. While the Koran tells us that all is in the hands of Allah, we have it on the authority of the Prophet himself that while we should trust in Allah, He enjoins us to tie our camel first.[13]

Bearing in mind the points brought out by the above analysis, a useful framework around which a personal protection profile might be organized is suggested as follows.

Personal History—This segment of the profile should certainly contain all the basic information referred to above, for example, all names by which the person in question is presently known or may have been known in the past[14]; date and place of birth; past and present nationalities; family ties; marital status and history with pertinent dates; places of residence; mother tongue and other languages; honors and distinctions; military service; other public service; occupation and occupational history; title.

A concise note should be made indicating how much of this information concerning the subject is in the public domain and the sources, biographies authorized or otherwise, *Who's Who*' and similar entries[15], periodical publications, etc. from which it was derived. It is useful to establish a discreet means for identifying information from privileged sources.

A physical description, with particular attention to appearance should be essayed here. This exercise is not intended for the purposes of identification, but, rather as a means of evaluating the importance of this factor for security purposes. The impact made upon others by appearance is often overlooked as a factor in security evaluations. To one of anti-semitic predispositions, for example, a certain appearance or mode of speech might well be a catalyst for violence. Public figures often accentuate, for understandable reasons, certain features of their personal appearance, to mark them out from the crowd or to capitalize upon their prominence. It is axiomatic that the easily recognized can, thereby, be the more easily targeted. This is the dilemma of every public figure, one heightened, moreover, by the demands of the activity in which he or she engages.

There is, too, an artificiality about this process which must be recognized; the "real" person may be quite different from the public appearance presented, but it is this which commands the attention, good and bad alike. Other manifestations of appearance are less thoughtfully advanced. A display of patent affluence amid stark poverty, the Marie Antoinette syndrome, can be very dangerous and must be allowed for in designing personal protection programs.[16]

These points are of particular importance for those having protective responsibilities for persons in the entertainment field. Sometimes, a business or economic interest is served by cultivating a certain strangeness of appearance rather than courting popularity, but security problems may be an unwanted by-product.

Personality is scarcely less important than appearance from the perspective of those providing protective services. A certain kind of personality—abrasive, combative, contentious—tends to attract trouble in the exercise of whatever is undertaken. Success and trouble are not necessarily mutually exclusive, and such people are sometimes enormously successful notwithstanding their confrontational style, sometimes indeed on account of it; they are simply able, for the most part, to overcome opposition by the sheer force of their personalities.[17]

A sincere, objective appraisal of these qualities must be undertaken by the personal protection specialist. If the person protected is inclined to make enemies by reason of his or her personality and the impact of it upon others, it is as well to know and allow for this in advance. If your principal lives by the Law of the Jungle and aspires to be a King of the Beasts, you must adapt yourself and your methods to the dictates of the situation. Personality traits must be carefully considered and detachedly described. You do not have to like or admire people to be able to work for them efficiently, But you do need an unusual degree of detachment to be able to describe them fairly and in useful, professional terms.

It is here that an ample, exact vocabulary comes in handy, for the task is, perhaps best undertaken adjectivally. Make a list of those adjectives that you feel best describe the impressions your principal makes upon you and others: mean; forceful; domineering; kind; thoughtful; penetrating; persuasive, etc. Do not try to establish some preconceived image or frame into which to insert the person, but, instead, allow a free flow of associations to develop so that a picture of the person starts to emerge of its own accord. When this is reasonably well developed, it should be dispassionately examined to see what security problems are suggested by it.

Attitudes and **beliefs** are important components of any personal protection profile. These are the ideological flag under which the individual travels through life. An attitude is a position or stance assumed by a person towards all matters that may affect him or her in any department of life. It may be principled or otherwise, rational or otherwise; many attitudes can be determinative of the way certain matters are handled in the security area but, perhaps even more important here, attitudes can generate security problems. An indifferent or callous attitude toward others can produce unfavorable reactions.

Prejudices are particularly dangerous attitudes, for they are often deeply ingrained and, as the name implies, have a core of opposition, which stems from prejudging someone or something to their disadvantage.[18] Antagonistic attitudes can give rise to their mirror image. A protected figure can have a bad attitude towards personal security generally, defying risk and eschewing measures designed to improve margins of personal safety. Attitudes generally manifest themselves in terms of behavior that requires cautious, skilled interpretation: what, for example, is betokened by a strong silence?

The attentive provider of protective services will carefully watch and catalogue his or her principal's attitudes as they are exhibited in the ordinary course and will allow for them accordingly. This is more than simply watching out for likes and dislikes, approval or disapproval. It involves managing them from a security perspective so as to reduce or eliminate the special hazards they might generate. Perhaps the most difficult person to protect is one who is insensitive. The provider of protective services must make up for the deficiency, as non-judgmentally as possible.

Beliefs are opinions or conviction, and are often the raw material out of which attitudes are fashioned: I can't stand the English (attitude), they are always so God-damned self-assured (belief). While belief systems in general are relevant subjects for consideration in the present context, it is those beliefs that bear most directly upon personal safety that are of immediate concern. A principal, for example, may believe him or herself to be in no danger and, accordingly, take the attitude that security measures are superfluous. Continued survival may well depend upon such a belief being correctly founded. Problems arise when strongly held, personal beliefs of this kind clash with the contra-indications of professional advisors.

Those who do not believe in the efficacy, desirability, or necessity for measures of personal protection in their particular case are very difficult to serve; every day that passes without incident tends to reinforce them in their own beliefs. Such beliefs are a cruel kind of handicap for the provider of protective services. It is generally a waste of time for the provider of protective services to try radically to modify the attitudes and beliefs of his or her masters; those who try too seriously are likely to find themselves out of a job!

Attitudes and beliefs held by those who are served can never be ignored. The extent to which they need to be taken into account will vary from case to case and situation to situation. In any event, the clearest picture of the more enduring ones should be quickly developed for operational use.

A special kind or category of beliefs that must always be taken specifically into account by those providing protective services are the personal *preferences* of the principal. Indeed, it is not too strong to say that these are ignored at your peril! Preferences may range from modes of address through all kinds of complicated arrangements and transactions. Careful attention must be paid to those having security implications, especially knowledge of them that may be in the public domain. Preferences are often a kind of habit, and are usually designed to serve some aspect of assumed self-interest, such as a seating preference in a theater or restaurant.

People tend to prefer that which they believe best serves them in some way or another and which experience suggests as giving them a certain measure of satisfaction. Thus, people take preferred routes to work, plan their activities to a preferred schedule, and generally select, where they have any choice in the matter, some things over others (soft centers over hard in the box of candy). We do not always exercise wise choices and some of our preferences may not be good for us. Choice brings into play a competition of possibilities.

From a security perspective, we must again take the jaundiced view, for the exercise of a preference, without due consideration for the security implications may be a very dangerous thing. Forming a catalogue of the principal's common preferences, with some indication of their respective strengths and the frequency with which they are exercised is a very necessary undertaking. The personal protection specialist who is familiar with his or her principal's preferences can weigh, professionally, the consequences of their exercise and if he or she is unable to intervene in the matter, it may yet be possible to take into account the effect of such preferences given the security situation. If your principal *must* stay in the penthouse suite, you can, at least, do whatever may be necessary to ensure a smooth and safe evacuation should this be forced upon you.

Like preferences, *peculiarities* can pose security problems unique to the individual concerned. A peculiarity, in the sense the term is used here, is any distinctive, personal characteristic which is an obvious, though not necessarily marked, variance with the norm. It may be a mode of speech, behavior or appearance. We all have our little peculiarities (eccentricity is not the exclusive prerogative of any particular class), but for the most of us, these are inconsequential. For the Rich and Famous they can become a definite security hazard and a particular nightmare for those providing protective services.

Peculiarities range from the quaint and endearing to the bizarre and embarrassing. Their variety and potential are endless. It is an important part of the duty of those providing protective services to see that their charges are not embarrassed or ridiculed, the more especially so on account of any personal peculiarities they may consciously or otherwise exhibit where this might expose them to danger. The peculiarities of your principal may cause him or her to make fools of themselves in public and that is clearly their prerogative. It becomes *your* responsibility when these peculiarities translate into foreseeable harm: if your principal insists on wearing cowboy boots while visiting the mosque, you had better have a fast getaway car nearby and protected routes to it and away from the scene.

Peculiarities may revolve around behavior or beliefs. Your principal may be an ardent devotee of astrology, prone to cancel carefully advanced trips on consulting the heavenly portents, at a moment's notice, leaving no time for alternative arrangements of equal quality from a security standpoint. Knowing these peculiarities allows for anticipation. The public idol who insists upon exhibiting his or her feet of clay may need special, sensitive protection while this endeavor is in progress. Again, peculiarities must be accepted, objectively, for what they are. The personal protection specialist ought not to sit in judgment on his or her principal's peculiarities, but he or she does need advance warning of their manifestation if the right course of action in the security field is to be taken.

The personal protection specialist should be thoroughly familiar, so far as is prudently possible, with his or her principal's *personal health* and any security problems to which this might give rise. It need hardly be stressed here that this is a most sensitive area of responsibility and nothing should be done even to hint of health problems to outsiders e.g. my principal needs plenty of fresh air as he has a breathing problem. Many persons are understandably unwilling to admit to disabilities or infirmities, however slight, in stressful business or social situations and the knowledge of them in the care of the provider of protective services may tactfully be used to guard against over exertion or situations posing a security hazard. A record of all medications ordinarily taken should be included in the personal protection profile, as well as a note of any special requirements for such life-threatening conditions as allergies of certain kinds.

The provider of protective services should endeavor to be on familiar terms with the principal's health care professionals and should try to coordinate the appropriate aspects of his or her own work with theirs. The personal protection profile should also contain a note of those persons who are to be immediately contacted in the event of a serious emergency involving the health of the principal and who can act in his or her stead in case of incapacitation of any kind.

Life-style is another important item requiring definition and inclusion in the personal protection profile. A reclusive principal may not be much fun, but such a life-style does tend to pose fewer challenges for those who provide protective services. An active life-style calls for matching qualities on the part of the personal protection specialist. If the principal likes to go for long, early morning horseback rides, the personal protection specialist had better be a competent equestrian as well as able to discharge his or her primary duties from the saddle. Showing the appropriate degree of enthusiasm for the task is also desirable if the principal is to be kept happy.

Some principals are workaholics, regularly spending incredibly long hours on the job—and expecting the same of their employees. Others would rather play than work and their recreational activities assume a major importance in the make-up of their life-style. They are great socializers, gregarious, party-loving, with all that implies in terms of mischievous possibilities, and incidental security problems. Some have a life-style that is in conformity with their affluence, while others, no less wealthy, maintain an almost miserly existence. There are those who live in opulence in a multiplicity of different dwellings around the world while others who could certainly afford to emulate such indulgences live in modest surroundings with little or no advertisement. The elements of these diverse life-styles as they are encountered in fact must be carefully catalogued on the personal protection profile in a way that enables their implications from a security perspective to be assessed and taken into account operationally.

A mobile life-style, with a principal constantly on the move will demand different skills and resources from the provider of protective services than will a relatively static one. A high-profile life-style carries with it risks that the seeker of anonymity need hardly contemplate.

Akin to life-style, indeed, an integral part of it, are *activities*. What does the principal do? How does he spend his waking hours—and nights? Broadly, activities may be divided for our purposes here into two classes: work and play. The personal protection specialist must be prepared to cover both, although there may be an attempt (always unwise, but understandable) to exclude him or her, professionally, from the latter. From the perspective of personal safety, some activities are clearly more dangerous than others. Any illicit or irregular liaison is always a special security hazard. Those with amorous or romantic undertones or implications are, perhaps, the most hazardous of all. The Nora Astorga solution[19] may always await the over-confident or the unwary. The defense against the vulnerability of the boudoir is all too often denial, an unfortunate reaction offering no protection at all.

Travel, especially to foreign, unfamiliar places presents a variety of problems for those providing protective services. Frequency of travel (jet lag, adequacy of advance arrangements, availability of services and personnel); style (discreet, notorious, ostentatious, etc.); activities *en route* and at destination; type of accommodations and services utilized abroad, form a complex pattern that needs to be recorded in its specifics and profiled for the purposes of the personal protection implications.

Protective services, although provided routinely, must always be designed with special situations in mind. Playing a round of golf, for example, may be just what the doctor ordered, but not if the golfer might be ambushed on the green. Messing about in boats is very pleasurable, but those who provide protective services need special knowledge and the means to apply it if the experience is to serve its intended purposes and not those of persons who would harm the principal.[20] An activity profile is almost an end in itself and it will amply repay, operationally, the time and care bestowed on its construction.

Associations constitute the final segment of the personal protection profile but this assignment by no means signifies the order of importance attaching to this component. While the personal protection specialist will obviously seek to avert harm to his or her principal proceeding from acts of nature, so far as this is humanly possible, the prime source of danger lies in association with other human beings. The provider of protective services should try to apprise him or herself of the security implications for the principal of all human contacts, transitory or extended, distant or intimate, business or social. The nature and meaning of each known or projected association must be carefully considered: does it have security implications for the principal? An encounter with an unfriendly business rival may not lead to an altercation or physical violence, but it can be embarrassing or give rise to a health problem in a susceptible individual.

There are delicate shades of risk to be measured and appreciated in all associations with other human beings. The closest, and potentially the most dangerous association of all is between the protected person and those whose obligation it is to protect him or her. The personal protection profile should contain a careful note of all who have served in a protective capacity in the past, the circumstances of their leaving their position, and their present situation. From a security point of view, all associations may be significant, past, present, and prospective. It is all too easy to ignore or overlook the seeds of harm that may have been planted in the past. All of us can number among those with whom we associate or have associated, the friendly, the not so friendly, as well as the vast mass of the indifferent. Those important or exposed enough to require personal protection for themselves and their intimates can be expected to have more than their fair share of enemies.

The personal protection profile should contain something in the nature of an 'enemies list', giving specifics where appropriate, or general indications where the animosity is diffused among as yet unidentified subjects. While cleaving to the fundamentals of brevity, this section should be thorough and comprehensive, giving indicia that can be followed up as necessary, e.g. X, bankrupt former partner, disappointed in law-suit, made certain threats on such and such a date. The arrangement of the data will be suggested by its amount and currency. Associates may perhaps, most conveniently be divided into categories, ranging from those closest to the principal, to those of a more remote and casual kind. Harm may come from any quarter, but those who are closest obviously have greater opportunity for exercising any malevolence they may harbor than those whose contacts are less frequent and hedged about by formalities and other restrictions.

The Golden Rule is: only those can count themselves totally secure whom no one wishes to harm. The profile should be constructed to show those who *might* wish to do some harm to the principal, and an appreciation of their respective opportunities for accomplishing their purposes.

In a very real sense, the personal protection profile is always provisional, never complete. New information is constantly being penciled in while the old is reviewed and revised as required. Yet it should never be overlooked that the objective is, operationally, to produce a useful, recognizable outline rather than a burdensome, comprehensive dossier. The project should never become over-ambitious in scope, an all-consuming end in itself, absorbing too great a portion of the time and energies of those engaged in it. Ideally, the profile should provide a sharp-edged picture that can be carried in the mind's eye of the personal protection specialist going about his or her daily tasks. It is a sort of *aide memoire* to orient what has to be done to keep the principal free from harm, annoyance, or inconvenience.

The personal protection profile is a *point of reference* rather than a *work of reference*, and this distinction should be clearly understood. It should be nicely balanced, well-rounded so that the principal can be properly seen from every angle. It should never be one-dimensional, but, rather, resemble the human individual to whom it refers. This means that as the subject changes, takes on other aspects and tints from his or her context so too, over time, does the profile and the way the needs of the subject require to be seen from a security perspective. Change, can, sometimes, be very abrupt; the subject can go from low to high-profile overnight. Withal, the personal protection profile is a working tool, a means by which information and analysis is organized so as to enable those who provide protective services to do their job to the best of their ability.

Perhaps the greatest value lies in the process itself, the putting together of the personal protection profile and the discipline this imposes upon those who engage in it. It is an intellectual exercise of great power and portent. It forces those who do the job to look at it and what they know that will assist them in doing it in a thoroughly systematic way. The pattern of their own professional thinking becomes impressed with the process in which they engage so that they carry with them, at all times, an image of the composite their endeavors have fashioned. The personal protection profile remains a permanent record of the process and a necessary operational instrument in its own right while the hard work that has gone into its making lives on in the skills' enhancement it has engendered. It thereby serves a dual operational function of actually increasing the store of relevant knowledge and providing a sound basis for its useful employment.

NOTES

[1] *U.S. News and World Report,* June 20, 1988, page 28.

[2] "The unprepared mind plays tricks on itself." New Rules, Daniel Yankelovich, New York: Random House, (1981), page 189.

[3] "To protect you I can't be limited to just a few hours. I must be with you and next to you as often as needed during the day, the evening or at night." *The Devil Tree,* Jerzy Kosinski, New York: Harcourt Brace Jovanovich, (1973), page 188.

[4] "The first rule in keeping secrets is nothing on paper: paper can be lost or stolen or simply inherited by the wrong people; if you really want to keep something secret, don't write it down." *The Man Who Kept the Secrets: Richard Helms and the CIA,* Thomas Powers, New York: Alfred A. Knopf, (1979), page 130.

[5] On this, see, "Electronic Moles and Their Trojan Cousins", H.H.A. Cooper and Lawrence J. Redlinger, 3 *Competitive Intelligencer,* Num. 2, August 1988, pages 1-12.

[6] ". . . information is a commodity which can be traded." *Colonel Z,* Anthony Read and David Fisher, New York: Viking, (1985), page 122.

[7] Those for whom the exercise is unfamiliar would do well to begin their education with the excellent work *Office Politics,* Marilyn Moats Kennedy, Chicago, IL: Follett, (1980).

[8] "The single most important thing about any piece of information is where it came from." *The Amateur,* Robert Littell, New York: Simon and Schuster, (1981), page 133.

[9] It has been sagely observed that ". . . powerful people are seldom good at keeping secrets." *Power! How to Get It, How to Use It,* Michael Korda, New York: Random House, (1975), page 27. The same author offers the perceptive advice that ". . . it is important to give up the self-indulgent habit of talking about oneself." id. page 259.

[10] "When a woman commits an act of violence—especially against those she is assumed to love and expected to nurture—she upsets our deepest notions of sexual and social order." *Wild Justice,* Susan Jacoby, New York: Harper and Row, (1983), page 186.

[11] "When judges are asked what they would do in a sentencing procedure, their answers do not correspond with what they in fact do." *Influencing Attitudes and Changing Behavior,* Philip G. Zimbardo, Ebbe B. Ebbesen, Christina Maslach, Reading MA: Addison-Wesley, 2nd Edn. (1977), page 88.

[12] For an in-depth review of some of the problems involved from a different perspective, see *Catching Spies,* H.H.A. Cooper and Lawrence J. Redlinger, Boulder, CO: Paladin Press, (1988), pages 71-118, "Backgrounding".

[13] So important has this wise precept always seemed to us that we employed it as a headnote in *Target Terrorism,* Richard W. Kobetz and H.H.A. Cooper, Gaithersburg, MD: International Association of Chiefs of Police, (1978), page 160.

[14] "He had discovered already that a name is a life, which meant that two names were two lives." *A Spy for God,* Pierre Joffroy, New York: Harcourt Brace Jovanovich, (1969), page 19.

[15] It should not be overlooked that many directories publish information provided by the individual to whom it refers and that individual often pays a fee for inclusion in the publication.

[16] "The rich had learned that no good comes from flaunting your good fortune—and much bad." *The Von Bulow Affair,* William Wright, New York: Delacorte Press, (1983), page 50.

[17] Great men are not always wise: neither do the aged understand judgment." *Job,* 32:9.

[18] For some interesting thoughts on this, see *The Robert Half Way to Get Hired in Today's Job Market,* New York: Bantam Books, (1983), pages 52-53. There is a great deal in this book worthy of careful study by the personal protection specialist.

[19] For an interesting security perspective on the late Nora Astorga, U.N. Ambassador of Nicaragua, see "Participation of Women in Terrorist Groups," Deborah M. Galvin, Ph.D., presented at the 11th Annual Meeting of the International Society of Political Psychology, May, 1988.

[20] On this, see "Advanced Protective Program in Baltimore Sails On . ." 5 *Nine Lives Associates Network,* No2, Winter 1988.

THREE

An Introduction to Providing Protective Services

by Robert L. Oatman

THE CONCEPT OF providing protective services has become complex indeed. The challenge of protecting the principal in today's environment involves complex elements not present in prior years. What remains unchanged is the fact that the would be assassin/kidnapper/terrorist/crazy chooses the time, the place and the conditions in which to strike your protectee. In providing protective services there will always remain the human instinct of the Personal Protection Specialist (PPS). There is no machine, no computer and certainly no tool that will accomplish this mission. These highly trained specialists work from instinct. The only way to succeed is to have a solid foundation of training, backed by experience and supported by more training and expertise. So when the time arrives to react, it will become an automatic response.

The United States Secret Service concept of the three rings of defense is called the concentric theory of protection. The inner most ring deals with the personal protection of the principal and the choreography of the protection detail. The second ring deployed can consist of uniformed police officers, standing posts, barriers, etc. The third ring of defense is less visible, i.e., roof top surveillance posts, counter assault teams, perimeter control points, etc.

In providing protective services you must stay at the edge of technology, testing and re-testing sophisticated hardware and electronic systems. This technology can provide a safer environment for your detail. Keeping in mind that technology is only a tool and should never be relied upon to provide the first ring of defense which is, again, human instinct.

As we begin to look at this human dimension and study assassinations or those attempts at such, we need to understand the transition from the one-person assassin to the ever present threat of terrorism. In this profession, you are limited in some respects to a reactive stance since the PPS is dealing with the protectee's life-style, his work environment, and his social norms. All of these pose an every day challenge to protection. As we explore the professional side of this business, we need to understand that knowledge, skills and abilities are all needed to respond to the potential threat.

Therefore no computer, no machine can accomplish this task at this time. The mission of providing protective services is to limit the risk and to prepare a plan of action if that threat occurs. To be effective in this endeavor, an understanding of all facets of protection must be clearly understood by the practitioner.

The concentric ring of protection will never change. We must provide a constant 360-degrees of protection at all times, whether it involves protecting the President of the United States with hundreds of Secret Service agents and police officers, or the opposite end of the security spectrum, one protection specialist. Understanding the objectives and goals of protection will limit your expectations in the dangerous world in which you work.

As in any profession there are terms and definitions an individual should understand and be able to articulate. If you consider the full scope of your protective services mission, the following roster represents a sizeable cross-section of your areas of responsibility and concern:

Risk Assessment
Advance
Security posts
Protective Intelligence
Protecting the Principal/Choreography
Motorcade and Route Security
Ten Minute Medicine
Command post and Security Briefing
Explosive Ordinance and Detection
Self Defense Tactics
Firearms Training and Control
Identification

To understand the overall mission of providing protective services you must identify your objectives.

1. To prevent assassination or intentional injury to the protectee.
2. To prevent kidnapping or your principal from being taken hostage.
3. To prevent unintentional injury to your principal, accidental or otherwise.
4. To prevent a medical injury from becoming more serious, even fatal.
5. To prevent embarrassment to the person you are protecting.

In order to be successful in this mission you must employ good sound reasoning and common sense. You should also consider taking on the role of a potential assassin or kidnapper. When you are able to identify potential weaknesses, your own limitations, it will be the only time you will tighten your security net, possibly avoiding failure. Your basis of knowledge in this arena is the long list of prior assassinations and ongoing attempts that take place each day around the world. There is also a copy cat mentality that exists when these kidnappings/assassinations take place. There is no room for complacency, if your detail consists of more than yourself, it is teamwork which will prove successful. You learn from each other's mistakes so that you and your protectee will not become a statistic for other professionals to examine and critique.

Your first objective then is target hardening. It sends a clear message to your adversary, "We are prepared and we are professional, therefore, move to another target." Time and time again the would-be assassin has moved to a softer target because the PPS has been attentive and professional. A case in point involved Arthur Bremer in Bowie, Maryland on May 15, 1972. His real aim was to assassinate President

Nixon, but he selected Governor Wallace. Was it the look of the agents or the teamwork which thwarted Bremer's plans?

You never know when you have been visited by the would-be assassin. After each detail, it would benefit the team leader to critique the operation and look for the team's vulnerable points, constantly trying to improve upon your mistakes. You will never learn from your success stories only your mistakes. The success of these details hinges on team work and cooperation and leaving your ego at the door.

First, it is essential to dispel the myth of our profession. The word "bodyguard" is an immediate turnoff and invokes the image of a bull in a china shop, where brawn replaces brains and force takes the place of reasoning. You should strive in this field to blend into your environment and not stand out. Many PPS's have been mistaken for the CEO or a rising young executive. Those in the field that project the "bodyguard image" make it difficult for the profession to be taken seriously. Your mannerism, appearance, and overall attitude and sense of mission is the key to your success. If you are working a protectee and you are always told to stay in the car or stand outside you need to take a close look at yourself and ask the tough question, "Is it me?". Corporate executives are now seeing the professional side of protection and are hiring the right look and the right mentality. Finding the right PPS has become a challenge for many personnel directors because of a limited supply of true professionals.

In examining the role of the PPS, other myths need to be dispelled. It is highly unlikely that you will ever have to pull out your gun or drive a car in excess of 100 miles per hour. You may never execute a boot-leg, a J-turn or worry about defusing a bomb. In reviewing many assassinations and attempts, few case examinations have allowed the PPS enough time to get out his or her hand gun and kill the assassin. Professionals must understand and accept firearm's discipline and their role in protective assignments.

Examine the most recent assaults on principal and you will see that the PPS never had a chance to take out his weapon, let alone shoot at his would be attacker. FBI statistics indicate that most police shootings are over within 3 seconds. If you examine the attempted assassination of President Reagan in 1981 outside the Hilton hotel in Washington, DC, Hinkley, fired 6 rounds in less than 2.8 seconds. Not one agent pulled his gun out during the assault. After Secret Service agent Jerry Parr heard the shots he reacted instinctively and put the President into the limo. Agents and police pulled their weapons out after the incident. It is over before you can think to react with a firearm. If you spoke to Parr, he would probably tell you it was instinct and years of experience coupled with training that made him react as he did.

It is this next stage that identifies the true protection specialist. Understanding the considerations if an assault occurs.

1. Arms reach
2. Sound-off
3. Cover
4. Evacuate

For each individual, the first step is a personal choice. Depending upon the size and agility of the PPS, this process of arms reach will be different for each person. If you feel that you can react instantly and be effective then go for it. If you have to think, then in most cases it will be too late. You recognize the assault and by instinct and training you attempt to neutralize the perpetrator.

Sound-off can be difficult, but very effective in alerting the principal of danger and gaining assistance from others on the detail. If you identify the danger and you are able to spot the weapon, calling out the type of weapon and direction will cause alarm to the suspect and locate the threat. A prime example would be the assassin with a knife coming after your principal from the left. You call out, "knife at ten o'clock." This alerts the other team members to move your protectee out of harm's way and alerts others to the location of the assault.

In the next step, you are now in the protective mode of cover. In identifying the threat, if you are in close proximity to the principal, you will move into his body space and use your body to block the assailant. Reaching up to grab the principal by the belt and controlling his movement, at the same time moving him away from the threat. You have simultaneously brought the principal's head down, thus reducing any exposure to a vital area of his body.

Evacuation is the next step in completing your process. Moving your protectee into a safe environment, out of harm's way. You are not in the business of confrontation. Evacuation is your top priority.

If an assailant comes at you with a gun, knife, club, etc., you should always push the weapon down and away. If possible controlling the weapon and disarming the suspect. This gives the principal time to escape to freedom or, in a team situation, it allows the cover agents to move quickly to safety.

The only way to succeed in this business and to live to talk about it is to practice the above considerations over and over again. When the time comes, the PPS will react to instinct and training. During the assault on President Reagan, Jerry Parr did not hesitate but reacted as a true professional. The driver of the Presidential limo reacted to the threat and with the direction of the detail leader, he evacuated his principal to safety. Again, team work cannot be over emphasized.

The next lesson that a PPS must learn in this business of providing protective services is choreography, working the principal. I have always found this job fascinating and enjoy watching other protection details move their principals in and out of cars or into buildings. It is easy to identify those who know the business from their opposites who are an embarrassment to their CEO's. Movements should be executed with ease and blend effectively into the environment in which you work. It involves staying close to the protectee but not becoming an obstacle in his way. A CEO of a Fortune 100 company was asked by his protection specialist how close he should walk to protect him. The CEO responded by stating, "Close enough to protect me, but not close enough to where I have to introduce you to everyone I meet." This should give the PPS an understanding of body space and movement. There are numerous formations that can be used to protect your principal. The box pattern, the diamond, and the modified diamond, for example, have a single objective, to support the concentric theory of protection, providing 360 degrees of constant protection. In the private sector, you normally work by yourself. If you are working the protectee, stay off to his right shoulder in close enough proximity to react accordingly. You must constantly be aware of your surroundings. Ask yourself, "What if this were to happen? What would I do about it?"

In providing protection, you must also remember that this is a service industry. Too many in this field are disappointed because of the demands placed upon them. In many cases, you will be asked to do menial tasks which may be beneath you. Anyone who has survived in this career has taken care of those types of tasks. You are providing a service to the person that you are protecting and many people in this line of work lose track of this requirement. They believe that their sole responsibility is to be a hired gun. That is far from the truth. Your job is to provide a service, whether you wind up walking the dogs or buying theatre tickets. In this type of work you hurry up and wait. You do a lot of standing around. Where PPS personnel make their mistake is that they become complacent because of the routine. Once you have arrived at your destination, you should immediately begin thinking about your next movement. This job can become very boring if you let it. Routine is boring but it is also very dangerous.

Before you enter the field of executive protection you should identify with the type of people you intend to protect. If you don't like kids, stay away from a principal with children. Your very reputation is on the line, if you work for a gangster you will be identified as a gangster. This holds true for any principal, do your homework before you take on the job. Perform a risk assessment and a personal perspective on the principal, his life-style, personality, etc. Keep in mind that you may be with this person 24-hours a day and be involved in his professional career and his leisure activity. You should also understand your limitations. A principal who enjoys the outdoor life, tennis, running, horseback riding, etc., is not going to hire someone who is out of shape. You would not want to work for a CEO who enjoys sailing when you get sea sick and hate the water.

Another concern is the personal life-style of the principal. If he is an alcoholic or a drug abuser, or a child molester. There are numerous horror stories about principals who lead double lives. You must draw the line when it comes to employment. It should be understood prior to taking on a contract that you will not violate the law or allow the law to be broken in your presence. It again falls back on your professionalism. Conduct the proper profile before you accept employment.

Regarding the cost of executive protection, many articles have described it as "exorbitant", "not cost effective", or "only for the rich and famous." Talk to most accountants and they will tell you that it is not cost effective to employ a PPS. However, if the Chairman of the Board of a Fortune 100 company was kidnapped or assassinated, what would be the impact on the company? The stock market? Keeping him safe and getting him to his meeting on time can be shown to be a cost effective program.

The real plus for the principal we protect is our role as facilitators. We are able to get the principal to his/her destination on time and in one piece. Having a PPS with the president of a company allows that person to have peace of mind about his day. He does not have to worry about his safety, his transportation, his accommodations or his space being violated. He has a comfort zone established by the PPS so that he can do what he does best, be an executive and make money and decisions.

Among the most common daily challenges in our profession is the responsibility to prevent embarrassment to our principal. A trained PPS is always cognizant of the press and the public when he is working with a principal. If you have gained the trust and admiration of your protectee, he will take your advice in situations that could be potentially embarrassing. Discretion in today's environment is extremely important to the executive. When you examine the catastrophic consequences of Senator Hart's campaign and the media blitz that destroyed his chances for the Presidency, this point can't be made any clearer. A trained PPS would have recognized the pitfalls and warned the Senator of the dangers. There are many examples that illustrate this point. The black tie affair where a guest has had too much to drink and the VIP is cornered into an embarrassing moment. A pre-arranged signal needs to be worked out beforehand when your principal needs assistance. The PPS can go up to the executive and excuse himself, advising of an emergency call or an important meeting that must be kept. These are the times that make you indispensable to your protectee.

In 1986, Coretta King came to the Towson State University to give a talk to the Student Government Association. Everything was going smoothly because the advance team had done an excellent job laying down the foundation. It was 8:00 P.M. She was taken into the hall for her speech and the lights were dimmed for effect. As she was going up the metal stair and onto the stage, a microphone cord had come unattached on the floor. She came very close to falling. The protection officer who was sitting on stage noticed the cord and very discreetly covered the cord so Mrs. King would not become entangled. This may seem like a very minor problem but it would have been very embarrassing to the principal if she had fallen.

When you begin to examine all of the facets of protection, you realize that this job is not as simple as you first suspected. You are in a constant state of alert, always examining your environment so that you will make the right decision when the time comes. Too many PPS get caught up only in the assassin mentality. Understand the probability of fire, an explosion or, lights going out in a large concert hall which can lead to a mass panic. It will be during these times that you will have to make split second decisions and remove your principal to safety.

To be effective in this line of work you need to have a good all-around personality. You won't survive in this business if you look like you have a chip on your shoulder. I get more accomplished by saying "please" and "thank you" than trying to play hard ball with people. Your personality will be a direct reflection upon your principal as well as the company or agency you represent. You are an ambassador of good will. People in general will do as you ask them but understand not everyone thinks you are as important as you may begin to think you are. Don't unnecessarily put your hands on people, it constitutes assault. You have no authority to push, shove, or man-handle the public. You will cause confrontation, not avoid it.

What constitutes a good personal protection specialist? The following traits should be considered:

Good common sense
Excellent Communicator
Excellent mental and physical health
Team player
Punctual and outgoing
Good sense of humor
Drug and alcohol free
Honesty and integrity
Positive attitude towards the job
Disciplined
Dedicated
Willingness to be further trained

When you look at all of these descriptive phrases, you get a better understanding of the true PPS. Not everyone possesses these attributes but those in the business who are successful certainly have the majority on their side.

It is important to be able to accept criticism when you make mistakes and build upon those lessons for the future.

Before President Reagan received United States Secret Service protection, and while he was campaigning for office, he visited Baltimore County in 1979. The advance motorcade security at the hotel and other arrangements were going as planned with only minor problems. After the President was secured in his room and the various security posts were manned, a briefing was held in the command post to begin the second phase. This entailed a large cocktail party and reception outside the ballroom, then a formal sit down dinner. At the briefing, emphasis was placed on maintaining the protective circle. At 7:30 PM, President Reagan left his suite, protected by PPS's using a modified diamond. The staff had arranged a roped stanchion so that the principal could walk along the path, greeting and signing autographs. Once inside the area, the noise of the guests was so loud that radios were not very useful and so the detail depended on eyesight and signals to keep the detail tight. In crowds such as this, everyone is pushing and shoving in an attempt to get close to your protectee. Four additional protection specialists worked the back of the crowd so that they could move in if an incident occurred. As he walked along, he was very gracious. He signed autographs, shook hands, and was pleased at the enthusiastic response. A young white male with a newspaper folded in his hands was attempting to get close to him without success. At the end of the stanchions, the detail made a turn into a secured area and then into a pre-arranged holding room. The plan of action was once the crowd had cleared and gone to their tables, President Reagan would be taken into the dinner.

When he reached the end of the corner, he was greeted by a small army of photographers. They had set up a press area and he was faced with a barrage of flash bulbs. The detail was completely blinded. Everyone had spots before their eyes and heard loud popping noises going off from the sound of the flash bulbs. When it all stopped, a police sergeant (assigned to the detail) was seen carrying the young man with the newspaper away. The guy's feet were dangling in the air. If he had a gun, there was no way he could have gotten to it since his arms were pinned to his side and the sergeant was controlling his every move. He moved him away from the crowd and he was soon joined by two other officers. The young man told the officers he was unarmed and it was only a folded newspaper. He was bored and wanted to see how close he could get to President Reagan in order to guage the proficiency of the protective detail.

If the subject had pulled a gun, he would have been stopped by the alertness of the Sergeant. The crowd was oblivious to the action because it was done effectively and in a low key fashion. Still the press area location and the breakdown in radio communications proved to be major obstacles.

After the detail ended and President Reagan was on his way to his next destination, the detail critiqued the operation and better understood its deficiencies. In about a week, a letter came from the Director of the USSS saying that President Reagan had complemented his agents for a superb job they did on his visit to Baltimore County. He wrote back to President Reagan and explained that Baltimore County was the agency responsible. No better complement could be extended than for the Baltimore County Police detail to be compared to the Secret Service.

Providing protective services is a challenging and rewarding career. It takes someone who is willing to give 110% and to risk their life to save another. In order to be successful you must understand the complexities of this business and be aware of the changing times in which we live. To have a professional title of Personal Protection Specialist you must earn that right and meet the demands placed upon you. You can find hundreds of jobs advertised in the newspapers around the country and abroad looking for bodyguards but few fit the professional profile of the Personal Protection Specialist.

FOUR

Establishing a Command Post

by W. Thomas Levering

THERE ARE TWO TYPES of command posts, fixed or permanent and, field or mobile command posts. The fixed command post is housed in a permanent facility such as a cottage on estate grounds and it is used solely as a command post, with limited access for non-security personnel. Remember, a command post is a concept not a physical entity. A field/mobile command post can be located in a temporary facility such as a hotel or motel room. Any vehicle, even a large sedan, can also be employed for this purpose, but only for short-term assignments. Whether fixed or mobile, the command post serves as a protective detail's nerve center. If the principal travels to another state for a one-week convention or business meeting, the protection team would set up a command post in the hotel, possibly in one of their rooms, or preferably in a separate room, operated 24 hours a day.

If the executive is going to travel by car several hours away from the home base and out of the base's radio communication range, a vehicle is appropriate for this purpose.

PURPOSE

A command post should coordinate the various functions being carried out by detail personnel as well as record and monitor all communications and detail activities. The command post serves as a control center for monitoring smoke, fire, intrusion, panic and power-interruption alarms. The command post may also serve as the storeroom for any equipment needed by the detail and as a CCTV observation center.

LOCATION

Ideally the command post serves as a hub. It is located near the center of activity. It should be in close proximity to a principal's residence and his office or suite of offices. Security personnel who may be assigned to the command post should see it as a crossroads, a repository for keys and assignment/incident logs and a crisis management center. In addition, on most estates, the residential quarters for security personnel are attached to the command post with an emphasis upon both a degree of privacy and rapid response time in the event of an emergency. The command post location should be secure and designed to ensure an unbroken flow of communication, inbound and outbound. The command post is the control point—for both estate and corporate settings—where all incoming mail, deliveries and service personnel are screened, logged in and processed. Signal integrity and strength is important, and the command post should be equipped with a back-up power supply that is tested on a regular basis. Like a firehouse, it is where vehicles are not only kept, but kept under control.

The command post should either be well hidden or configured in the least visible fashion. This will help limit the number of curiosity seekers attempting to discover just what goes on at that location.

A command post will preferably be found in the most secure location, a spot where protection activity is highly concentrated. Suppose that a protective detail provides service to an executive at his or her office and residence. If an office is already manned on a round-the-clock basis with security guards and monitored by CCTV, then logically, this is where the command post belongs if at all possible. Thus, the protective detail can secure the command post using systems and other hardware already in place.

The command post itself must be secure at all times. In the event the command post should be made inoperative. All communications and control functions would be wiped out and the activities of the detail would be almost impossible to coordinate. In addition, there may be valuable equipment in the command post which you do not want stolen or lost as well as any sensitive biographical or medical data which could compromise the staff, or the protectee or the protection detail. This could include important and confidential phone numbers, sensitive corporate data, a safe for visitor's valuables, itineraries, schedules, locations and types of security devices and systems.

COMMUNICATIONS

All communications involving an executive protection detail should be directed through the command post, and logged. If the detail leader and another member of the team needs to talk to each other over the radio, they should first get permission from the command post to communicate directly with one another.

Only essential messages should be transmitted on the radio. Idle chatter will clog the radio channel, taking up valuable time if an emergency should occur. At no time should names, locations, itineraries, or details on number of security personnel be divulged on the air. This precaution reduces the possibility of the security of the detail being compromised by persons monitoring conversations.

The suggested mode of communication is the use of a very simple code or alpha-numeric identification system for any topic to be discussed. All posts should be assigned a number. An easy method of referring to the principal is by code. Security personnel can be identified by number, based on their credentials. Routes, locations and intineraries are easily coded, the simpler the better. All codes should be recorded and maintained in the command post. Consider changing them on a regular basis.

Personally designed/molded earpieces are recommended. This prevents radio transmissions from being overheard by bystanders, and the molded earpiece is most comfortable for a personal protection specialist especially when radios must be carried during long shifts.

Limiting the information that goes over the air regarding the number of personnel on a detail can be reversed to the protection team's advantage. If the detail leader suspects that the channel is no longer secure and he wishes to give the image of strength in numbers, he can instruct the command post to do a roll call check of post numbers, reading off two numbers for every post that actually exists. Advise each team member during the briefing to acknowledge standing at two posts each. This gives the impression that a detail is twice its actual size. Such deception could deter a possible threat by making a detail seem to be virtually omnipresent, even if it is a hoax.

PERSONNEL

There should be an experienced, senior personal protection specialist or supervisor in the command post whenever possible. Many important decisions are going to be made from that location, proper accountability must be established. For example, what should be done if someone gets left behind or if an appointment is missed? The fixed command post is generally the command, control, and coordination center for the entire protective operation.

The proper number of personnel should be assigned to the command post to operate all technical equipment and monitor alarms, CCTV and so on. Scheduling should be arranged to allow for the relief person to be briefed on the previous shift activities. Alternates should be on stand-by in case of illness or change of plans.

Absolutely *no one* but security personnel should be allowed in the command post except when absolutely necessary. *No staff members should see the inside of that command post unless they have direct responsibility for security.* The last thing you want to do is compromise your security system by allowing unauthorized personnel to see what you have in place. The information they gather could be used by them to compromise the detail's safety or effectiveness. It could be used as a valuable product for sale. Or it may be inadvertently passed on, during a conversation overheard in a restaurant, or on a trip or in the form of idle gossip.

SUPPLIES AND INFORMATION

Several factors determine the type or amount of supplies and information contained in the command post. The size, location, and security of the command post is governed by the security department's budget and imagination. Below is a sample of items which may be kept in the command post:

Information
- Maps
- Telephone Numbers (police, fire, key corporate personnel, all security personnel)
- Code Key
- Standard procedures book and logs (SOP)
- Emergency/contingency plans
- Pre-selected routes for destinations
- Vital information on principal and expected guests
- Visitor's log
- Intelligence files/look outs
- Detailed diagrams of the entire area/security posts
- List of vehicle locations
- Itinerary

Equipment
- Spare keys (cars, buildings)

- First aid/burn kit
- Weapons/ammunition
- Batteries/flashlights
- Emergency generator
- Creature comforts (toilet, sink, refrigerator, coffee pot)
- CCTV monitors/alarm station
- Base radio/hand units/battery chargers
- Telephones/books
- Fire extinguishers

This list is by no means complete, but it spells out the basic components that make up a well equipped and responsive command post.

Remember, a command post in some form should be maintained at every site that a principal frequents on a regular basis for an extended period of time. These alternate sites will have command posts that are very primitive in comparison to the elaborate facilities at the estate or at the corporate headquarters; however, their purpose never changes regardless of size or sophistication.

Also, a command post will always serve as an immediate point of contact for any protective services personnel who have been left behind, regardless of the circumstances, or in the event that a scheduled activity, appointment or whatever has not taken place as planned. The command post serves as a multi-purpose clearing house for all information that impacts upon or relates to the principal.

The photo above shows a fixed command post ideally located near the principal's residence with ready access to a waiting vehicle.

FIVE

Team Dynamics:
Working Together, Working Smart

by Peter J. Brown

THE TEAM/TEAM APPROACH

ALL TEAMS, regardless of their size or purpose for being, are required to be aware of certain ground rules. In terms of the mission of providing protective services, teams should be able to perform a variety of tasks in a professional manner as well as in any number of circumstances. This rule applies to both the more visible functions as well as to the vast number of behind-the-scenes procedures, especially during travel-intensive assignments.

Every profession has its own supply of acronyms. Here, we can start with the TEAM/TEAM concept which has been developed to help security personnel understand the true nature of the business. Every protective services team must possess four essential characteristics.

TOUGH ON TIME. This implies that punctuality, careful preplanning, precise time management and, of course, setting aside time for personal pursuits—are all integrated into the team's standard operating procedures. And speaking of routines, it is important that enough redundancy exists to allow for a smooth transition in the event that any member of the team is taken ill or otherwise incapacitated.

EAGER TO EXECUTE. This should not be somehow confused with the sense of being "eager to evacuate" which indicates a total commitment to a defensive stance. Having the right attitude to all the tasks involved, major and petty alike. Lots of minor time-consuming details must be addressed, and these can often be a real source of irritation. Avoiding headaches is preferable, and one easy way to minimize them is to accept that the job does not simply involve providing security, rather it requires that security-conscious measures be injected into all of your principal's activities in the least disruptive manner.

ALERT AND AWARE. The need for this part of the equation should be obvious. Any team member who comes to the job without a clear head can become more than just a burden. He or she can jeopardize everyone in the detail. Steps can be taken to patch holes; however, lingering problems—both physical and/or personal—should not be left untreated for long. Team members should recognize that while it is important to be able to cover for someone who is temporarily under the weather, it is even more important for the team to act quickly and decisively in the event that one member of the team is incapable of pulling himself or herself out of a troubling and often self-destructive behavioral pattern. In cases of drug or alcohol abuse, often a stress-related phenomenon, drastic measures may need to be undertaken.

MACHINELIKE YET MORTAL. In short, while it would be nice to be superhuman, performing flawlessly round-the-clock, recognizing one's limitations and strengths, while tapping team members so that each individual's talents and skills are used wisely, leads to a smoother operating unit. Surprises and challenges will never disappear entirely, but they can be kept to a minimum with good advance work and precise planning—getting back to our initial thrust of the need to be tough on time. Being mortal is simply accepting the fact that as long as you walk around thinking, "Nope, it can't happen to me," you can bet that it just might happen.

HERE COMES THE "C" TEAM

When you think of the protective services profession, you can put aside the paramilitary potential of the "A Team" and you can omit the academic depth of the "B Team"—an alien concept anywhere outside intelligence circles. You can always trust the "C Team", because it covers just about the whole spectrum of protective services concerns.

Being part of the "C Team" means that you have the CAPACITY TO COPE WITH CONSTANT CHANGE, to provide CONCENTRIC CIRCLES OF PROTECTION, to maintain strict CONFIDENTIALITY, and, no matter where you go or who you deal with, COUNT ON COMING BACK. Don't forget your CAREER when you accept an assignment or when you undertake a risk assessment.

And there is a lot more, like above all being COURTEOUS. Other equally important components of the "C Team" includes:

COMMUNICATION	COUNTERMEASURES
COORDINATION	COMMAND/CONTROL
COOPERATION	CORRECTNESS
CONFIDENCE	COMFORT
COMPETENCE	COOLNESS
CAUTION	CALMNESS
COMMON SENSE	CAPABILITY
CONSISTENCY	CANDIDNESS
CONTINGENCIES	CHARACTER
CAMOUFLAGE	CHOREOGRAPHY
CLANDESTINENESS	CHRONOLOGY
CRIME DEFLECTION	CLASS
CLEANLINESS	CLEARHEADEDNESS
COMPLIMENT	COMPUTERS
COMPREHENSION	COMPRESSION
COMPOSURE	CONDUCT
CONCISENESS	CONDITIONING
CONFIRMATION	CONNECTION
CONSCIOUSNESS	CONSERVATION
CONSIDERATION	CONSOLIDATION

CONTACT   CONSTRAINT
CONTAINMENT   CONTRACT

A little CLAIRVOYANCE might help too. The list is far from complete, and finally, COMPLACENCY must be avoided at all costs.

In the above brief descriptions of the TEAM/TEAM and "C Team" concepts, an obviously over-simplified attempt has been made to address team dynamics. Many protective services personnel will see things quite differently. For example, some details will challenge the notion that the ability to cope with constant change is important. Their routine might be the exact opposite, a never-changing pattern of events and daily routines. Such details exist.

THE BENEFITS OF TEAMWORK

Personal protection requires patience, discipline, and an ability to work well with different groups of people in widely varied settings. Your attitude and your willingness to get along with people—identifying and striving to reach a common goal—is an essential prerequisite. You cannot succeed in this or any other people-related business if you come to work with the wrong attitude. This line of work is too demanding in terms of the routine and a constant interaction with people. Sure, if your principal lives in total isolation on some remote island, you will not have to worry about meeting people or frequently making schedules and mapping out itineraries. This type of assignment is the exception, not the rule.

You will discover that your life as a personal protection specialist will quickly break down into a series of encounters. The challenge inherent in this profession is to eliminate the element of surprise—the unknowns at the dinner party, in the hotel, passing through the airport or wherever. Coping with all these scenarios by yourself is impossible, and the go-it-alone approach will certainly lead to an ultimate destination, a classic case of burn-out. Your job performance, enthusiasm, spirit, motivation, and dedication will be enhanced through successful teamwork.

Learn to work with people in all kinds of situations and settings. Mobilize and motivate people to perform as many tasks as possible. Delegating responsibility is not the same as simply abandoning your professional approach and substituting in its place a loosely structured series of assumptions such as, "Well, I can relax now because so-and-so told me that everything is going ahead as planned." No, your job requires more than that, much more. You cannot take things for granted if you are going to be effective, efficient, and responsive.

You must learn to "recruit" people in a polite, courteous, professional, and direct fashion. Before you ask yourself, "Can I trust this person to carry out his or her assignment?", you should be asking yourself a more important series of questions. "Why should this person respond in a positive manner to me? Am I reliable and trustworthy? Am I conducting myself in the right way? Did I make a strong, positive, and longlasting impression or did I leave a group of unhappy and disgruntled people in my wake?"

Recruiting people becomes a matter of adding resources to your protective detail. You might arrive at a hotel, for example, with one or two other people in your protective detail. By adopting the right attitude from the start, you can begin to augment your detail's scope of operations and resource base by contacting the hotel security manager, the head housekeeper, the maitre d', the bell captain, the head doorman, and, of course, both the hotel manager, and his night duty counterpart. These people become part of your detail. Why? Imagine your stay at a hotel—regardless of its length—if anyone of these key people is not on your team.

So you introduce yourself and you present your list of special needs in an appropriate manner and—this is critical—on a "need-to-know" basis. After all, if your principal is intent upon slipping into a particular hotel and he wants his profile kept lower than a ghost for the duration of his brief stay, you may elect to book all the rooms in your name—actually a common procedure anyway. You can always elect to say little or nothing to anyone. Otherwise, get ready to alert key hotel staff to your specific, and special, needs. Be prepared to tip people when you check out, a process made much easier if you know their names, and titles in advance so that your "thank you" and a gratuity arrive together in the right hands. Your objective is not to "buy" people, but rather to suitably "reward" them when their work is completed in the way you had wanted it done and at the precise time you expected it to be done. Remember, you can count on coming back. That is a safe assumption as well as a smart one.

JOINT SECURITY DETAILS

Just as you plan in advance to establish good relations with hotel staff, you should also be prepared to interact effectively with other security details. If you happen to come together at some location with one, or perhaps more, additional security details, you should establish contact immediately and attempt to work out a system that enables you to share certain responsibilities such as grounds/perimeter patrol, watch over vehicles and/or aircraft and hall duty. Egos may prevent or prohibit you from achieving an ad hoc shared security system.

Communication is crucial. You can maintain your autonomy, keep your principal happy and, even get a little extra rest, if you lay out a few common ground rules. First, get names and faces matched up. Get to know the identities of your fellow security personnel, and find out immediately who is in charge. A shared command post is a good idea, especially in a sprawling resort-type complex. Each detail can retain its own command post in whatever room they select. The flow of scheduling requirements of the joint command should be kept to an absolute minimum.

In the joint command post, as in any command post, you want two separate logs: assignments and incidents, with the time in the left column, name of contact or assignee in the center column and the details—type of assignment or incident-related details—in the right hand column. Also, a list of emergency contacts both on and off the premises should be available along with the usual room/phone roster.

Third, fix a time—preferably in the evening—when all the detail chiefs can put their heads together and evaluate the strengths and weaknesses of their joint endeavors. Be open and be honest, talk about the good and the bad, and do not let yourself fall into the trap of being silent, while an incompetent detail or an unacceptable situation goes uncorrected.

If you think a working agreement or relationship like the team approach being spelled out in this chapter does not happen in the real world, you are mistaken and misinformed. A clever and astute detail leader can use a situation like this to his team's advantage. By complying with the prearranged guidelines, by sticking to a tight schedule and by consolidating efforts, the job gets done accordingly. And you can always renegotiate or make alternative arrangements if everything falls apart. You are not relinquishing either your direct involvement with your own principal, nor are you over-committing yourself and your detail to the extent that you lose control of your own protective role. You are simply attempting to minimize redundancy during the more predictable and less hectic evening hours in particular. If the assembled principals hold collective meetings during the day, this is also a convenient and controllable set of circumstances which can be handled effectively on a joint detail basis.

Difficulties will arise, you can count on it. You should not expect a flawless or a perfect track record. Your goal should be to make the joint effort as simple as possible. What if one of the details does not speak English? So what, be polite and offer your assistance. That is what really counts, the fact that you held out your hand. This situation may not occur frequently in the U.S., but in Europe and elsewhere overseas, such encounters are hardly rare or unusual.

What about radio traffic? Here again, a little common sense and flexibility goes a long way. The most basic and yet most responsive approach involves the use of each respective team's command post to feed vital information back to the joint command post where, in turn, it is disseminated down to all the other command posts. How is it done? Easy, by phone. Personnel cannot be expected to carry four or five portable radios. At the same time, few details carry enough spare radios so that they can leave one in the joint command post. And finally, multiple radio contacts—not to mention keeping track of your own detail's radios alone—can get confusing and frustrating. So, if something unexpected occurs and everyone needs to know about it, PPS John Doe calls his command post on his portable, his command post immediately contacts the joint command post by phone, and in turn, the joint command post instantly issues an alert to all the other command posts, mobilizing the collective security apparatus.

The automatic sequence of events should not be reduced to chaos, and a collapse of the collective support network is avoidable. Your first priority is the safety and security of your principal, and your initial response to an alert will be a swift enhancement of the inner-most protective ring around your principal. You should expect the other details to act accordingly. That is natural; however, once an all-out mobilization has taken place, detail chiefs can congregate quickly. At that point, a decision should be made so that a collective pool of available manpower is directed en masse to the trouble spot. Remember, this is also a good time to float a second or even third team in the event that the incident you are responding to turns out to be nothing more than a diversion. If you take the time—not too much time—to organize your details instead of reacting in a panic-stricken burst of activity, you might be less vulnerable to whatever happens next.

What if no attack is underway, and you are dealing with a hotel fire—not to leave aside the possibility that the fire was intentionally set to flush you out? A coherent and collective response brings more manpower together at a prearranged location, where the cluster of protection specialists acts as a strong deterrent in itself.

The hotel fire scenario is a valid one, and a nightmare if you are ever unfortunate enough to experience it. Imagine a hotel fire with the crowded stairways filled with terrified guests fleeing for their lives, and the smoke-filled halls. No, this is not a reminder of the need to brush up on your evacuation plans, although, it is worth considering. Instead, it is offered as a means of reinforcing the advantages of working together and working smart with other details. This is a business where you are supposed to react to emergency situations with rapid countermeasures, and well thought out plans so that you control the outcome as opposed to being overwhelmed and defeated by the sequence of events.

Can you conduct a realistic training exercise that simulates this cooperative effort? Sure, but it requires both elaborate planning and an independent team of observers who stage the various phases of the exercise. It is not easy because you want to come face-to-face with people who are total strangers, often with big egos, who have command authority, and who may be more than a bit skeptical about the concept of shared duty or a joint command structure of any kind.

RECIPROCITY

Protective services personnel, who have worked on large private estates where visiting principals and their details are frequent guests, know full well that it is routine for the host detail to retain full control over all activities on the grounds. Guest details are given the opportunity to sit back and relax for the simple reason that reciprocity is expected and anticipated. In other words, whereas this time you might be the guest and its your turn to relax, some time in the future, this detail will visit your principal's residence. During that brief stay, you will be expected to run the whole show while they relax until the time they depart.

It is more than a common professional courtesy, it is common sense. Just as you know the layout of the grounds around your principal's residence, the location of emergency medical facilities, and other details about your area that are essential to your day-to-day operations, so you can be assured that your professional counterparts are in a similar state of preparedness, on their own turf.

In addition, making all the relevant background information available and taking all the time to brief another detail like a conventional advance can be not only a pain in the neck—a brief overview is recommended—but it is unnecessary, impractical, and inefficient. Every principal visiting your principal's residence, regardless of the length of his or her stay, is protected by the existing, fixed security facilities and manpower that operate there 24 hours-a-day. This reality is distinctly different from the circumstances surrounding the decision-making at any off-premises site such as a hotel or resort complex.

The above-mentioned recommendations and suggestions hinge on your determination that the other security details measure up to your standards. Rest assured that you and your team will be scrutinized in the same way. It is part of the profession. You also have to make a rapid determination because you often do not have the time to conduct a thorough screening of your cohorts. Do you simply assume that your fellow security personnel are up to par? No, of course not. Trust your instincts, proceed cautiously and yet remember that you may not be the only one with doubts and concerns about getting the job done right. Quality control can be a sticky issue.

While interaction and cooperation with other security teams or on-site staff has been the focus thus far, nothing is more critical than your own team's ability to work together as a unit, mutually reinforcing and complimenting each other. The relationship that binds each member of your team together relies upon a good number of different qualities starting with a strong sense of respect for one another.

You need to recognize and acknowledge your own strengths and weaknesses, as well as those of your compatriots. No one single personality trait dominates this business. Skill and competency go only so far. You need privacy, time alone, personal space, recreational pursuits, and relationships that are totally separate and apart from your professional life. Your roommate, shift partner, assistants or whomever else makes up your team, requires the same.

PART II

Advance Work, Unwanted Visitors, and the Role of Technology

SIX

Advance Work, Travel, and Hotel Security

by Jerome H. Glazebrook and Charles H. Blennerhassett

ALL OF US are familiar with the U.S. Secret Service, the witness protection program, and numerous other cabinet-level protective details. All of these involve virtually unlimited resources, support, and authority. In most cases, we in the private sector, lack the assets to provide that level of security. Many former government security professionals join the private sector only to find that the game is played very differently. Their principals are often more interested in personal services and in convenience, than in security. Unfortunately, this is the reality of the corporate and private sectors. It is difficult to make a protective detail cost effective. Seldom does management look at the possible problems that could occur in the event of the injury or death of a CEO. Granted kidnapping and assassination are two significant concerns but the percentages strongly favor personal injury.

In developing your protective program, your first priority is to assess your threat level. Structure your team accordingly, with the capability to up your protective level quickly and efficiently. Camouflaging the security personnel into the lifestyle of the executive or private family is very effective. Some examples of how this can be accomplished will be covered here.

There are a number of different ways to approach a protective detail. You can camouflage protective personnel as executive assistants, as grounds staff on an estate, and as in-house staff for a private family. You are much more effective if you can't be identified as protective personnel in the private sector. One exception to this approach involves entertainers that use security for crowd control and their own personal security. Often their security staff is recruited from the local gym for the purpose of intimidating crowds and fans. In short, they are nothing more than a physical barrier, in most cases with little or no training in the most elementary procedures. This is especially true for touring rock groups. The major concerns are crowd control and access control whether at the concert hall, when moving from the hotel to the performance, or at the airport.

Business titles allow you access to meetings and settings where security people would not usually be found. At board meetings, the security people are often improperly positioned to be of any assistance either for a physical or medical reason. If you are identified as the executive assistant to the chairman of the board or the president of the corporation, chances are you are going to be in a much better position to respond regardless of the need. You are going to be in a position to not only provide a better level of security for your principal but you are also more accessible if an emergency arises.

Today's executive protection specialists find that they have more than one role. You become a combination of an executive or special assistant, a valet, a chauffeur, and even a nanny if children are involved. How can you possibly do your job if you are carrying these other titles? We all would like to be able to say, "Security is our only responsibility." On the other hand, we are in a service profession and we should accept the fact we will be expected to do many personal duties and errands for our principals and their families. While this may help to solidify our position, it also tends to draw us away from our paramount responsibility, protecting our principals. In fact, most of our days are spent providing personal service and not security. The most difficult thing is learning to anticipate the needs of our protectees and taking care of these needs without jeopardizing our security responsibilities.

Proper planning prevents poor performance. The five p's. If you anticipate problems and do what is required, you won't be drawn from your principal. Suppose you know that his dry cleaning goes out at 8:00 in the morning and that he is going to send you off with it. If he jumps in the car with the chauffeur while you are at the dry cleaners, you are not much good to him. However, if you suggest to him that you want to take the dry cleaning, that night, you have anticipated the problem that is going to make you ineffective the next day.

By practicing the 5 p's, you can minimize problems and irritations. It is going to make your job easier on a day to day basis. You say, "My job is security." Not exactly, your job is to ensure the security, safety, health and well-being of your protectees. You enable them to function properly and to perform their daily responsibilities in the most efficient manner possible. You enable them more time to concentrate on their business without being concerned with many day to day details. Learn to anticipate your protectees needs.

If you are moving into a hotel suite or you are going to the mountain or the lake house, anticipate the things that you are going to need there. Food, clothing, medical supplies, telephone numbers, maps, and recreation equipment, to name just a few things you may want to consider. Set procedures and checklists to ensure that nothing gets overlooked. If something is needed, rest assured that security will be sent to obtain it. Every principal has his own idiosyncrasies. Some principals require special bed linen and items such as bottled water or a particular soap. You don't want to be driving around at 2:00 in the morning trying to meet the needs of your principal.

When you initially select a team, look for appropriate skills as well as the candidate's appearance. Does he blend in to the profile of your principal? A 280-pound weight lifter is not going to blend in with a 58-year-old corporate chief executive officer. He would draw attention and you want to avoid drawing attention. Do whatever is necessary to blend in with the principal.

Discipline is paramount. You must control your vices and desires. Both you and your principal can easily be compromised through a lack of discipline. It happens all the time in protective services. Affairs with wives, daughters, or secretaries may happen more often than you think. Avoid smoking and alcoholic beverages when you work. If you have to use force and you had one drink that day or had one drink in a night club, by the time it's all over you have actually had ten. Everybody there is going to say that they saw you have a drink. So if you have one drink, it is going to be ten if there is a confrontation.

Stay away from alcohol when you are on assignment. Drink soda water or coke, but make it your established rule so that there is never a question when you are on assignment that you might have been drinking. It is even more dangerous if you are armed. If you have to use deadly force and you take one drink, it is going to be detrimental in court. The attorney is going to use that against you. Always establish a "No Alcohol Policy" as one of your rules of operation, whenever you are on assignment.

Smoking shows a lack of discipline. If you are standing around smoking a cigarette on assignment, your hands are occupied. Smoking is obviously one of the best ways you can think of to curb the pangs of hunger. Lots of times when you are on private details, it gets hard in between meals. Smoking helps a little bit, but it shows a lack of discipline.

Be aware of the protocol and etiquette of your particular position. It is your job to be aware of the cultural differences and idiosyncrasies that could turn into an embarrassment for you or your principal. You are always a direct representative of your principal. If you project a negative image and a lack of self-discipline, it reflects immediately upon your principal. Team members who behave in an unbecoming manner should be replaced. It is a reflection upon every man on the team. You may not be particularly bad at your job but you are not projecting the image that is necessary for that particular principal or you as a professional.

Your conduct off duty is also important. You would be amazed by how many people are not only aware of who you are, but also who you work for. You may have a low profile or use a camouflage approach, but there are always people, especially local law enforcement, who will know who you are. If you are making a spectacle of yourself in a bar, believe me, it spreads like wildfire. If you are overindulging in the bar, that spreads. If you are having an affair in town, everybody will know about it. Conduct, again, is a direct reflection on your principal and you as a professional.

There is personal assistance and there is personal assistance/security. A man that is good in his job will know when to say "no" and to say "no" effectively, when it is necessary. If your principal has any respect for you as a professional, when you say "no", he is going to know that there is a sound reason for it. There is a real difference between providing personal services in an efficient professional manner, and, bowing and scraping. As a professional, you will have to determine on an individual basis just how far you will and can go.

Maintaining your skill levels and fitness, that is your profession. The fact that your principal has not been assaulted does not mean that you can cut down on the gym time, sacrificing your level of fitness. Training and constantly updating your skills are at the core of this profession. It changes constantly. What might have been acceptable on the protective services margin 5 or 10 years ago in the private sector, is no longer adequate. The quality of personnel is changing very quickly. People are becoming very aware that there is a critical difference in quality levels in protective services.

Your relationship with your principal can be ever changing as you fulfill the roles of protector, friend, confidant, employee, or special assistant. If either confidence, dependability, dedication or trust is absent, your relationship with your principal won't last very long. Trust and dependability are most important. Honesty and integrity are also essential elements. You will have to advise your principal of his particular threat level constantly. You cannot afford to have him ever question your character.

At social functions such as cocktail parties, official functions, sporting events or dinner parties, you should establish procedures and stick to them. Be aware of guest lists. Be aware of problem people that are going to be on the guest list that could cause confrontations with your principal. Be aware of who is expected and who is not. Control access even if you have to station yourself in the doorway simply to open the door. It will look like you are providing a function as far as the guests are concerned, but you are able to screen people as they come and go. You have a reason for being closer to your principal. He may not want you at a party or a social event, so "door duty" puts you closer than you would probably be otherwise. Establish procedures that are effective for each particular set of circumstances. We have all seen situations where the protective personnel is right up in the back pocket of the principal. That is not possible in the corporate world in most cases. As a matter of fact, you are lucky if you are going to be a couple of arm lengths away, let alone in immediate reach. You have to maintain visual contact. You have to be able to strategically place yourself in order to respond quickly. Keep in mind your risk assessment. The chances of someone assassinating your principal are probably slim, but there may be a possibility you will be needed to respond to an embarrassing situation.

On one-on-one situations, you have to constantly be moving and jockeying for position around your principal without looking like a jack rabbit. It should look natural. If this means moving around the room with a club soda in your hand, do it in order to position yourself effectively. Blend into the party or function that is taking place. If it is black tie, wear a black tie. Don't show up in a blue blazer and gray slacks. If it is morning coat, wear a morning coat; don't show up in a blue suit. The whole idea is to blend so that you are more effective. You don't want to be singled out as security once you are identified. You will surely be dealt with first should there be a serious threat against your principal. Blending into the environment is more important than one might think.

Be aware of the body language in the room, any threatening profiles or revealing eye contact. Be aware of what is happening around you in the room. Learn to develop peripheral vision, looking through a room and picking up movement without making any eye contact. Eye contact can be used to intimidate in some cases but it can also force a confrontation. Remember, good judgment comes from experience, experience comes from doing. You usually see protective personnel wearing sun glasses. Sun glasses are effective but it also may immediately identify you as security. Try to be aware of the small details which could make you stand out, particularly in what you wear, how you stand and how you conduct yourself.

Develop a signal system for your principal, use prearranged signals or codes. I have found it most effective in a one-on-one situation. Have signals that he can flash when he is in a distressed situation. If he is having problems with someone he is talking to or if he sees someone in a room that he wants to avoid. If you see a confrontation developing, approach your boss and say "Excuse me, sir, I just want to remind you of a meeting that you wanted to make at 9 o'clock." It is not threatening. You can slide out of the situation. Or try, "Sir, you have a phone call." There are a number of different lines. That is a much better way to deal with a confrontation than jumping between him and his potential assailant—doing that is only going to fuel a confrontation. You are not effective tied up in a physical confrontation.

Another example is, think about being in a night club, not one that you are particularly familiar with. You are with your boss and his lady friend. You are having a confrontation because there is a person bothering the lady. How do you deal with it? Ask her if she would like to dance. That would cool the situation. Or "Come on sis, it is time to go". Do something that is simple and elementary. It cools the situation quickly. Dealing with someone's sister is not the same as dealing with another girl in a bar.

You have to be confident in order to avoid the confrontation. You have to discuss signals that the principal can give you when he or she feels distress or discomfort. He doesn't want to say, "I feel uncomfortable" or "I am getting out of here." Instead he puts his hand to his chin or pulls out his handkerchief. Subtle signals such as requesting a coke when you know that he always drinks Perrier can be used. How do you develop the signal system? It will depend on how well you communicate with your principal. Communicating with your principal is very important, especially in one-on-one or two-on-one situations. (To assume your abilities are far superior to anyone else is a mistake. Sooner or later you are going to fall.) Good judgment and finesse are more effective than physical confrontation. In any one-on-one situation, if you are tied up in a confrontation you are not being truly effective with your principal.

If you advise your principal not to do something, or discourage him, be prepared to defend your judgment. Be sure that you have your act together. You should have a good solid explanation. Don't fall back on, "Security reasons, sir." Be prepared. Your principals are bright and quick. If you can't respond in an effective manner, you are wasting a lot of his time. Hopefully you have developed an environment of trust. Strive to keep it. Suppose you are walking in the city of New York and you take a short cut through a back alley where a confrontation is lurking. It is not unmacho to change your route to keep away from the problem. Maintaining distance from a danger zone is why you are there. Avoiding the problem and foreseeing a problem is much more effective than a one-on-one confrontation.

BIOGRAPHICAL INFORMATION

Monitor the health and fitness of your principal. Maintain up to date health information on your principal and have it available when you travel. Know his physical limitations, medications, and allergies. Encourage a physical fitness program for your principal. Try to make arrangements so you can work out together.

Today, the state of the art is a microchip which allows information to be stored and recalled with a touch of a finger. Just a few years ago you had to carry your principal's records in a small porta-file in order to quickly access necessary medical files, detail records and other needed material. Now you can keep all his personal data on a microchip, worn around his neck or a bracelet or carried in his wallet. If he is injured and he goes into surgery all that information will be instantly on call to the surgeon. Microchip-type medallions as well as medical information cards—the size of a credit card—are very important when traveling overseas.

The kind of information that you want is very basic. You want to compile a list with your principal's complete name and address (both residence and office) personal and official telephone numbers (listed and unlisted) and radio call signs for any corporate or personal boats and aircraft. Be aware of how to make a land to air call. Know what the procedure is. If you are on the Atlantic side and you are calling from an aircraft, it has to be routed personally.

A complete physical description for both principal and family members is absolutely necessary. You can also use a tape or a dictaphone if necessary in the office to obtain a voice stress sample. In the event of a kidnapping, it can be compared to a ransom tape. It can also be used to measure the degree of stress and duress your principal is under. Handwriting samples are easily accessible. The same is true of finger prints. Know the blood type of your principal and whether or not he is allergic to anything. If he is in an accident and if he is allergic to penicillin, he could wind up in shock or worse if he is given the wrong medication. Be alert to possible critical problems that could result in stressful situations, adverse cardiovascular responses or occurances that could affect an ulcer.

Record credit card numbers, physician and dentist numbers, both home and office. Most physicians and dentists have unlisted numbers. If you cannot access microchips or the credit card sized medical files, be sure that you have prearranged access to alternate file sources. You must have 24-hour access to all essential documents if there is a medical emergency.

FAMILY

Know the schools attended by the children and key administrative personnel as well as emergency contacts at the school. If you need to withdraw the children during an emergency situation, you need to know who has been designated at the school as your emergency contact. Establish a prearranged signal to confirm your identity. These things have to be prearranged and predetermined, if not you are going to have trouble during any emergency situation. Be aware of the route traveled by the children to and from school. If a boarding school or college is involved, be aware of travel routes and availability of trains and aircraft. Keep track of travel arrangements and be familiar with their schedules in case you have to get in contact with them quickly.

Be aware of the outside activities of the family members as well as the names, addresses and telephone numbers of principal relatives. In many private family corporations, specific individuals have immediate access to cash accounts. Other members don't have that authority. Be aware of who has that type of control. Who has the authority to move Heaven and earth with just a phone call? Junior may have a great title but he doesn't always have the necessary clout. Be aware of the principal players in an organization and what type of influence they have.

Keep current registration numbers and a roster of recreational and personal vehicles. If your executive spends a lot of time in the wilderness hiking, camping, motorcycling, off-road trail biking or water skiing, be familiar with the area and all emergency services. You should keep abreast of the weather and the terrain. How will emergency procedures be affected by these variables?

Compile current lists of weapons from family members and know where weapons are located in the house. In the event of an emergency, nothing will make an impression like the moment you turn a corner and find your boss confronting you with a weapon you knew nothing about. In an emergency, you will need to know what is available for response. In some country estates there might be a weapon hidden in every room. If there are weapons in the house, be aware of where they are located, keeping in mind that those same weapons would be available to anyone else. If so, be sure that the principal and his family are qualified to use them.

Keep diagrams of all family residences, floor plans as well as utility maps. A utility map should include electrical wiring, outside access to telephone wires, cables, conduits and power switches. Identify and secure underground pipes that would allow someone to gain access to the house. Air conditioning and exhaust ducts have to be secured. People will spend thousands of dollars on security guards, alarms, and armored cars—then neglect to secure accesses. Consider a back-up power source to thwart any attempt to shut down your primary power source. A $100,000.00 alarm system is useless without a back-up power supply. One bolt cutter can neutralize a vulnerable system, no matter how much it costs.

The maps mentioned above must be current. People are constantly adding on to their houses, properties, and staff quarters. Be familiar with who has access to the house and office, as well as the boats, vacation houses, etc. Safe rooms are also worth consideration. These are rooms in which your principal can secure themselves while calling for assistance. The master bathroom adjacent to the master bedroom is an ideal site for such a safe haven. If a home has more than one level, you should consider safe rooms on each level.

You can't be with the principal 24-hours a day, especially on one-on-one, two-on-one details. You are going to have to sleep. If there is a problem in the house, your principal can flee to the safe room and secure himself inside. If the room is properly built and maintained, it is going to give him enough time to get help from the security team or the police. It can boost your principal's confidence if he knows that somewhere in his house he or she can be totally secure for a period of time.

It is easy to convert a room to a safe room. First, select the room, even a bathroom. It should have only one reinforced and secured window. Bathrooms are excellent because they have a water supply already. You can reinforce doors, add a telephone (perferably cordless) connected to the police and security system. A two-way radio should be considered also. Communication is not a problem because today's cellular telephones have a lot of capabilities. They are relatively inexpensive and they can be preprogrammed to an alarm system company. They are inexpensive to install without a lot of wiring and extra work on the room. Fortifying the doors and windows should not result in the construction of a fortress. Your objective is to create a sanctuary that is going to give your principal enough time to wait out of harms way until help arrives. This is particularly useful when the security team is not assigned round-the-clock.

Maintain an up-to-date threat assessment file. Keep a log on all threatening telephone calls or "bomb calls" to home and office numbers. Compile all the hate and threat letters that are directed at your principal along with derogatory and negative-type newspaper or magazine articles. Constantly update your file and keep it current. This may be your only source of the history of the threat and record of prior contact with unstable persons. Note especially the ones who start with nice letters and, over a period of time progressively get nastier.

Also, if you ever need to go to the authorities for special support because you have decided that the threat assessment is rising quickly and that someone is out to do harm to your principal or his family, this file can substantiate the need for police support. If you can produce a current file, you are much more likely to get the kind of support you need from the local authorities than if you go in and say your employer is getting threats. An accurate updated file can establish both the existence and the changing nature of any immediate threat to your principal.

TRAVEL

Brief executives before going overseas. This type of material gives the executive and his travel companions some insight as to what they can expect. Overseas briefings are designed primarily to identify problems in advance and inform the traveler of possible pitfalls that could jeopardize his project, safety, or health. You are not preparing a political report for your boss. It is a capsule overview, a familiarization and not an intelligence report. Focus on basic information.

Start with the country's general characteristics such as terrain, climate, natural resources, major industries and people. Many security people from private corporations fly off to a country without the foggiest idea as to where they are going or even what countries surround the country they are enroute to. Watch the climate, do not arrive in the middle of winter wearing a summer suit. You should be able to tell your principal what to wear and what to pack. Dress so that you blend in with the native people, do not stand out.

Know the country's natural resources, export and import items. Most important of all, know procedures, law, educational level, monetary exchange, and visa requirements. Be aware of the shots needed (and how far in advance of the trip), sanitation, hygiene, and the name, address and telephone number of an English speaking doctor. Seek out British or American-trained doctors. Be sure you are aware of their qualifications. Overseas doctors may not be as well versed in the latest medical advances. Know what medications to bring with you and which are commonly available. Prepare and pack for yourself a medical comfort and first aid kit. Obtain a copy of the directory, *International Association for Medical Assistance to Traveling,* (736 Center Street, Lewistown, NY 14092).

Know the government in power, the politics, the opposition, and who heads the opposition. If you are going there to meet with business executives, try to be aware of their political attitudes and affiliations. If you visit a corporate head in a foreign country, be aware of their threat factors. You could become caught up in any monitoring of this executive because he has an affiliation with an extremist group that is in opposition to the party in power. It takes a lot of homework.

What is the overall political atmosphere? The state department has a number you can call and get the address of its offices. If you are going to use this resource—it is available to everybody—be aware that you are going to get the same information from that desk officer as everyone else. You won't be receiving any classified information or classified insight into the political situation. If you have done your homework, you would probably reach a similar conclusion. Many consulting firms in Washington D.C. and New York City specialize in this type of information. Many firms provide very good foreign country briefings, both political and nonpolitical insights. You have to pick out the one that is best for you.

Be aware of security procedures as you travel. If you travel with a family that has several kids, discuss details with the children. Going to the bathroom, the gift shop, and the newsstand, need to be covered. If one goes, everyone goes. It is impossible to work in a one-on-one situation when Junior is running through the comic books and Sally is running through the candy stand. Sally has got to go to the bathroom and Junior has got to go to the bathroom. What is going to be the procedure at the hotel when the children want to go swimming and the Mr. and Mrs. want to stay in and read? These are some of the scenarios that need to be discussed. What is going to be your game plan?

This should be included in your briefing. Try to provide a do's and don'ts list, lists that the kids understand that cover basic security procedures and elementary security precautions for everyone on the trip. You must establish these procedures before the trip, particularly if it is a one-on-one situation. Depending on your particular threat situation, you might want to establish a check in system for the kids. You don't have to follow them. You can just establish a simple little thing like, "When I come down the hall at 11:00, I want to see your 'no maid' card stuck under the door on the right side." You don't have to bother anybody. Establish recognition, a code to confirm that everything is OK. That is really simple and elementary. It may be a situation in which you might want to physically have phone checks before everyone turns in.

What is going to be the procedure when traveling in a crowded aircraft or boats? What are the S.O.P.'s? What are the plans for dealing with scuba diving, snow skiing, rock climbing, just to name a few? If you are water skiing, how many people are going to be required to be on the tow boat or will you be using a chase boat? Those are the things that you want to assess. It is your job to provide a secure and safe environment for your principal. Some of the information you should have on hand when traveling with the family is as follows: emergency telephone numbers, hospital, doctors, hotel, (if you are staying in a hotel) physician or nurse, hotel dentist—kids always lose fillings on vacation or they break their teeth. You are going to be the one to deal with these problems because the secretary is not going to be there to pick up the slack for you. Know the nearest embassy or consulate and its emergency number.

Be alert to any active terrorist groups operating in the area, especially when traveling overseas. Sometimes, it is not the terrorists that you have to worry about so much as the locals. Thieves and pick pockets pose a threat too. You can make your advance work as complex or as detailed as necessary depending upon your particular travel needs. If you are going on a domestic trip, adapt your briefing accordingly, but try to keep to the same format so it becomes an established routine.

HOTELS

When you start to travel overseas and domestically, begin a log. Keep this information compiled in a loose leaf book. You will use it over and over again. It contains the kind of information that you need. It holds the basic telephone numbers, country codes, names of hotels, their telephone numbers, their telex fax machine numbers, street addresses, and contact persons at the hotel. Who is there that can take care of any particular special requests? Who is the manager, assistant manager, and the security director? Most bosses will prefer particular suites or penthouses. Know which ones they are. If you are going to use another name in booking the hotel arrangements, be sure all the details are covered such as billings, handling phone calls and visitors. In some cases you have to be aware if they take pets, especially dogs or cats. Some hotels will take 20-pound dogs but they won't take 50-pound dogs. Baggage handling is critical and it can become a real headache. How is baggage going to be handled at the hotel? What services are available: Western Union, Telex, shops. Are secretarial facilities available? What about typewriters or copying machines? Are they available after hours? If they aren't, can you arrange for them to be? Who were the reservations made by? Did the secretary handle them or do you? Verbal or written confirmation of reservation? If you phone and get a verbal confirmation, have them telex you a confirmation. When you arrive, you will have something in your hand, proof that you made a reservation.

If you use a hotel on a regular basis, it is better to arrange direct billing to the company instead of using credit cards. Avoid headaches. Why wait for an account to be set up at the hotel desk when they could just put all the bills under an account in the comptroller's office? Delays in checking in or out are avoidable if you make your arrangements in advance.

You might want to be the one that makes the wake up call while at the hotel. Are there going to be any special events while you are there? Are there going to be any conventions? It might bring added confusion for the hotel staff. Tell the security director of any problems that have been encountered in the recent past and ask him if he has had any special problems. Most security staff in large hotels can tell you which workers work which shifts. They know who is in or working the crowd, such as pick pockets, thieves, prostitutes and con-men. As for safety deposit access, many hotels limit access after 11:00 PM. If your boss's jewelry is in there, you might want to be aware of that if you are going out or coming in. You may have to make arrangements for greater access. Know the number of security personnel on duty at all times. Some security directors will assign extra guards in your hallway. Know your specific needs.

The doormen at major hotels, especially in Europe, literally buy their positions. You would be amazed at how valuable these positions are. They also control the very valuable 3 or 4 parking places that are under the canopy at that hotel or club. Those are the kind of things to be taken care of. These doormen determine who parks where. It makes it possible for you to maintain surveillance of the car. The chances are less likely that anyone would tamper with it under their noses. If you are working one-on-one, you can only be so many places at one time. Your principal generally will not give you enough time to search that car, so it must be secure. It's just like the security of a room or any communication system you use. You can have the room electronically swept, and the phones examined, but once you walk away from them—if it is not maintained under 24-hour guard—security has been compromised. Unless you are willing to place them or your vehicle under 24-hour guard, surveillance and protection will be compromised.

When advancing, don't forget that the hotel shift changes. People work different shifts. If you do your advance on Tuesday, the shifts might change. What is the basic overall attitude of the hotel staff? If you give them money, be sure that they are going to be there on the curb for your arrival. Be sure to ask about the parking area. What is the procedure for baggage distribution to the rooms? One of the ways you can do it involves the use of filing dots. You can say, "OK, gentlemen, all the bags with red dots go to 204, all the bags with the blue dots go to room 205." Use some identifying code, but don't use name tags. This will only help to identify and locate your principals should anyone be monitoring you. If you are dealing with a high profile, high risk target, you are certainly not going to leave bags unattended. All the bags are going to be escorted. Keep in mind what the level of your threat is.

Be familiar with all the exits and entrances to the hotel and the location of rest rooms and telephones. Check the fire escape stairwell, check to see if the doors lock behind you; that could save you an embarrassing moment later. Check the edges of the doors, the evacuation system, and ladders. In hotels today, you really might want to seriously consider what floor you are on. In case of fire, you might not want to be quite so high up. Check the fire extinguisher and the elevator. When were they serviced last? Check the fire detection system. Check the door locks, the window locks, the cords on the appliances, and lights. If you see frayed cords, tell the hotel to replace them with new ones because it is a fire hazard. Look for things, especially in the children's rooms, that they could injure themselves on. As soon as they are in that room by themselves, it's a Romper Room. Be aware of furniture, especially glass table tops that can be broken. Be careful about balconies when you are locating the children.

Travel with smoke hoods. Smoke hoods are easily carried in your suitcase. They are usually sold in a storage package that is ideal for travel. Some of the best ones I am familiar with are made in the U.K. They are very inexpensive. If there is a hotel fire you can put these on and it is going to give you five minutes to get out. Otherwise you might suffocate from the smoke. Be familiar with ways to deal with smoke such as wet towels or evacuation. Establish a procedure on what is going to be the drill if there is a fire, or any other type of an emergency. If you are traveling with a family or a business executive, place number cards by every phone in his suite. On his note pad or on 3x5 cards put the room number where you can be reached, all the family members and the house emergency number, if there is one. Be sure they are familiar with the dialing procedure for the hotel. Be aware of the nearest police station, fire department, and emergency services such as ambulances. Ask the security director what was the response time the last time they had to call an ambulance to the hotel. How long did it take them to get there?

RESTAURANTS

With restaurants; addresses, telephone numbers, and the names of maitre d's are most useful. Knowing the fact that they are closed on Mondays, for example, could spare you and your employer an embarrassing moment. Keep a record of the kind of restaurants that you visit, their style, decor, and specialities. You will find it very useful over the years as you accumulate this information. You can go back and save yourself a lot of grief by being able to flip through to a city and see the hotels, restaurants, and airport information. It goes a long way to have a log or travel book that you can look back on. Keep it periodically updated.

AIRCRAFT

Get your facts straight when traveling by corporate or private aircraft. Know the name of your crew members and what hotel they are staying at. Many times they stay at a different hotel then the rest of the group. They often prefer hotels that are closer to the airport. Have a way to contact them, keep their telephone numbers close at hand. Be aware of noise restrictions at small airports. Are there any restrictions? Some airports, especially in the New York or New Jersey area, have curfews and noise limitations. Some private aircraft aren't equipped with noise suppressers for the engine and can't land after 11:00. Do you know all the limitations? You have to be aware of them. You have to be aware of how long the runway is. Will it take your particular aircraft?

As for helicopters, you should be aware of the type of helicopter and its capabilities. People often forget that ceilings make all the difference in helicopters. Rain, snow, overcast, and flying around mountains are among the factors that influence helicopters unlike larger fixed-wing aircraft. Be familiar with the seating and luggage capacity of different models. Keep a list of the companies that you are doing business with in that particular city, including addresses and telephone numbers. If you are fortunate enough to have a contact with a security man or a secretary at the company you are visiting, try to get as much information about landing facilities as possible to insure a smooth visit.

AIRPORTS

Know the airport facilities that you are going to possibly use in a particular city or country. Know where the bathroom, telephone, gift shop, newstands, and restaurants are located. Know the handling agents and if you are dealing with a private aircraft, any telephone number and telex number as well as the contact person. What is the nature and scheduling requirement of the customs and immigration facility? Some foriegn airports require 24-hour notice for you to land and receive proper customs and immigration clearance. Otherwise you may just sit on the airplane until the next morning, They won't let you off.

Be aware of the location of the airport security, police office, and first aid station. If you are using a commercial flight, know the exact location of the terminal that you are going to use. In New York, for example, the shuttles serving New York City and Washington, D.C., are in different areas. Where are you going to drop off both your principal and luggage? Predesignate this point. The airport police can assist you with special parking and security arrangements, crowd control, and terminal escorts.

The ticket counter will have a customer service manager. You can get special VIP handling by using these people. People don't use them enough. Most people aren't even aware that they exist. They can do a great deal for you like get special handling for the baggage, move you through checkpoints to the VIP lounges, take you through to holding areas, and expedite transportation and luggage between flights. They can assist to make your life easier. They can approve extra baggage for overhead storage. They can keep a seat open by your principal until the last minute. They can keep a seat reserved as long as the flight is not full. Also, if you are traveling with a government official, they can box seats off around your principal for security reasons. If seats are available, this can be done for the private individual VIP as well.

Try to avoid confusion at the security check points. It saves you a lot of grief if you approach security before you come through, for example, say "Listen, I am going to be coming through at such and such a time with a brief case full of jewelry. I don't want to open it here at the detector and let everyone see what is in the briefcase, so I'm mentioning it now. Can you check it in a room so I won't expose all this jewelry?" If you are a federal agent or if you are traveling in a law enforcement capacity, prearrange weapons, auto, and personnel passes. It will save a tremendous amount of headaches. Be aware of and prepared to deal with new or temporary security measures utilized at some airports, such as having to plug in computers, VCR's, and electronic carry-on equipment in order to observe the fact that they are operable. Don't wear things that are going to set off the metal detector. You see some personnel traveling in a protective detail with gold bracelets, necklaces, and rings. This only draws attention to you and your principal when the metal detectors are activated. Maintain a low profile.

With commerical flights, have some idea about how long it takes to sign in, to get food service, and to get from the gate to the car. Have an idea about how long it is going to take you from point A to point B in case someone may ask you. Know the location of security personnel on the flight. If you are traveling with a large detail, you might want to strategically place them and spread them out. Try to be aware of other details which could be traveling on the same flight. You can clear with the airport police to make plane side or ramp side pickups. Remember, if you are handling a government personality, this same information is available to the other side. Get the floor plans of the aircraft, as well as the terminal. These are free and available at most airports.

If you are dealing with a high risk, high profile target, you will want to become more familiar with counter sniper and building surveys, particularly from the airport to your destination. Know exactly what time you will be arriving at the hotel or facility where your principal is scheduled to be. How long it takes to get to your destination will depend on the traffic flow. Are you arriving during morning or afternoon rush hour? It is very reassuring to tell your employer that arrival time from this point is 22 minutes. Or, for example, if you have ever been to Tokyo, it can take you two hours to get into downtown Tokyo during rush hour. Even with light traffic there, it can take an hour.

VEHICLES

What car service will you use? Try to establish a regular driver, one that handles you whenever you come in. Avoid switching drivers. It also gives you a chance to do a background check on him. That particular driver gets familiar with the places that you go, the restaurants, and the appointments that you make. By using the same driver, he becomes familiar with your needs and the places you are likely to go. Time is not wasted locating addresses. Of course, if you are advancing these sites that is another matter. Request telephones in the cars and be sure they have the capability for long distance calling. Now, most car services have them. Do not use limousines, use a full size sedan such as a Lincoln Town car. It has lots of room, luggage space, and a very low profile. It looks like all the other cars you are going to see on the road.

Get the home telephone number of the driver along with the type of cars your office arranges for and any billing details. At the end of the trip, you can avoid coping with credit charges if you can pre-establish a billing arrangement. If you are preoccupied with billing problems, you are not in control of the situation. If you are using a car service when you are traveling or if you are using a corporate car with in house staff then at least you have the benefit of having a driver to assist you. Hopefully he has been trained well enough to use the car effectively in an ambush situation.

The driver should stay with the vehicle at all times when it is being used for transportation of the principal. When he takes it home at the end of the day or back to the garage, he must be able to determine that the vehicle will be kept secure. When he returns to the vehicle in the morning, he will still do a search before he picks you up. Many companies are only fooling themselves by employing a single so-called chauffeur-bodyguard, rather than two men. For most companies, this is their weakest point. Their principal's most vulnerable point is during transport. It is amazing how many company chauffeurs are unaware of this vulnerability. Many companies harden offices and home sites, but then they neglect to give their drivers, who are responsible for one of their companies most important assets, the senior executive, the proper training.

[Please note detailed checklists included in the Appendix with respect to advance work and actual protective movements.]

SEVEN

Interviewing Unwanted Visitors

by Taylor R. Rudd, Jr.

ANYONE WHO REQUIRES a protective detail is going to attract people who want to visit, call, write, or in extreme cases, to harm the protectee. The numbers of these people are directly proportional to the protectee's visibility. More people will try to contact the President of the United States than will try to contact a governor or a chief executive officer.

How a protective detail handles these people is a critical part of the entire protective effort. Too often the protective detail is understaffed, on the move, or otherwise too busy to take the time to interview a person who attempts to contact the protectee. The point of this chapter is to emphasize that it is imperative that these people be interviewed if at all possible because a great deal may be learned from them. It will enhance the overall protective effort.

These people may attempt to contact the protectee at any time or place. When someone appears with the statement "I will not leave until I talk to . . . ," the protective detail must be prepared to handle this person and a good interview is an essential first step.

TYPES OF VISITORS

For the sake of simplicity, unwanted visitors may be divided into three broad categories: the curious, the nuisance, and the potentially dangerous. The first problem the protector faces is how to determine which is which.

CURIOUS

Most people are interested in seeing prominent people. Often times the protective detail or a motorcade will be enough to attract a crowd. Most rational people know that they cannot have an interview with a protectee and they are satisfied to stand back and just get a glimpse of him. Some may want to shake hands or get an autograph but if rebuffed, they realize that further pursuit is useless.

NUISANCE

The nuisance is a person who persistently tries to contact a protectee even though the protectee or staff has offered no encouragement. Many of these people may write, call or even visit on a regular basis.

The President may have ten individuals who write two or three letters a day, every day. As protectors, it is not uncommon to encounter someone who tries to call, write or visit your protectee daily. Often the nuisance will have a problem, idea, or complaint which was factual in its origin, but has now become an unreasonable obsession. It is very reasonable to him! Perhaps, for example, someone is focusing on your principal because his family farm was condemned. It was needed for a cloverleaf on the interstate. He has complained to everyone that his family was not adequately compensated for the land.

The nuisance will rarely persist to the point where he may be a threat to the protectee, but he can be a real pest. There is not much that can be done as long as no laws are broken. His picture and brief biography should be distributed to all members of the protective detail, staff members and the protectee's family.

POTENTIALLY DANGEROUS

Determining who these people are and what to do about them is a primary function of the protective detail. The protectee really needs no protection in situations involving the curious or the nuisance as they pose no threat to his personal security.

It must be assumed that someone who would try to harm a protectee—or anyone else—probably has a mental problem. Any individual who attempts to contact the protectee should be treated with extreme caution until it is determined by interview which of the above categories he falls into. He may appear obviously unbalanced, or he may appear quite normal. The task placed upon the protective detail is how to determine who is a danger to the protectee.

Anyone who has an unusual interest in the protectee and is abusive, obscene, or threatening should be of particular interest to you.

THE INTERVIEW

Remember, your objective is to find out if the individual is a danger to your protectee or to you or anyone else, including himself. You are not trying to determine guilt or innocence; you want to find out if the subject will harm your protectee. If he has broken a law, he may be arrested, or if he is mentally ill, he may be committed, but some day he will be released. Will he then try to harm your protectee? So you are concerned with the long term outcome as well as with what he may do today.

The best time to interview one of these people is when the first contact is made. In the vast majority of cases, he will initiate the contact because he wants something. He wants something from the protectee or he wants to give him something such as information or advice. He is far more receptive to a good interview because he has not been rebuffed nor has he been arrested. As the old saying goes, "He may be crazy, but he is not stupid."

The primary difference between this type of interview is that you want the subject to talk about himself as much as possible. You want to find out if he is a danger to your protectee, you, others or himself.

Always assume that anyone you interview is potentially dangerous and act accordingly. At the outset of the interview, get enough personal information to have a co-worker conduct a name check. By telling the subject that before he can see the protectee, he must be positively identified. You can obtain at least his full name, address, date and place of birth, and social security number. While a co-worker is conducting whatever name checks are possible, encourage the subject to talk. Why does he want to contact the protectee? What is his background? How did he come to decide that the protectee can help him or that he can help the protectee?

The way to find out this information is to encourage the subject to talk. No matter how outlandish his statements are, be sympathetic and understanding. If he is mentally ill, he may say some things that are utterly impossible to believe and at times very funny to you. Be professional and learn to be understanding. People who are mentally ill don't need to be told that they are crazy. They have heard that before from family members and others. If you listen to them and even encourage him to talk, he will trust you and in most cases, will tell you anything you may ask.

You cannot let him wander too far afield in his talking. Don't cut off his conversation, but gently ask him to elaborate on something he said previously.

One good way of encouraging him to talk and to assist you in obtaining your objective is to ask questions requiring more than yes or no answers. Such as:

1. Why do you feel that way?
2. What does that mean to you?
3. Who else have you contacted about this?
4. What response have you gotten?
5. If (protectee) can't help you, what will you do?

Be alert for evasive answers, anger or other signs which may affect your judgment and your questions. Any statement indicating a propensity for violence in any direction should be pursued to its fullest. Be patient. By now you should have his confidence and by asking questions in a low key manner, you will be surprised at the answers you may get. Some will tell the most intimate secrets of their life and what their intentions may be. There have been cases where people have been asked what they intend to do if the protectee will not help them and they have answered "I'll blow his head off." This should certainly be a clue to the interviewer that until proven otherwise, this person is a real danger.

Some visitors will claim that they have a high level of knowledge in a particular field. It may be that they are a Ph.D. or a pilot or perhaps an astronaut. Usually you will not have the resources to verify this type of claim beyond asking for some type of documentation.

One method which has proven effective is to conduct reality testing. You do not have to be an expert to do this. You simply ask the subject to explain to you what is involved in the claimed field. Many who make claims such as this have a superficial knowledge of the field, but on closer examination, will expose themselves as frauds.

When he tells you what his field of expertise is, tell him that it is very interesting (whether it is or not) and ask him to elaborate. Keep asking him to explain various aspects of the claim including educational and practical experience. Don't be afraid to ask for details about technical claims, even if you don't understand them. The more questions you ask, the more likely the subject will trip himself up. Of course, if he answers all of your questions satisfactorily and with authority, maybe he does have the expertise he claims. In either case, this is valuable information for you to have.

Don't get hung up on note taking. You must take some notes but do your writing when he is talking about something innocuous. If you take notes every time he shows anger or when he is talking about his expertise with weapons or how much he dislikes your protectee, he will pick up on what you are doing and may stop talking.

After you have obtained all of the information from him that you feel you are going to get, and you feel that you can place him into either the curious, nuisance, or dangerous categories, then ask about his personal history. Has he an arrest record, history of mental illness, or relevant family history? Is he on medication of any type, etc.? Some of these facts may have come out during the interview and may be expanded on now.

You should make a decision as to how dangerous the subject is. If he is just curious, you probably should not pursue any further investigation. If he appears that he may be a nuisance, you may want to conduct a follow-up investigation to insure that he has not "conned" you and is really a dangerous person. It has happened more than once before. If you feel that the person is dangerous, you want to find out as much as possible.

Fortunately, most of the people you are going to interview are not going to be dangerous. How do you know unless you have interviewed them and conducted a follow-up investigation, if necessary? Profiles should be established for the people who are dangerous. You must be aware that voluminous files become useless. Only files of the dangerous few should be given priority and carried with the protective detail in transit. The files of the nuisance types should be kept at the residence and office, or carried in the form of an abbreviated name list for quick identification. These people are probably known to the protective detail and staff anyway.

THE MOST DANGEROUS

Based on past history, the person who is most likely to harm your protectee is "the loser." While the professional killer should not be overlooked, you will probably never get an opportunity to interview him until after the fact.

The loser can usually be identified through a good interview. He or she will usually have unsatisfactory relationships with the opposite sex, trouble holding a job, few if any close friends, low self esteem (although they may try to hide it through bravado or aggressive behavior), and a general feeling of despair.

Many times "the loser" will feel that by harming a prominent person, he may get the recognition (although negative) that has eluded him during his entire life. He may feel that if he can harm a protectee, he will willingly forfeit his own life or freedom in exchange for that recognition. Often he will show signs of being suicidal during the interview. Be very wary if he shows these signs. Many psychiatrists feel that "a suicide is a murder looking for a place to happen." When a person contemplates suicide, it is because he is trapped in a dead end. He can see no way out of his predicament. Certainly not all suicides want to harm anyone else before they die, but in your interview, be alert to anyone who feels that your protectee is either the only one who can help or is the sole cause of his problems. Also, take note if someone is seeking recognition which he believes has been due him. Any undue direction of interest toward the protectee should be considered with caution.

ACTION

Be familiar with state, local, and federal laws in your area of operation. Contact the local and state police where your protectee works and lives. Explain your responsibilities, capabilities and limitations. Predetermine how these agencies may be of assistance to you. Find out what local laws covering mental health, trespassing, loitering and/or threatening statements and actions will allow you to do, and, how the police may assist you. When possible, this should also be done when the protectee is traveling.

If your protectee is a national figure, contact the U.S. Secret Service and FBI offices and let them know your protectee's scheduled itinerary. They may have information that will be of use to you. Emphasize that you are providing this information for information sake only unless you have a specific need for assistance.

FOLLOW UP UNVESTIGATION

If a person has threatened your protectee and he has been arrested or committed for mental observation as a result, chances are that he will be back on the street in a short period of time. If you have conducted a good interview and determined that he is dangerous, you should conduct a follow-up investigation to either confirm or refute your assessment. The follow-up should not be restricted just to those who are locked up or dangerous, but whenever possible. Do not overlook subjects who you feel *may* be of interest to the protective detail. The consequences of ignoring someone far outweigh the expenditure of resources needed to either confirm or refute an assessment.

The following are a few minimal steps in the follow-up investigation:

1. Obtain a photo.
2. Do a police records check.
3. Check for mental hospitalization.
4. Interview friends, relatives and people he has tried to contact.
5. Keep your own up-to-date records of people who are felt to be dangerous and abbreviated lists of known nuisances. These records should be accessible to the protective detail at all times.

SUMMARY

No protective detail can afford the luxury of not interviewing anyone who displays an inordinate or persistent direction of interest towards their protectee. Due to the restrictions of manpower and other resources, it is often difficult to give these people the time and attention necessary to make a proper evaluation, but every effort to do so must be made.

A good interview, combined with a follow up investigation can identify people who constitute a danger to a protectee as well as those who are not a danger.

By conducting the interview in a patient and understanding way, the visitor will often give the interviewer all the information he needs to make a judgment which will benefit the entire protective function.

EIGHT

Portable Protection Technology

by Professor John I. Kostanoski, CST

LAW ENFORCEMENT, corrections, and security officers have tended to react to protection-related problems in the past by making procedural and/or personnel adjustments. Today, however, increasing numbers of practitioners are attending a variety of physical security seminars in order to acquire a new type of skill—silicon rather than carbon-based—that offers capabilities previously unavailable. The current trend in the security field entails a much greater reliance on technology. Technology is impacting on the criminal justice and security professions in significant ways. The following are just two examples:

1. Improvements in technology are rapidly being incorporated into police, corrections, and security operations to enhance service capabilities. For example, approximately 2300 prisoners are now supervised by electronic monitoring devices in their homes. State corrections, probation and parole authorities in 33 states were using these systems in 1988, three times the total in 1987.*

2. New technologies and novel tactics to control and prevent crime are evolving. An example is robotics. Robots can patrol, detect, report and respond to threats. They can control crowds, handle bomb and toxic disturbances, climb steps and lift objects many times their own weight. Either fully autonomous or remotely controlled, they can go into areas that human counterparts cannot or will not go.

Throughout their careers, security professionals, including personal protection specialists, will encounter further advancements in technology. It is the latter group for whom this chapter on portable protection systems has been written. These systems have been designed for personnel who don't know all the technical details but who desire to reinforce their ability to handle and manage protection assignments with a technological advantage. These devices are easy to operate, take less than five minutes

---

*See Schmidt, Annesley K., "Electronic Monitoring of Offenders Increases", *NIJ Reports*, Rockville, MD.: National Institute of Justice, U.S. Department of Justice, January/February, 1989, pp. 2-5.

to set up, even less time to remove, and they can be used in a variety of settings indoors and outdoors.

Courtesy of Executive Protection Institute, Berryville, Virginia.

INTERSECTOR-RF Indoor Protection System.

INDOOR SYSTEM: HOW IT WORKS

A wireless sensor detects the presence of a person and transmits a radio frequency signal to a receiver housed in an attache case. This signal is re-transmitted to a pager-receiver carried by a security person or the signal is used to activate a siren. The signaling process takes seconds to complete. There are five types of sensors that are standard equipment on the portable indoor system: hand-held transmitter; executive pen transmitter; detector cell; magnetic actuated switch; and passive infrared detector.

Sensor ———— 150′ ———— Attache Case ———— 2 miles ———— Pager Receivers

Siren

HAND-HELD TRANSMITTER

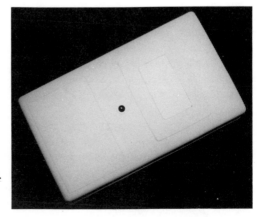

Hand-held Transmitter.

This transmitter can be hidden in a soft pack of cigarettes. It produces a silent alert when its user is in a threat situation. It does so unobtrusively.

APPLICATIONS:

Hospital Nurse: A female nurse had been receiving threatening phone calls. She informed security that she was leaving for the day. As she approached her car she encountered a stranger who threatened her. She activated a hand-held transmitter in her coat pocket whose signal was received by a security officer on patrol. He responded in seconds.

Police: Narcotics officers were planning to make a buy and subsequently arrest a drug dealer. The drug dealer specified the location for the transaction which was to be a certain street corner. The buyer was provided with a hand-held transmitter cleverly disguised inside a soft pack of cigarettes. The buyer completed the transaction, pulled out his pack of cigarettes and in doing so alerted the stake-out team to make an arrest.

DETECTOR CELL

Detector Cell Sensor.

A momentary type switch can be placed under any object that weighs at least two ounces. Removing or lifting the object activates the cell. Computer terminals, typewriters, books, and even drawings, for example, can be protected with detector cells. Also known as a "theft button."

APPLICATION

Hospital: A hospital suspected that a head nurse was entering patients' rooms to steal cash and personal items. Security placed a wallet containing identifiable money in a selected patient's room while the patient was in surgery. A security officer waited in a room nearby. The moment the wallet was picked up, a signal prompted the officer to walk in on the suspect. The surprised employee was subsequently caught in the act of stealing.

University: A major university had suffered substantial losses of computer terminals. To put an end to these losses detector cells were placed under those models known to have a high resale value. Shortly thereafter security received a signal that a terminal was being lifted. They responded and caught the thief. This is another instance in which portable protection technology has enabled security to react instantly and eyewitness a criminal act.

MAGNETIC ACTUATED SWITCH

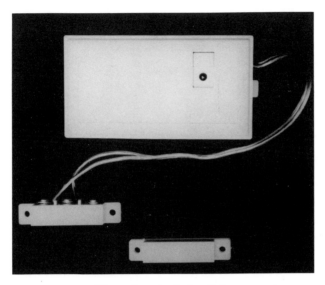

Magnetic actuated switch.

A switch that consists of two separate units, mounted in a fixed position (door jam, window frame, desk drawer frame) opposing the magnet, which is fastened to a moving door, window, or desk drawer. When the door, window or desk drawer is opened the magnet moves with it and away from the actuated switch, thereby removing the force holding the switch closed, and so it opens. The change in the switch's position activates the transmitter.

APPLICATIONS:

Business Office: Someone was entering an office and stealing items from the desks of various secretaries. The door and desk were temporarily protected with magnetic actuated switches. An employee entered the office after hours and triggered the magnetic actuated switch on the door. Security was alerted and dispatched an officer to wait outside the office. The employee then opened a desk drawer, triggering another switch. Security walked in on the employee who was caught in the act of stealing.

Airline: Airline passenger luggage was being removed, opened and items were taken. The thief would close a suitcase and allow it to continue on its journey to the passenger pick-up area. Passengers, once home, would discover their loss and report it to the airline. Security placed an expensive-looking suitcase onto the conveyer belt with a marked camera strapped over a detector cell and a magnetic actuated switch affixed to the locking mechanism. When the thief opened the suitcase security received an alert signal and stationed themselves outside the exit area. The second sensor signal meant that the camera had been lifted off of the detector cell. An employee, within one minute of receipt of this signal, was observed leaving the exit area with camera in hand. His employment was terminated.

PASSIVE INFRARED DETECTOR

Passive infrared detector.

This battery-operated (9v transistor type) detector takes in what a human sends out, infrared energy or what we know as temperature. In as much as it receives and does not emit energy, the term "passive" is used. The detector operates in much the same way as our eyes, which sees light; specifically, the visible light portion of the electromagnetic spectrum. The detector "sees" the infrared portion of this same spectrum. The detector continuously monitors the infrared energy or temperature of everything within the range of its field of view, and as long as the particular room's or zone's background temperature remains constant, nothing happens. If a human being enters the detector's field of view, the difference in his or her body temperature will cause the detector to activate a RF transmission. The detector is sometimes mounted on the ceiling, camouflaged as a smoke detector. It creates an invisible screen that surrounds a valuable object. A thief moving into this invisible screen to reach the object sets off the detector. Some models may also be used with a mirror. They can "see" infrared energy reflected in a mirror and thus can offer additional investigative-surveillance-personal protection applications.

APPLICATIONS

Brokerage Firm: The security staff of a financial house had been utilizing CCTV to counter its employee theft problems. The need for the services of an outside electrician, the need for a well lit field of view, the difficulty of identifying the thief on the video-tape, and the inability of this equipment to function adequately in outside areas undermined this approach. Portable protection technology changed all that. The first time it was used, it caught a thief removing an expensive electronic typewriter. The moment the thief walked into the invisible beam, security was put on alert. By lifting the typewriter, the thief activated a detector cell and security moved in.

Corporate Espionage: An international corporation suspected that their computer tapes were being copied. A portable passive infrared detector detected entry into the computer room after normal business hours. It also detected re-entry into the computer room five hours later. Apparently cleaning personnel entered the computer room, took the tapes to be copied, and then returned them.

Courtesy of Executive Protection Institute, Berryville, Virginia

INTERSECTOR-EXT outdoor protection system.

OUTDOOR SYSTEMS: HOW IT WORKS

A sensor (outdoor passive infrared motion detector) senses movement and transmits a RF signal to a receiver housed in an attache case. This signal is re-transmitted to pager-receivers carried by security personnel or the signal is used to activate a siren. The signaling process takes seconds to complete. Standard equipment includes two outdoor passive motion detectors.

Sensor ——— 70' ——— Attache   Case ——2 miles——— Pager-Receivers

Siren

PASSIVE INFRARED MOTION DETECTOR

Outdoor passive infrared motion detectors.

This battery-powered (Three AA 1.5v) detector can operate during the day or night and it can "see" the infrared energy emitted by a person or object in motion. It observes this energy through its line of sight, and it is weatherproof for outdoor use. It is designed to operate for two years before its batteries need to be replaced.

APPLICATIONS:

Executive Protection: During a personal protection assignment, a principal, in this case a well known political leader, parked his limousine and entered a restaurant to attend a luncheon meeting. Personal protection specialists placed outdoor passive infrared detectors around the car. If anyone attempted to plant or conceal a bomb on the car the protection team would have been notified in seconds to counteract the attempt.

Campus Security: A college was renovating one of its classroom buildings. Security received report that students had been seen at this site drinking beer and "partying." The area was considered hazardous and a fence had been placed around it. Security also set up outdoor passive infrared motion detectors at the excavation site. Anyone entering the area would trigger the detectors and activate an on-site local alarm (siren). Simultaneously, a security officer assigned to patrol duties would receive a signal on his pager-receiver (remote alarm) and could respond at once.

CONCLUSION

Criminal justice agencies and private security firms will redouble their emphasis on the recruitment, development, and retention of quality personnel. As with other professions, technology is finding widespread use as a tool to aid security personnel in meeting increased demands for their services. The technology described in this chapter bridges the gap between traditional procedures and novel countermeasures. It is a transition that points the way to new standards of protection excellence. It represents the vision, as well as the journey, of our profession.

PART III

Fine Tuning Your Approach

NINE

Stress and the
Personal Protection Specialist

by Bruce L. Danto, M.D.

A SEARCH OF THE LITERATURE fails to reveal any study that has been done to date regarding stress for this type of professional, a personal protection specialist.

Yet, occupational stress as a general category is a well-known phenomenon. Many studies have been done on various types of jobs concerning the relationship between work productivity and special areas of occupational functions that give rise to stress.

Stress has become the battle cry of our modern world, in terms of the work place, the family, and even in play and recreation as reflected by the problems of athletes. The world was shocked when Donnie Moore, a former California Angels star pitcher, killed himself after seriously wounding his wife in their home in Orange County, California. Particularly stressful to him was the fact that he had pitched what became the home run ball to Dave Henderson, costing the Angels not only the game, but also the pennant race a few years ago.

GENERAL FEATURES OF STRESS

In all stress reactions, there are three stages of adaptation to stress. The first is *alarm,* the situation where the systems of a person are aroused to respond and all internal resources are focused on the stress factor. The second stage is *resistance,* where all systems react to bring the effects of the stress factor within tolerable levels. If the stress is not successfully resolved or reduced at this stage, then a third stage follows—*exhaustion.* In this stage, the defenses of all systems collapse, and the stress effects run wild. Chronic illness, psychosis, distressing physical symptoms or even death may result.

As happens with most professional workers who have a great deal of responsibility connected with their jobs and unending sources of frustration—in the profession most related to personal protection, namely the police officer—this type of individual has become subject to stress reactions, often with unfortunate and irreversible effects.

Cardiologists who specialize in stress effects on the heart have been able to obtain some scientific evidence of stress by questioning persons regarding their job situation while an EKG is running. For those who have experienced cardiac symptoms like chest pain on the job, the EKGs reflect serious and significant changes as the patient simply talks about his job. This was particularly true of cardiac studies of police officers.

POLICE STRESS

For purposes of background, since previous studies regarding personal protection specialists are not available for reference or contrast, stress for the police officer will be reviewed. The author has conducted a considerable amount of research in this area.

It should be pointed out from the very beginning that there are differences between police officers and personal protection specialists, as well as among police officers who are used to perform this role.

In the first place, the police officer is a part of a paramilitary organization and is trained to take orders from superior officers. The personal protection specialist frequently has to function on his own. He has to be flexible and make up the rules as he goes. Management guidelines evolve as he sees, senses and then determines what is appropriate behavior to protect the principal. The personal protection specialist has virtually no powers of arrest, like any other civilian, and he is in no position to command people to do anything. His function is to protect the principal. He reduces risk and prevents exposure to volatile situations, removing the principal if necessary.

Unlike the police officer, who has the authority of a badge and gun, the personal protection specialist is left to his own devices. The police officer, like the soldier, not only has a defensive function, but he also has an offensive function. He has to give chase to wrongdoers in order to apprehend them. The personal protection specialist's primary responsibility is to remove that protectee to a place of safety. His mission does not include apprehension of the wrongdoer, particularly if he is privately employed. Even a Secret Service protection detail is primarily concerned with protection of the principal. Other agents are used to make arrests. Local police agencies will assign officers whose responsibilities are protection, apprehension and crime containment.

The police officer is then subject to any resulting press coverage if an incident comes down. He may have to answer to a shooting board—if so, he may be suspended pending investigation. He may be assigned an evidence gathering role. If a crime has been committed. On the other hand, the personal protection specialist is not responsible for an investigation or prosecution of a crime, but is solely interested in keeping his principal out of trouble.

The personal protection specialist is not expected to return fire unless an assault makes it impossible to protect the protectee otherwise. On the other hand, the police officer, like the military, has an offensive role, which means that fire may be returned almost immediately and hot pursuit of the perpetrators will occur. The personal protection specialist should be free of this responsibility.

Aside from these differences, certainly, protecting life and property is a function common to both the police officer and the personal protection specialist. Let's review some of the features of work stress for the police officer and see whether or not any of these have some application or open up applications for study regarding the personal protection specialist.

The police officer is a work machine who has to live with a greater degree of accountability than any other professional, such as a doctor or lawyer.[1] The officer must answer to the press, the public, lawyers in court, citizen commissioner boards, supervisory personnel, neighbors, friends—everybody. He must patrol the streets, refrain from the use of force whenever possible, account for why he fired his sidearm, live in fear while working in areas of the community where citizens are hostile toward the police, and endure suspension whenever he is involved in a fatal shooting. He is scorched if he belongs to a union which does not support the mayor who is elected. He confronts political factors which are alien to a personal protection specialist. Politicians who decide on pay raises, fringe benefits, and who wield a lot of influence in the community, can be an endless source of trouble, and anxiety.

Despite these sources of stress, he is expected to be insensitive to all these events, maintain his duty assignment, pretend that nothing has really happened, accommodate overtime, which usually is not compensated even with time off, and must have his sleep habits interrupted by constant changes of shifts. In addition, he must be away from home during times of personal problems with children or marriage.

Working under such pressure reflects the basic attitude that a policeman is supposed to be big and dumb, function like a good soldier, fit into whatever the system demands of him or her. Obviously, this represents a dehumanized picture of a person, let alone a police officer. Everyone knows how many psychiatric casualties come out of war. It is not any different for the police officer who is a combat veteran of the streets, in an urban or rural environment.

It is well-known, in general, that under stress, a police officer can develop asthma, gastrointestinal distress, pounding headaches, hypertension, significant shifts in weight in terms of either gain or loss, muscle aches and emotional anxiety.

Dr. Hans Selye, a well-known scientist, has expressed the belief that, in nature, all creatures survive to achieve physical and psychological balance. This balance is called homeostasis. A person who feels stressed and tense will try to achieve balance by doing something about it. We call that coping. Many officers who feel stressed use alcohol to calm down, smoke too much, turn to sex, violence or tranquilizers. Some wind up committing suicide, with a rate of between 22 to 40 per 100,000 whereas the general suicide rate for the United States is 13 per 100,000.

Causes for stress for the police officer can be found in several different areas:

Administrative: The issuance of an order means that the problem has been defined, regardless of whether or not it makes any sense. All too frequently, a police department functions on the basis of rank, not wisdom.

Partner Assignment: If a partner is inadequate or poorly motivated, the officer may feel his life is in greater danger, either because the partner handles people poorly, or he provokes them into violence against the police. Perhaps the partner is frightened by street confrontations and will provide little or no back up.

Supervision: Perhaps the supervising officer has a college degree, but no street experience. His capacity to handle police problems or perform police assignments may be radically impaired if not totally inefficient. As a consequence, the police officer will be chewed out for mistakes, not the supervisor who either misdirected him or failed to give him competent supervision.

Shift Structure: Although shifts may change every 30 days, lifestyles don't. Most of us spend the first 21 years of our lives sleeping at night and working during the day. When the officer is sworn in after the academy, all this changes. It is hard to sleep during the day while making changes. If the officer is seen napping in his patrol car or a reporter or photographer shows a policeman slacking on the job he is criticized. Nobody appreciates the stress of accommodating to a constantly changing sleeping schedule.

Social/Personal Factors: Obviously, the officer is going to meet people like women in bars and will come into contact with other lonely people. He may find that his wife and family cannot really offer the support he needs to do the kind of job he is expected to perform.

He may find because of administrative stresses like being called in to work overtime or having a different shift, that his wife begins to complain because she is running different feeding schedules and does not have her husband available to help her with the problems of child rearing.

Deficient Equipment: Patrol becomes frustrating and even dangerous when the equipment that is used is not working. There may be a patrol car with no spare tire, no working first aid equipment, not enough gas with which to begin patrol, and the preceding crew of partners may not have cleaned or checked the shotgun.

Paperwork: Additional stress comes from the amount of the paperwork itself. Few guidelines are offered to help the officer write a meaningful report. The report may be filled with grammatical and spelling errors, and this may come to haunt the officer when he is asked to discuss his report in court.

Contact with Unstable People: Another problem concerns the type of citizens to be managed. Because of a general failure throughout the United States to appropriately address the management of mentally ill citizens, more of them are being brought into contact with police officers as they become involved in crime and are fed into the criminal justice system instead of the mental health system. Confrontations by these types of citizens become particularly stressful for the police officer because he is expected to handle explosive, unpredictable, and violent behavior with little or no back up from other agencies, or training in how to psychologically defuse such individuals.

Failure to Communicate: In the personal area of his life, the police officer is reluctant to share these concerns and work experiences with family members. In my judgment, this is a very bad mistake, but it is, nonetheless, a common practice. Officers are told in the academy to keep their business in the corner bar, where they will have the opportunity to deprogram and let off steam during the typical "choirboy"-type, "letting your hair down" exercises that police officers engage in from time to time.

Thus, the police officer is involved in a vicious cycle. He is reluctant to share his concerns and work with his family members. He becomes a part of the so-called police family to the exclusion of his own family. The officer's social circle begins to narrow. He becomes isolated from his family by the system, as well as from the mainstream of society. He is a policeman all the time and never leaves duty to gain a perspective about being a person, spouse, or parent, as well as a non-police officer/citizen.

Suicide, as mentioned, is frequently associated with guilt feelings and alcohol dependency. The divorce rate among officers is very high.

They take a beating from the press, feel embarrassment from neighbors and relatives if they are involved in some serious problem like death arising from a high-speed chase in which they have participated or a fatal shooting of a suspect who turns out to be a child.

With this type of exposure to public and neighborhood reaction, it gets mighty cold and lonely on top of the mountain, as far as the officer is concerned. He becomes acutely aware of the absence of any support.

Adding to his personal worries is the reality that the courts seem to more frequently protect the rights of the offender, rather than those offended against.

Technicalities lead to dismissal of charges. Less than 25% of all felony convictions end up in prison, and an increasing number of people get off with light sentences.

Political problems within the department such as Affirmative Action may be another stumbling block creating additional stress. In can inhibit his chances of promotion. He may score higher on the promotional test,[2] but still won't get the promotion—it is more than stressful.

Increases in psychosomatic distress, drinking, family problems, and dissatisfaction with police work can be traced to Affirmative Action-related conflicts.

There are other problems impairing promotion opportunities besides Affirmative Action. It has been well known that promotions may involve getting on the good side of some official within the department, and may occur despite questionable qualifications, particularly in large urban departments.

On the streets, officers have to maintain their constant state of alert, and this is definitely stressful. The officer has to be ready to employ physical force, maintain sharp awareness of what goes on around him, be prepared for danger at any turn. He must also contend with the boredom of routine patrol at 30 miles per hour.

It is quite apparent that stress produces a cut-off of emotions in the officer, who learns to keep his feelings locked up. Such tight control may break down at other times, causing poorly timed emotional explosions. It is at this point that arrests become inappropriately physical, and citizens who are arrested may show signs of prisoner abuse.

The problems of not being able to express feelings can trigger the development of psychosomatic problems such as racing heart, ulcers, diarrhea, colitis, breathing impairments such as asthma, overeating, weight loss due to undereating and anorexia, and increased smoking. Sexual dysfunction may occur or an effort to cope with stress physically may involve too much exercise or too much sexual activity in order to re-experience a feeling of potency through sex.

The net result is impaired concentration, slowed reaction time, irritability, exhaustion, increased need for sleep and low energy. Many officers have their families, or keep their families, but still become workaholics. They also become alcoholics. Some may become involved in drug abuse.

They develop high levels of cholesterol and triglycerides, both of which are precursors to heart disease. When they are accompanied with hypertension and smoking, there may be a 50% increase in cardiac disease.

From all this, it is apparent that the profession of police work has become more complicated and demanding. There are job-specific sources of stress in terms of how the job affects the personal life of the officer and his family. He cannot turn to his uniform, the badge and gun for the feeling that he has an important job to do and that he will be the recipient of respect. Similarly, the physician in our community is confronted with the same loss of self-esteem due to a general community depreciation of trust and respect for the role of the physician.

It is not difficult to understand why many may commit suicide early in their careers. The loss of highly experienced trained personnel could be due to an exodus from police work to the private sector, where stress does not have to erode away at the health and emotional state of the officer.

In a study of 12 police suicides in the Detroit Police Department, it came to light that factors preceding the suicide involved an officer group that was relatively young. They had relatively little service time, an abundance of marital problems, poor and diminishing service rating, and they expressed feelings of guilt about shooting incidents. The department structure and problems contributed to the frustration levels of these men, which failed to offer any management of the troubled and suicidal officer. It is apparent that the department structure had not prepared supervisors to look for warning signs of suicide. These were officers who, in addition to their lowered performance reviews, also had been involved in more physical confrontations with arrested citizens, and were involved in an increasing number of duty-related automobile accidents, as well as showing signs of increased drinking.[3]

The study showed poor relationships between the department and the families of its officers, where there was no line of communication open in order for the department to know that there may have been personal problems within the family.

Political problems have an impact on the members of the police department. In a study of political-induced stress in officers of the Wayne County Sheriff's Department, such effects were clearly seen.[4]

Well known to all who have been officers or studied the problem of police stress is the destructive effect of a police shooting on the officer who is involved.[5]

Prior to 1960, whenever a police officer displayed bravery by killing a thief, shooting an armed criminal, or waiting in ambush for Bonnie and Clyde-type criminals, his actions were either sensationalized in movies or newspapers or he was awarded a police medal. Even today, the Dirty Harry-type of police officer seen in television series like "Police Story" portrayed the officer involved in the shooting as a truly great hero. He was able to respond to the employment of lethal force as if he was either eating a hot dog, or felt perfectly justified because of circumstances. "Lethal Weapon I and II" fundamentally shows that shooting is a part of a full day's work. Policemen were always viewed as being big, tall, and if not bright, certainly courageous.

The idea of killing wrongdoers was consistent with the notion that crime does not pay, and that people who show disrespect for a policeman by placing his life in jeopardy should pay with their lives. For the policeman, killing such dangerous persons was a matter of public expectation and honor, and was a way of preventing the wrongdoer from becoming romanticized in the public eye.

Conversely, since 1965, there were not only protest movements questioning the courts and universities, but also many Americans asked questions about why we were in Vietnam. The same revolutionary trend of the 60's began to engulf the police officer where there were lawsuits and community action groups which generated negative, even hostile, sentiments towards the police departments regarding killings.

Rather than receiving the police medal today, the officer is suspended pending an investigation. He is the target of sensationalized publicity. He awaits the uncertain outcome of a departmental hearing, as a shooting committee investigates the shooting. He no longer wants to conform to the image of being big, strong and powerful, a cop who resorts to physical force to cope with everyday police reality. Instead, we find the officer is frequently a college graduate who has strong feelings about morality and the importance of human life and family.

The modern officer applicant expresses more value for human life in general. The courts and public echo this change and protest against the careless use of lethal force by policeman. Caution is the watchword.

Over the years, I have treated a number of officers involved in fatals. They are very definitely uncomfortable with what happens when they have to pull the trigger on somebody. Many of them become so distraught they have to leave the police department. In Stanton, California, for example, an officer accidentally killed a 5-year-old who had barricaded himself behind the television, and in a dimly-lit room, his small body size assumed the size of the proportions of a full-grown man. He also was pointing a toy gun at the officer.

Officers cannot emotionally tolerate taking a life, despite all of their weeks of training in the academy and the support of the officer group.

What happens is the officer gets known as a killer in the police group. Other officers will playfully play "quick draw" with him, and he will pick up the nickname "Killer" or "Wyatt Earp." In his efforts to be of service to the community, he seems to be appalled by the fact that all he represents is the image of a killer to his peers and to the community.

Many of the officers who are involved in a fatal shooting develop drinking problems, marital problems, become either very withdrawn or begin to apply for sick time due to some kind of somatic complaint, the kinds of which have been outlined earlier in this chapter.

Such an officer becomes very emotionally remote from others, distancing themselves in order to cope with feelings of anxiety and depression. He also tries to cover up for his fear that history will repeat itself, that he will be involved once again in another fatal confrontation.

Within the police department in this era, such officers are sent for routine psychological reviews. It has been my experience that such psychological support from a department psychologist is basically inadequate because the psychologists have no appreciation of what it is like to be a police officer. In my eight years of experience as a sworn officer, I was able to establish some degree of emotional sensitivity to officers and the kinds of stress they take.

The officer involved in a fatal shooting is as much a victim as the man he kills or shoots. It goes without saying that the corrections officer meets rather cold-blooded and vicious types of inmates from time to time. They may brag about their toughness and even may talk about details of the crime, but when it comes to taking them to court, they begin to play the role of choir boy and look like they spend most of their day helping little old ladies across the street. This is very frustrating because the corrections officer cannot participate in the trial or offer observations that might inform the jury of what kind of person the defendant really is.

Visits by relatives of the inmates can be very stressful to the officer when he sees a young women with her children trying to survive economically and emotionally while her breadwinner husband or boyfriend is incarcerated. There is little the officer can do to cope with this kind of stress except make a referral to a social worker. In most jails, this type of professional has still not arrived at the scene.

The jail corrections officer frequently develops psychosomatic complaints, particularly gastrointestinal ones with lots of gas. Some develop tremors and headaches and generally overeat because the only focus for many for boredom is food.[6]

This material briefly summarizes some of the research that has been done, what is currently known about police stress, how it develops and in what ways it manifests itself among law enforcement personnel.

PERSONAL PROTECTION SPECIALIST AND THE PROBLEM OF STRESS

It should be apparent for those of us who are personal protection specialists that there are real differences between the profession of law enforcement and our own.

The personal protection specialist differs from the police officer because his role is limited to protection of the principal. He is not on patrol. He gathers intelligence, and performs a comprehensive risk assessment. He has to maintain security for the principal round-the-clock not only during travel. He must be intimately familiar with business and residential layouts, routines, schedules, vehicles, aircraft and automobiles, to name a few areas of responsibility.

The personal protection specialist is not generally identified as such by the community, perhaps only radio equipment with an earpiece may distinguish him as a personal protection specialist.

The personal protection specialist is usually free of any kind of political influence. conditions in the community and public personalities do not dictate how he goes about his job of protecting the principal. His function also does not include any primary responsibility for court appearances or for pressing charges formally against citizens who may create problems for the principal.

There are no promotions—at least visible—involved in this work. There is little career advancement or upward mobility unless he becomes a supervisor for some protection agency or he forms his own private security firm.

The amount of risk to which he is subjected during the course of his job is minimized by proper and intensive planning, intelligence gathering and secrecy. The more nondescript he appears, for example if he looks like an administrative assistant, the less likely it would be that anyone would be interested in him. Attackers are primarily interested in the principal. If the personal protection specialist is injured, it is because he sustains an injury in the process of defending the principal.

His performance reviews are likely to come from the principal whom he protects, rather than from some administrative person although not always.

The weapon he chooses is of his own preference and specifications. He is not fundamentally bound by agency policy the way a police officer is bound by departmental regulation.

In the same vein, he lives where he wants to live and there are no residency restrictions within which he has to operate. He has no union to serve as his advocate. He is an employee who has negotiated his own pay and job benefits. His job will remain the same and he will not be reaching out for other kinds of assignments.

The likelihood that he will become involved in an armed response in the process of defending his principal is minimal compared to the likelihood that an armed confrontation will occur for the police officer.

If he is doing his job correctly, he will have little opportunity to meet any groupees or women who hang around bars where police officers are known to frequent. He will have nothing to do with guests at a cocktail party or the like, as his job is strictly defined. He is not there to socialize.

He will not be confronted with problems of Affirmative Action or minority employment, as there is no political competition that should interfere with how he does his job.

Responses to some questionnaires that were mailed out recently to protective services personnel revealed that the majority of subjects were in their late twenties, none were divorced, and all were male. All were married and most had at least one child.

None had been treated for alcoholism or drug abuse.

All were at least high school graduates. Forty percent had military experience.

All were taller than 5'11" and most weighed no less than 155 pounds. Sixty percent weighed in excess of 200 pounds.

All were actively engaged in some type of sports activities, the younger ones choosing weightlifting, and the older ones played golf or ran.

In terms of firearms practice, two were at the firing range at least every one to three months, one was once a year, one was once a week, and one was every six months. (All persons surveyed did carry firearms.)

None reported any kind of medical condition except an ulnar nerve relocation in one case, and another had some indigestion which was corrected the past three months and was associated with a weight loss of 50 pounds. For this person, his reported weight at the time of survey was 215 pounds.

Sixty percent denied any intoxication by alcohol or any use of street drugs, but one, who was 30, reported he would get intoxicated once a year.

Sixty percent indicated that the absence of normal socializing due to their profession was stressful.

Only twenty percent felt that the opportunity for adventure offset the lack of socialization, and the rest did not feel any reduction of stress due to the excitement of the job.

The number of reported complaints by family and spouses about the unavailability of the professional because of his job was rated by sixty percent as being insignificant.

Forty percent felt that the job interfered with normal bodily functions or control such as going to the bathroom, eating, social activities, etc.

Eighty percent agreed that a group plan for personal protection would help relieve stresses stemming from bodily control problems due to having to be available all the time.

In response to whether or not harm to the principal might be a stress factor on the job, forty percent responded with a "yes." Feeling special because of an assignment as a personal protection specialist was not a stress reduction factor.

A prolonged period of hyperalertness as part of working as a personal protection specialist and actually guarding the principal was considered by one hundred percent to be very stressful.

Sixty percent felt that constantly anticipating trouble, while at the same time attempting to prevent overreaction, was stressful.

Despite descriptions by former Secret Service agents that they found guarding a very popular celebrity or government official too stressful because of a need to focus the eyes and look for danger, causing the body to shut everything out even including climbing stairs, sixty percent of the respondents felt that the need to focus eyes and ears to look for danger causes the body to shut out everything else.

Constant critiquing of duty assignments was stressful to forty percent.

OTHER STRESSFUL FACTORS INCLUDE:

- Boredom
- Fear of not doing well on a job
- Anticipation of problems with the fear of not being able to handle them
- Working all hours of duty assignments and not being able to enjoy time off
- Working security for political campaigns and activities that required long hours and interference with sleep.
- Staying at different hotels with different room partners

- Not being at home to deal with the family problems
- Being away from home for more than 16 days
- Handling travel vouchers or ordering food for the principal
- Seeing a violation of the law by some persons connected with the principal, without bringing about his arrest
- Not enjoying the job or lack of motivation for doing the job
- The absence of feeling of accomplishment for doing this type of work
- Failure to actively plan for security detail so that all aspects of the security operation would fall into place
- Being in poor physical shape or getting too old for the job
- The lack of a restful night's sleep during a duty assignment
- Playing hide and seek and open rebellion by the principal toward the agents assigned to guard him and even humiliating them

CONCLUSION

Interesting is the fact that all the respondents were relatively homogeneous from the standpoint of being married, feeling that physical activity was important, and that they did not turn to substance abuse to deal with any area of stress they did acknowledge. This would certainly place the personal protection specialist in a position of marked contrast to many police officers, who deal with stress through food and alcohol indulgence.

In reflection, it is apparent that this very modest effort to explore stress among personal protection specialists does show that this type of profession is not free from stress. Efforts were made in this study to develop questions that would be effective in getting at the phenomena of stress among personal protection specialists.

At this writing, a more up-to-date research instrument has been developed and will be circulated by Nine Lives Associates to its membership. It has been distributed to over 600 men and women. The objective is to obtain more definitive information on this topic.

The factor of stress becomes important as the basic industry of personal protection increases in our society due to increased threats against important persons and the development of escalating levels of violence.

Those entering the profession of personal protection specialist should be well-advised to make sure they make provisions for reducing any stress which may appear and which may be revealed in this particular publication and any to follow. In other words, it is an up-and-coming area which should capture the attention of the entire private security industry.

BIBLIOGRAPHY

[1] Danto, B.L.: Police Stress. *Police Product News.* 3 (10) October, 1979, pp. 56-60.

[2] Danto, B.L.: The Effects of Affirmative Action. *Peace Officer.* 21 (5): 33-43, April/May, 1979.

[3] Danto, B.L.: Police Suicide. *International Journal of Police Stress*

[4] Danto, B.L. and Pitman, L.M.: A Study of Politically Induced Stress in Officers of the Wayne County Sheriff's Department.

[5] Danto, B.L.: A Psychiatric View of Another Survivor of Homicide. *The American Journal of Forensic Medicine and Pathology.* 5 (3): 257-261, September, 1984.

[6] Danto, B.L: Chapter 6. Dealing with Stress. *In the Jail Officer's Training Manual.* National Sheriff's Association, 1980, pp. 101-123.

TEN

Appearance and Dress

by John J. Bakie

APPEARANCE IS A VERY IMPORTANT PART of executive protection. It's probably the first thing that will get you hired or fired. In the Executive Protection field, ninety-five percent of the time the personal protection specialist is judged more on appearance than on ability. Take the example of the marine that stands at the steps to "Air Force One". This appears to be a very prestigious assignment. This marine looks sharp and squared away; however, this marine probably has just gotten out of boot camp with only six months in the Marine Corps and has never seen a battle or done anything heroic. But the one thing that pops into everyone's mind is "I wouldn't want to mess with this guy." Why? Because he presents an appearance of confidence, strength, knowledge and the ability to take care of himself. This assumption is based solely on the man's appearance. Do you begin to see the correlation to the personal protection specialist?

The most important item of clothing is the suit. A good suit is a suit made of a blend of wool and polyester. A good blend is 45% polyester/55% wool or 40% polyester/60% wool. A 100% worsted wool suit is an excellent suit but it's not one that can be worn year round. The polyester in a suit gives it it's strength and durability. The wool in a suit gives it a rich appearance. Avoid 100% polyester suits. Polyester suits tend to show wear quicker than a blended suit and they have a tendency to snag and wrinkle easily. A good suit should cost $300 dollars or more. When shopping for a suit, it's always advisable to shop in a reputable men's clothing store. The salesmen in these stores are professionals who can assist you with color selection and the proper fit in a suit.

In selecting color, one suit should be navy blue and the other grey. Staying with basic gray or blue suits makes shirt and tie selections much easier. The navy blue suit with a white shirt and tie with some red in it makes an excellent selection either for a business dinner or in the event of an emergency, when, for example, you may be required to attend a black tie affair and you don't have a tux. A man in a navy blue suit could blend in a lot better at a black tie affair than someone in a brown or beige colored suit. Gray is another good color suit to have. Blue and gray suits are conservative and present a professional appearance. Blue pinstripe and grey pinstripe suits are also acceptable.

If you are required to carry a weapon on an assignment, be sure that you carry that weapon when you're trying on a new suit. This will ensure the proper suit coat size and augment any tailoring that might have to be done. It is advisable to buy suits one size larger than you would normally wear to allow for proper concealment of a weapon. When having your trousers tailored, place items that you normally carry in your pockets (wallet, handkerchief, keys, etc.) Also, place your belt through the belt loops to ensure that the waist of the trousers falls where you normally wear them. The bottom of your trousers should rest on the front of your shoe causing a "1/2 break" in the front crease of the legs. Remember, dry cleaning shrinks clothes so you might want to leave a little extra length to your trousers.

When having the length of your trousers measured, be sure to wear the shoes that you expect to wear with that suit. The height of heels on many shoes varies and this will affect how the trousers rest upon the shoe.

Another important item for your wardrobe is suspenders. Suspenders are ideal for holding your trousers in place when they are being weighed down by your weapon and perhaps radio as well. Dress etiquette dictates that you don't wear suspenders with a belt. However, the personal protection specialist is an exception to the rule. In this line of work, you never remove your suit coat in public, so no one would know that you are wearing suspenders along with a belt. Because you have to wear a belt in order to carry your radio and weapon, suspenders are a great aid, preventing your trousers from creeping down your waist.

Again, wear the shoes you would normally wear when you are being fitted for a suit. When purchasing shoes, spend a little extra to get a good comfortable fit. Get a shoe with a low heel and strong arch support. In this line of work. you spend most of your time on your feet and a good shoe is a necessity.

Black shoes will go with any color suit except brown. Your leather should always match, black shoes-black belt, brown shoes-brown belt etc. A tie shoe is the most appropriate dress shoe, but loafers are also acceptable. Whichever shoe you decide on, be sure to keep them polished. Don't allow the heels to get run down and check the soles for holes. Avoid metal cleats on the heels of shoes. Instead, use a rubber cleat to help prolong the life of the heel. If your preference is for a tie shoe, be sure to carry a spare pair of shoe strings with you just in case.

Socks should be dark in color and should match the suit. Support hose will assist your legs from feeling fatigued. Regardless of the type of socks you choose, the proper length for socks is over the calf of your leg. There is nothing more disgusting than to see a man seated with his legs crossed and a hairy bare leg showing. So get a dark color sock that comes over the calf.

If you happen to be one of those lucky individuals with a normal build, you can probably get away with a shirt right off the shelf. If you happen to be somewhat of an odd size, you might want to find a custom shirt shop and have your shirts made to fit your build. You would be surprised to find that a custom shirt is only about ten dollars more expensive than a good shirt off the shelf. Usually your custom shirt shops will require you to order a minimum of four shirts for approximately forty five dollars each. Most shirt shops will offer free monogramming and french cuffs if so desired. A one-hundred percent cotton shirt is not only a comfortable shirt, it also looks great. White shirts are preferable after 6 P.M., and solid pastel colors are acceptable for day time wear.

Shirt collars vary from button down to the tab collar with or without a tie bar. Collars are a matter of preference. Proper laundering is essential, especially when your schedule is travel-intensive.

Spare no expense when buying a tie. A 100% silk tie is easy to tie and sharp in appearance. The style of knot that you select is determined by the shirt collar. For instance, a large windsor knot wouldn't look good with a tab collar. A tie should be conservative. Loud ties as well as bow ties and shoe string ties have no place in the wardrobe of the personal protection specialist.

Remember you should not outshine your principal, nor should you dress in a manner that sets you distinctly apart from others in your group. Your wardrobe should be adjustable as well as comfortable. This becomes more difficult to achieve in the case of a principal who is very active, not just socially, but also in terms of his daily routine.

Jewelry should be plain and simple. Pinky rings are out for the men. You are not trying to make a fashion statement, but rather blend in. Be sure to match jewelry. If you're wearing a gold tie bar, then a plain simple gold pin collar is appropriate along with gold colored cuff links.

Appearance may be the only thing you're going to be judged on. Make a good first impression. Don't forget that proper hygiene goes hand in hand with appearance. Clean and clip those fingernails, trim that mustache and keep your hair trimmed and neat.

The female personal protection specialist should dress conservatively. Plunging necklines and rising hem lines should be avoided. Dress suits of conservative colors are appropriate. A low heeled shoe such as a pump is more appropriate than a high heel. No fishnet or wild stockings should be worn.

Your hairstyle should be plain and simple as well as easy to care for. Make-up should be moderate and, when used, perfume should be light.

In conclusion, "You never get a second chance to make a first impression."

THINGS TO REMEMBER

1. You can always dress down but it's difficult to dress up.
2. Keep your jewelry plain and simple—no garish lapel pins.
3. Don't outdress the principal.
4. Some things you might want to consider carrying in a briefcase.
   a. Travel iron
   b. Sewing kit
   c. Electric razor
   d. Deodorant
   e. After shave (A subtle after shave)
   f. Toothbrush
   g. Spare shirt and tie, pocket square
   h. Fingernail clippers, emery board or file
5. Cover tattoos
6. When shopping for clothes, look for a store that specializes in men's clothes.
7. A wool blend suit may cost $300 plus, but the appearance they present and the wear that you'll get out of them make them worth it. YOU ARE WHAT YOU LOOK LIKE!

John T. Molloy offers these suggestions for the executive dresser. Some are new; others appeared in *Dress For Success* and are very valid.

Dress for the job you want, not the one you have. Decide which person in your company you'd like to be like, and emulate him/her a little.

Wear blue, grey or beige suits—or shades of those colors. Avoid brown and black. Wear wool or a blend, not polyester.

The darker the suit, the more authority it reflects. The most authoritative pattern is the pin stripe.

Wear a single-breasted suit, not highly fitted.

Don't wear a sport jacket to the office—and never a short sleeved shirt for any business purpose.

In major cities the dress code is set by the dominant corporations. If you're unsure what to wear in a small town, follow the lead of local bankers.

Whenever you buy a suit, buy shirts and ties to wear with it. The tie is the single most important status symbol. Buy a good silk one, or a blend. *Never* wear a bow tie—or a gaudy tie, except a paisley.

Don't wear colors that clash or are so monochromatic they fade into each other. Mixing solids is always acceptable and is the simplest, most effective clothing combination. Don't mix patterns unless you're an expert.

Stay away from multi-colored shirts. And, to avoid looking like a "gangster," make sure your shirt is lighter in color than your suit, and that your tie is darker than your shirt.

Don't wear trousers that are too short. The pants should just touch the shoes, breaking a bit.

The less jewelry on a man, the better.

Wear a beige—not a black or dark—raincoat. And, if you're short, never carry an umbrella.

DRESSING CONSERVATIVELY

SUITS	SHIRTS	TIES	BELTS	SHOES	SOCKS
GRAY OR GRAY PINSTRIPE	White	Maroon Stripe/Polka Dot Blue Stripe/Polka Dot	Black	Black	Gray
	Lt. Blue	Blue Paisley/Blue Stripe Blue Solid/Polka Dot	or	or	Charcoal
	Pink	Maroon Polka Dot/Paisley Maroon Stripe	Cordovan	Cordovan	Black
CHARCOAL	White Lt. Blue	Same As Above	Black	Black	Charcoal or Black
NAVY OR LT. BLUE OR BLUE PINSTRIPE	White or Lt. Blue	Maroon & Navy Stripe Blue Polka Dot Maroon/Red Paisley Maroon/Red Print	Black	Black	Navy Blue
BROWN	White Yellow Beige	Brown Polka Dot/Paisley Brown Regimental Rep. Brown Repeating Pattern	Brown	Brown	Dark Brown

ELEVEN

Manners and Mannerisms for Personal Protection Specialists

by Susan A. DiGiacomo

"Where do you come from?" said the Red Queen
"And where are you going? Look up, speak nicely, and don't
twiddle your fingers all the time."

Alice attended to all these directions, and explained, as well as
she could that she had lost her way.
"I don't know what you mean by *your way*," said the Queen:
"All the ways about here belong to me—but why did you come
out here at all?" she added in a kindly tone. "Curtsy while
you're thinking about what to say. It saves time."

Lewis Carroll[1]

A BRITISH HUMORIST, with a distinguished law enforcement background, has recently published in Canada a book with the engaging title, "Gorilla in the Garage"[2]. Alas, for many, the most evocative title for a book about the personal protection specialist would still be *Gorilla in a Business Suit*. This is an unhelpful impression. This is an ancient vocation that is struggling in a media-conscious age to present a new and more realistic image. This profession needs to pay special attention to the image it conveys. The purpose, here, is to examine some of the ways in which those needs might be met while getting the real job done with all the efficiency and dedication it demands. For all this is not simply a matter of impressions; there is an underlying substance that needs to be preserved and, where, necessary, highlighted.

Success in this profession, as in any other undertaking, depends only in part in being able to do the job in hand. The rest is a kind of illusion, the conjurer's art. It is packaging and presentation. In order to do the job and get credit for having performed well, first secure the opportunity to be able to show off your skills. In short, someone has to choose you, to display a degree of confidence in you, to trust you. We are not concerned here with how such opportunities might come your way. What we are interested in is being prepared to exploit them to the best advantage when they occur. Let us stress the point here: First impressions are very important, crucial perhaps. And, as the Head & Shoulders commercial puts it: You don't get a second chance to make a first impression.[3] The old Boy Scout motto should be firmly before your gaze: "Be prepared." What kind of preparation do you need?

A simple prescription is suggested here: **Accentuate the Positive and Eliminate the Negative.** It is perhaps easier and more convenient, to attend to the latter first. The very few who are perfect have no need of the advice being offered here. The wise do not look for perfection in any human being, only a constant striving for improvement. Almost any performance can be improved. The nirvana of self-satisfaction is to be avoided by the conscientious professional. Such indulgence leads to arrogance and obviously this can often irritate the discerning employer. Those who are very good have no need to boast; they ask only to be given the chance to prove their worth. The candidate personal protection specialist should exude a quiet confidence, the self-assurance of one who knows how to do his job well. It should be apparent in speech, dress, and manner. This is really an acting job.[4] Some, the lucky ones, do it naturally. Others have to work at it. An important pre-requisite is self-awareness. What do you look like to others?

How we look to others has three main dimensions: general appearance; dress; and manners. The first is an omnibus sort of thing, which we need to break down into its component parts. We tend to judge people by what we call their "appearance". The impression they make upon us when we first meet them can be a decisive factor in whether we take to them or not. How many times have you met someone to whom you took a dislike on sight? Without, perhaps, being able to put a finger on the cause for your own reaction, you felt a compelling distaste for something about them. This rarely has anything to do with what we would, frankly, term physical ugliness, although deformity can be as repulsive to some as it is attractive to others.[5] It is usually the result of some small item that somehow triggers your general dissatisfaction with the individual's appearance overall. Posture and bearing are very important. How you stand and how you move speak volumes about yourself to the knowledgeable observer. These elements of appearance not only speak to what you may be feeling, experiencing internally; they are useful indicators of what you really think (or don't think) about yourself.

The proper study of mankind is man and those who intend to make a serious study of the subject need to learn body language, how to interpret those overt signals that people give off about their inner state. Part of our early socialization is to learn, by appearance, when others are angry, pleased, indifferent, and all the other moods affecting human interaction. Many of us neglect a study of ourselves. What are we projecting?[6] How is this seen by others? It is useful to be able to look fierce in a situation where the manifestation of such an appearance is socially appropriate, in justifiable defense of some interest for example. It is both burdensome and counter-productive to go about looking fierce all the time. This, obviously, is negative. It is something easily enough corrected—once it is perceived. Many simply do not see the negative, whatever it may be, because they lack what is needed to appraise their own appearance objectively.

Those who take their business seriously (as do successful C.E.O.s in the corporate world) are turning more and more to professional evaluations in these matters. Media consultants these days do a lot more than advise their clients how to part their hair and to wear a red tie when appearing on television. They study the general appearance of their client and consider its impact on the viewer. Before they can sensibly remake it, they must work at *Eliminating the Negative.*

A good appearance is one that is appropriate to the circumstances.[7] How do you feel about a TV anchorperson who tells of a horrible disaster while smiling. People took Walter Cronkite seriously, they *trusted* him and what he said because of the image he projected on the nightly news. He was grave when gravity was called for, and yet he had a lighter touch when this was in order. None of this was accidental; it was all part of a conscious production undertaken with great flair and naturalness.

Those providing protective services must assume they are under scrutiny from the moment they offer themselves for the job. They are *always* up for inspection. They must accept this without being self-conscious; it goes with the job. It is not something that can be doffed, like a business suit. The truth is that those who take these positions of confidence can *never* afford to let down their guard, even among their peers. This is a hard rule, but rule it is, and you disregard it at your peril. When they start to say of you, "he/she is a different person off duty", you know there is something wrong.[8] All you can hope for is that no-one who really counts sees that other you when it might matter.

Appearance is a collection of small but relevant details all adding up to a general impression. Eye contact is very important. We are always suspicious of those who will not meet our gaze. Whatever the reason fear, shyness, unsociability, untrustworthiness, or plain indifference—these are hardly qualities that suit someone in a position of confidence.[9] But eye contact, too, has its proper measure of appropriateness. It can all too easily be overdone! It can easily turn into a piercing, uncomfortable stare. The *way* in which you look at others carries with it your own sense of self, and how you see yourself in relation to others. Those providing personal protection need to cultivate an easy awareness of what is going on about them. The Clint Eastwood Look may have its place, but a negative characteristic is the wandering glance. We do not readily take to those whose gaze is elsewhere when we expect them to be paying attention to us. Sometimes, in this business, your eyes *do* have to be everywhere at once. Try to avoid having a serious and meaningful conversation with someone while engaging in such an exercise. The eyes, it is said, are the "Windows of the Soul." Nothing rivets human attention so effectively as good eye contact.[10] Learn how to use the eyes not only to observe what is going on about you, but to convey an impression of who and what you are.

Cleanliness, so they tell us, is next to godliness. Whatever the case, we are rarely impressed by those in positions of responsibility whom we perceive as dirty, scruffy, or just plain careless with their appearance. There is a contradiction, here, that does not often escape notice. Those who provide protective services cannot, in the nature of things *always* look like the Palace Guard—but that in no way dampens our expectations that they *should*. Again, it is the detail that commands out attention. Fingernails should be clean and neatly trimmed. Hair length should be appropriate. The personal protection specialist of a rock star might well present, in this regard, a different appearance from one providing protective services for the sedate C.E.O. of a low-key Fortune 100 corporation. In this area, the key word is *care*. If you are careless about your appearance, you are really making a very unappealing statement about your attitudes towards those you presume to serve.

You are saying, in effect, "you must take me as you find me". A moment's reflection should convince you of the monumental arrogance of such a position. Even in the thinnest of markets, prospective employers do have a choice. And they are not going to exercise it in favor of those who display what is really a quite fatal flaw in their make-up. How would you feel about putting your life or the lives of your loved ones in the hands of one who is not only careless, but who doesn't care who knows it? If everything about your appearance and demeanor makes the statement *I care*, you are more likely to be given the opportunity to serve regardless of any deficiencies in terms of your experience or technical qualification.[11]

Such carefulness comes naturally to those who take a real pride in their appearance. Others must take a more systematic, methodical approach. It is useful, for these purposes, to make a checklist so as to ensure that nothing of importance is missed or overlooked. Those who provide personal protection must be ever ready to adapt to their surroundings and what is required of them by their principals.[12] There are those who have a cruel malicious streak in their natures which often manifests itself in the form of a number of demeaning episodes involving their staffs. President Lyndon B. Johnson's treatment of his Secret Service details comes readily to mind in this connection. It is, of course, a very unwise indulgence, rather like needling troops that you are soon to lead into action against the enemy. For the most part, principals tend to be benevolent but indifferent towards those who render them these important services. It is not that *they* do not care, but rather that they do not *see* it as a personal obligation to enhance the general education of their protectors.

A select few employers do, indeed, take a personal hand in shaping those they employ, in molding them to their own liking. This can be a very rewarding experience for both parties. Those who aspire to provide protective services must have a real desire to learn without envy. Providing protective services opens new and fascinating worlds to those who engage in this work. It is heady stuff and can easily lead to a kind of giddiness. Those suffering from this malady simply forget their place. Encouraged perhaps by lonely or anxious principals with the wherewithal to indulge themselves, their fantasies are fed to the point where they can over-estimate their true worth. They strut, preen, and draw unwelcome attention to themselves—and their principals. Neither party is served by such behavior.[13] The personal protection specialist, like the Queen's Consort, should walk modestly two or three paces behind his principal— unless a present danger impels him to assume a more prominent position.

The provider of protective services is something of a chameleon. He takes on the protective coloration of his surroundings, he blends in. He must have a special sensitivity to his principal's needs, appreciating them, before they are directly communicated to him. To look the part, he must dress the part.

Those providing protective services must have a sense for fashion as it applies to each occasion.[14] The principal can afford to ignore the fashions of the day; those who provide protective services for him or her cannot. In earlier times, Soviet diplomats and intelligence officers under diplomatic cover were ridiculed on account of what they wore and how they conducted themselves in the society in which they had to work. The personal protection specialist must be fashionable without being ostentatious. He must never—and this is worth repeating with additional emphasis—never outshine his principal. He should carefully study his principal's style and sense of dress, in small matters as well as in large; what could be more embarrassing than turning up at an important function wearing a prominent accessory, a tie, say, identical to that worn by the principal? It might be handy to carry a spare tie ready for a quick change act off-stage. The personal protection specialist should wear good, well-tailored, generously cut clothing in keeping with the climate and the occasion.[15] If he has to carry the tools of his trade, weaponry or communications equipment, these should be capable of artful concealment without giving rise to suspicious looking bumps and bulges. Clothing, of all kinds, should be functional, durable and apt for the occasion. It should be easily maintained and free from extravagances. If protective clothing is worn, it should be adequate for the level of risk anticipated and never obvious. Particular attention should be paid to footwear. Shoes or boots should be comfortable, well broken in and in a good state of repair. Worn heels give a poor impression of the wearer.

If the job requires much travel overseas, special attention should be paid to the clothing required to function efficiently under all conditions. In some parts of the world, there is a marked variation between day and night-time conditions. Clothes must travel well and be wrinkle-resistant. They should be carefully packed so that they are immediately available. A good clothes brush, a lint remover, and a traveling steam iron should always be taken along, as should an electrical adapter for small appliances. A portable steamer is a useful piece of equipment. Wash and wear garments are a must for the personal protection specialist on the go. Remember, it is hard to look fresh in tired clothes. A clean shirt and a change of tie will do wonders for both appearance and morale. If heavier clothing cannot be freshly laundered, you can get the wrinkles out by hanging it in a bathroom where the hot taps are left running.

Personal hygiene is important at all times but never more so than when traveling. Anti-perspirants are essential, but they are no substitute for soap and water in liberal proportions whenever the opportunity arises.[16] Toilet preparations, including soaps and shaving creams should be discreet in fragrance. Good luggage that will travel well is another indispensable item of equipment. Frequent travelers know that all baggage is subjected to rough treatment; few pieces retain their pristine look for more than a few hours. Solid leather luggage is very handsome and durable, but is far too heavy for practical use, especially for air travel. Waterproof canvas or synthetic luggage with a hardwood frame and leather trim is probably the best buy. It looks expensive, travels well, and doesn't require the use of a fork-lift truck. A good looking briefcase completes the ensemble. Checked luggage is delayed and sometimes lost. The wise personal protection specialist is equipped with a carry-on garment bag and a briefcase. He can then leave quickly and efficiently so as to assist his principal. Those traveling abroad in private aircraft can still profit from following the same regimen.

A bad attitude may so affect performance that even if the goal is attained, the credit for the accomplishment is diminished or displaced. Those whose manner provokes an unfavorable reaction may get the job done, but they are unlikely to win any brownie points as a result. Poor performance can nearly always be traced to an attitude problem.[17] The person afflicted by it does not like what he or she is required to do—and it inevitably shows. All human beings have their particular likes and dislikes. This is one of the things that shapes them as individuals. There is nothing intrinsically wrong with exhibiting them appropriately. Sometimes, indeed they are better exhibited than bottled up. No-one should consider a career in providing protective services unless he or she understands the true meaning of service and is prepared to serve.[18] Those who see this as just another job would be wise to seek gainful employment elsewhere; it is simply the wrong attitude. Service requires commitment and dedication. It demands the disciplined subjugation of one's personal interests to those of the person in whose name the service is performed. All this is much easier to deal with in the abstract than by reference to harsh reality. Those for whom protective services are provided are themselves human beings. If they are wealthy enough to need personal protection, they will have developed certain attitudes of their own towards the "hired help".[19] Their own manner may not always, or even usually, be very pleasant. They, however, are the customer and, as such, are entitled to these indulgences (the wise do not argue with the Red Queen). There are, of course, principals for whom it is a joy to work. They are understanding, considerate, and helpful in every way to those who work for them. In the nature of things, they are unlikely to be in a majority. Another thing is worth noticing. Security is never a popular item in anyone's budget. The expense is often resented, and while the need for personal protection may come to be recognized, and grudgingly accepted, some of these feelings inevitably rub off on those who provide it. Thus, the groundwork for a happy and profitable working relationship is not always there. Nothing erodes performance so quickly as discontent. And nothing, in this area, so quickly produces discontent as unhappiness with one's employer.

The principal is entitled to his or her money's worth. This means entitlement to the best performance those employed are capable of giving. The wise employer knows the importance of motivation in securing and maintaining optimum performance. Good results don't just happen. But there is no obligation on the part of the employer to do this; he or she has only to keep their own end of the bargain. Even where these obligations are formally spelled out in a written contract, only rarely do they touch upon those matters most likely to generate employee discontent. Money is not usually a major issue, and long hours without additional compensation are to be expected in this business. Many principals are, indeed, very generous in these matters and recognize and reward good service accordingly.[20] The true sources of discontent often seem trivial to those outside the relationship, for it is the nature of that bond itself which tends to produce and exacerbate these problems.

The relationship between those who provide protective services and those in receipt of them is of a very close nature, sometimes involving a degree of intimacy approaching that of immediate family. Even in the best regulated of families, such closeness generates friction and antagonisms disturbing to harmony and equilibrium. Some employers do regard members of their work force as a kind of extended family. Selected retainers are often rewarded with a confidence and trust not accorded any member of the immediate family circle. But those upon whom the benefits and burdens of this status are conferred are not *family* (although they may marry into it) and the status is a privilege, not a right. It will only, in a crunch, bear so much weight. Ideally, both sides should realize this, but principals do not often take kindly to instruction. It is left to the other party, therefore, to make such a relationship and to avoid stepping over the bounds.

In terms of manner, there are some important consequences of all this. Those who provide protective services should remain appropriately deferential at all times, regardless of the nature assumed by the relationship. They should never allow themselves the liberty of letting down their guard in this respect; familiarities breed contempt. Those who become overly familiar with their employers often come to regret the indiscretion. Sooner or later, the employee will receive a put-down as a sharp and unpleasant reminder of who he or she really is. **Rule Number One** in this business should be: **Never forget who is the Boss. Rule Number Two** is a corollary of the first: **Never forget to treat him or her as the Boss.**

It is the obligation of those who provide protective services to set (and maintain) the tone of the relationship. Those who aspire to the recognition and respect accorded the true professional must learn the techniques and subtle nuances of this delicate area of interpersonal relations. Some working environments are considerably less formal and more relaxed than others. There are those which positively invite informality and which, in consequence, have special hidden pitfalls for the unwary. It is possible to maintain a pleasant, comfortable and relaxed manner without doing damage to the essential functions of the business of providing protective services. A certain coolness and degree of professional detachment is demanded. Anything that gets in the way of this outlook or approach is distinctly negative. The ideal personal protection specialist is a "take-charge" kind of person. Taking charge does not mean being over-bearing or indulging in exhibitions of authority. It is more a matter of manner with the establishment of a kind of presence that commands respect. To command respect, one must show respect. This sets an example that others find easy and agreeable to follow. Those who consistently demonstrate that they know what to do, no matter how unfamiliar the situation which they face inspire confidence. They are not only "self-starters"; they go off in the right direction. Calm is always reassuring. A calm, efficient manner in a crisis, whatever its nature is a treasure to be valued.

A mannerism is a kind of flourish, a personal signature, though not necessarily anything very original. It can be valuable, an accentuation of the personality. Mannerisms, then, are far from being all negative. Great performers are remembered for such eccentricities. Some mannerisms have a charm of their own. They affect those who observe them differently. Many of the more provoking mannerisms of ordinary folk are not conscious and have a closer resemblance to the nervous tic. There are those who act for a living and they rely upon a carefully designed professional construct employed for effect. Calculated mannerisms should be left for those who have professional need of them. They have no place in the armory of the personal protection specialist. Indeed, they might well prove to be a loose cannon of heavier than ordinary caliber. They should be resolutely sought out and stoutly tied down.

The unconscious mannerisms are, invariably, those that pose the greatest problems. They can be little more than inappropriate behavior. Once more, we are faced here with the familiar problem of seeking out and eliminating the negative. If you do not know you have a problem, you can hardly prepare yourself to address it. Some of us have quite irritating mannerisms. Many of these mannerisms are triggered or exaggerated by nervousness or anxiety. This is doubly unfortunate because we are often most anxious to make a good impression when we meet someone for the first time. The finger-twiddling syndrome has a thousand variations, few of which are helpful to the afflicted. It is the professional's job to detect and correct these little—yet vitally important—inadequacies.

These days, a personal protection specialist needs, at the very minimum a basic set of social graces.[21] These are as important to the job as having the "right" clothes; they are part and parcel of the tools needed for this kind of employment. If you are employed by royalty, you need to learn how to present yourself in a befitting manner. Certain behavior will be expected of you and there will, equally, be certain things that you will be required to avoid. The Golden Rule is: **"When in Rome, do as the Romans do."** But there is the *right* class and kind of Romans in every instance. Fortunately, we are not without guidance in this area.

The code by which our actions are informed is called manners.[22] What are good manners? Appropriate social behavior dictated by a particular set of circumstances. Good manners are the rules by which social transactions are mediated, a way of getting through (and even enjoying) the amenities of regular social intercourse. Manners are a code of transactional behavior. They are based and formulated on subtle notions of power and hierarchy. In another important sense, manners are a kind of *recognition* of the facts of social life and of certain kinds of social situations. Manners are a kind of protective apparatus the purpose of which is to avoid embarrassments when people are brought into contact with each other.[23] Manners are ritualistic; they are formalistic. **The Rule of the Rules is that there should be no surprises.** Manners are designed to let us know what to expect of others; they are a special defensive way of allowing us to get close to others without overt defenses.

Good manners establish what is expected of us. We occasionally say of someone, "He is one of nature's gentlemen," meaning thereby that the person concerned seems to have been endowed with good manners as part of a natural inheritance, i.e., he was born that way.[24] What is important to acknowledge is that good manners are and can be learned, that they are not the exclusive province of any particular set of persons to be worn as a kind of class badge. The key to success in the learning endeavor is in knowing what is appropriate for the time, place, and occasion.

From the present perspective, it is worth reiterating that those who provide protective services are, almost invariably, of a *different* socio-economic class from those who employ them. *Their* milieu produces its own, distinctive criteria of good manners. It is incumbent upon those who provide protective services to bridge the gap, to learn what is expected of them in the service of their employers, and to conform accordingly. This may well be a daunting, multi-dimensional task. It will involve considerable self-instruction, but it is really all part of learning to do the job.

There are many good books that lay out, succinctly, how to behave in different social situations and indeed, in different societies at home and abroad.[25] Study them carefully. Then adapt them to your own style and station in life. Good manners should be worn as unself-consciously or naturally as a well-fitting suit of clothes. The legendary English Butler is prized for his impeccable sense of occasion. His gracious manner lends special significance to the most mundane of encounters.[26]

Above all he conveys a sense of service with dignity; his manner puts others at their ease. Knowing that you know how to behave imparts a special kind of self-confidence. Good manners help you do your job more efficiently.

It is worth reflecting a moment or two on the subject of bad manners. Certain kinds of behavior by others cause us to experience a variety of unfavorable emotions from mild embarrassment to outright disgust. It is bad manners in itself, to ignore or disregard the sensibilities of others. Bad manners set people on edge. It is clear that, to a large extent, it is attitude that governs manners. And attitude, as we have seen, tends to manifest itself through or impress itself upon certain types of behavior. Bad manners are really the expression of our contempt for the feelings of others. There is an unpleasant arrogance about those who consistently exhibit a lack of good manners. This unfortunately is throwing out a challenge. He or she is saying, in effect: "This is how I am—take it or leave it." One has to be exceedingly affluent or self-sufficient to be able to engage in or sustain such self-destructive behavior. All this is negative in the extreme. It certainly does not commend itself to a prospective employer.

All this may sound very trite and, perhaps, a little overdone. Surely, the wiseacres will say, if you are smart enough and you want the job badly enough, you will watch your manners at least until you are hired. It is equally trite, of course, that those who hire on such superficial terms can fire just as easily—at the first exhibition of manners that does not suit their fancy. Bad manners are not something superficial; they are, more usually, symptomatic of a deep-seated malady, whether it be ignorance or design.[27] Sooner or later the bad will come out.

Manners are a lot more than learning the correct knife and fork to use at the table. They shape and define out social relationships with other beings. Good manners are a token of respect for those with whom we interact. Bad manners are an affront, and obstacle to social harmony. The good news is that the bad can be eradicated by the application of diligent effort, we can eliminate the negative.

The term, "Sprucing up the Image" has taken on a somewhat unfavorable connotation since the recent revelations of Larry Speakes concerning his ill-advised endeavors to do public relations wonders for his boss, President Reagan. We must always be careful that our work does not cause us to engage in making a silk purse out of a sow's ear. Accentuating the positive means taking that which is already good and making it better. It is not invention, but, rather, a renovation or improvement. As with home improvements, a lot can be done with self-help. The last few years have produced a profusion of popular literature for the determined do-it-yourselfer in this field; however, there is a lack of specifically relevant reference materials. We do not yet, for example, have a "What the Well-Dressed Personal Protection Specialist is Wearing" on the best-seller list. For guidance, we must turn to general works that offer useful application and this calls for a certain amount of discrimination. The watchword, here, must be adaptation, not imitation.

Those who provide protective services are seeking to establish their own distinctive style, something for which they will be recognized in their own sphere of endeavor. Such a style *might* come as a incidental product of the work effort, a sort of trial and error spin-off. Most of us develop our style in life in just such a way. What is suggested here is that there is another, more methodical (and quicker) way of going about the business, the development of a plan. It is a task to be taken very seriously and with complete honesty. Form is less important here than content. Take a sheet of paper and with pen in hand, mark off two columns. Head one "Positive", the other "Negative". Then, under each heading (honestly, mind you) record what *you* see as your positive and negative attributes.[29] Check those out with someone you can trust (do you think I'm a loudmouth?), or preferably with greater subtlety and guile. You are not trying to develop an encyclopedia; keep it simple. With this inventory, you are in business.

Armed with this evaluation of yourself, you are now ready to begin to **Accentuate the Positive and Eliminate the Negative.** You must create a standard, or envision a role model, an idealized provider of protective services endowed with all the virtues of the profession and none of the vices.[30] Keep it simple. Opinions may differ on some of the attributes and their degree of importance, but on others there would certainly be broad agreement. Without trying to establish precise standards, few would disagree that those who provide protective services should be physically fit and trim. If you are twenty pounds overweight with a substantial spare tire hanging over your belt and you are exhausted climbing a couple of flights of stairs, you are clearly in no shape to face the demands of this job. But, at least, you have a simple enough standard against which to measure yourself. You must have clear guidance as to where to begin. The command is plain; only the prescription for attaining the goal is lacking. Discipline, a regimen of diet and proper exercise should suffice for the purpose. This is, of course, an extreme example chosen for the illustration of the point. Every case is different, and must be examined on its own merits. Some of those providing protective services set and attain for themselves commendably high standards of physical fitness and athleticism. It is commendable. What you are aiming at is **personal improvement** within the parameters of your own capabilities. After examining yourself in all the necessary departments, you should be able to say, "I need to work on this or that" or "Such and such needs attention."

The true elite of this profession are quite widely known. They serve as useful role models for others who would aspire to join that elite.[31] What is it about them that makes these persons outstanding members of their profession? How do you measure up? What qualities do you have in common with them? It is here that you must begin to **accentuate the positive.** Whatever is good in your self-appraisal can be made better. And with the knowledge of that improvement will come an overall strengthening of confidence and a sense of achievement. This will not only stimulate you to further personal growth, but will lend stature to your efforts and your performance. At the same time, make a conscious effort to **rid yourself of anything negative** to which you have admitted. There is something holistic about this exercise, for out of the combined endeavors will emerge the new, improved you. If you do this exercise conscientiously, you will build integrity.[32] In the final analysis, it is this personal integrity that is the most valued item in the armory of any professional. If you can to your own self be true, your principal is indeed a lucky person to have you in his or her service.

NOTES

[1] *Through the Looking Glass and What Alice Found There,* in *The Annotated Alice,* New York, Forum Books, (1971), Page 206.

[2] Don Hepworth, Erin, Ontario: Boston Mills Press, (1987).

[3] "First impressions are not only the beginning of social interaction, they are one of its major determinants." *Social Psychology,* Jonathan L. Freedman, J. Merrill Carlsmith, David O. Sears, Englewood Cliffs, N.J.: Prentice-Hall, 2nd Edition (1973), page 30.

[4] An actor converts all life experience into an art form. For a unique insight into what is professionally involved, see the autobiography of Sir Alec Guiness, *Blessings in Disguise,* London: Hanish Hamilton, (1985). At page 285, he records a poignant, instructive incident. While in Cuba with Kenneth Tynan, the drama critic shortly after Castro's revolution had taken place, Tynan said to him, "They are shooting a couple of sixteen-year olds. A boy and a girl. I thought you might like to see it. One should see everything, if one's an actor."

[5] See, for example, Freedman, Carlsmith, & Sears, op. cit supra note 3, page 78.

[6] See, "Perception and Self-Image" in *Speak Easy,* Sandy Linver, New York: Summit Books, (1978), pages 49-65.

[7] An interesting observation by Sir Kenneth Clark in *Civilization,* New York: Harper & Row, (1969), page 18 neatly underlines the point. Of Charlemagne, he writes: "He was a commanding figure, over six feet a walrus moustache instead of a beard."

[8] This is really another way of making a statement about personal integrity. The English actor, Kenneth More, put it very well in his autobiography: "In an upside down world, with all the rules being rewritten as the game goes on and spectators invading the pitch, it is good to feel that some things and some people seem to stay just as they were." *More or Less,* New York: Hodder & Stoughton, 1978, page 233.

[9] "Like a mouse eyed hungrily by a cat, you are being looked over and evaluated. If you seem calm and confident, this makes an impression on the other side." *Salary Strategies,* Marilyn Moats Kennedy, New York: Rawson, Wade, (1982), page 91.

[10] "Authentic audience awareness must come from an impulse within you to genuinely focus your attention outward and establish contact with as many human beings as possible within the room. Ideally, it means relating to each member as an individual and opening yourself up to him". Linver, op. cit. supra note 6, page 31.

[11] A quote from the job-hunter's bible, *What Color is Your Parachute?* Richard Nelson Bolles, Berkeley: Ten Speed Press, (1987), page 210, is apposite here. "Luck favors the person who is trying hard to be 'a special type of person' in this world, treating others with grace and dignity and courtesy and kindness."

[12] On this see, *The Professional Image*, Susan Bixler, New York: G.P. Putman's sons, (1984).

[13] There are some very primitive dynamics involved in this. See, *The Human Zoo*, Desmond Morris, London: Jonathan Cape, (1969).

[14] See, *Executive Style*, Diana Lewis Jewell, New York: New Century (1983).

[15] A good basic grounding in these matters can be obtained from *Dress for Success*, John T. Molloy, New York: Warner Books, (1978).

[16] The therapeutic value of a hot bath (or shower) should not be overlooked. Again, Kenneth More: "Whenever I feel lonely or depressed, I run a hot bath and lie back in it, remembering days when I could not afford such indulgence." Op. cit supra note 8 page 228.

[17] The wise counsel of Marilyn Moats Kennedy is worth pondering. "If you don't care, or refuse, to accept your boss's attitudes as reality, you'll have no options except to gripe about the system. This will make you monumentally unattractive to everyone around you and may eventually result in termination. It is called having a poor attitude, and it will show in everything you do." *Office Politics*, New York: Warner Books, (1980), page 176.

[18] Few books have expressed so well, and succinctly, what is involved in this concept as *Think and Grow Rich*, Napoleon Hill, Greenwich, CT: Fawcett Crest, (1960), pages 116-119.

[19] It has been observed that, "It is not enough to have power, one must be observed to have power." Morris, op. cit. supra note 13, page 46.

[20] ". . . the giving of favors requires an expert hand." Morris op. cit. supra note 13, page 50.

[21] "If you want to belong to our society, you must play our game." *Psychotherapy East and West*, Alan W. Watts, New York: Pantheon Books, (1961), page 37. Thus, all books on manners are really rule books for the societies to which they refer.

[22] "We gave you the opportunity of doing it," the Red Queen remarked: "But I daresay you've not had many lessons in manners yet?" "Manners are not taught in lesson," said Alice. "Lessons teach you to do sums, and things of that sort." Lewis Carroll, op. cit. supra note 1, page 320.

[23] That acute social observer, and first curator of the Royal Ontario Museum of Archaeology, Dr. C.T. Currelly recounts in his *I Brought the Ages Home*, Toronto: Royal Ontario Museum, (1976), page 26: "I never knew people to laugh as much as the Indians, especially the women, and the men were merry, too. But the instant a stranger came every face instantly went stiff. This was a matter of politeness."

[24] The great statesman, Edmund Burke noted: "Somebody has said that a king may make a nobleman, but he cannot make a gentleman." Letter to William Smith, January 19, 1795.

[25] Any list given here would of necessity be incomplete and misleading. Excellent guidance to the specific literature required for the purpose can be obtained from the reference section of the public library of any major city. The librarian should be advised that you are seeking information about the manners and social customs of the particular society about which you are inquiring.

[26] Although some tended to overdo matters. The distinguished rhymester, Hilaire Belloc wrote:

> In my opinion butlers ought
> To know their place, and not to play
> The Old Retainer night and day

[27] William Shakespeare wrote:

> "Men's evil manners live in brass; their
> virtues we write in water."

[18] We are reminded by Voltaire that "All styles are good except the tiresome sort." Preface to *L'Enfant Prodigue*, (1738).

[29] "Look around the habitable world! How few know their own good; or know it to pursue." John Dryden, translation of *Juvernal*.

[30] But, be warned, "Comparisons are odorous; palabras, neighbour Verges." William Shakespeare, *Much Ado About Nothing*, Act III, Scene V.

[31] "If one may measure small things by great." Virgil, *Georgics IV*, 176.

[32] "Trust is a matter of balance." *Vipers' Tangle*, Francois Mauriac, New York: Image Books, (1957), page 195.

TWELVE

Dining, Etiquette, and Protocol

by Jetze Beers

ETIQUETTE IS MUCH MORE than a fixed set of guidelines or a list of firm rules. Customs obviously vary from country to country. These enormous cultural differences will affect the way in which you interact with others, especially if your principal travels to Europe, or the Far East. Regardless, formal entertainment in particular is conducted within a framework of rules and you must become familiar with some of the more basic rules.

In your profession, it is very important to remain almost incognito. You have to develop an awareness of social skills whenever you are organizing parties or any kind of gathering, and when you are traveling with your principal. If you do not know, you may make mistakes. If you are familiar with "Old World" manners, then you can be effective without being conspicuous because you do not want to be noticed, but you want to be there.

One of the greatest pleasures in life is the art of entertaining; however, it requires creativity, common sense, discipline, and planning. The better a party is planned, the better the guests and the hosts will enjoy it. Therefore, the hosts and the hosts' representative—and that's often you—must be aware of everything that's going on.

Many of you, due to your special role and area of responsibility, will be the ones who have to keep an eye on everything, not just security. You are often the organizer, and you often establish the first liaison with corporate contacts that your principal values. You must have the correct information. You want to make sure that there is an easy, comfortable flow of events and no surprises. And that involves more than the correct table settings.

In practice, you will often be involved in making arrangements for parties, banquets, or reservations in a restaurant. Your principals will certainly have guests, and you will have to make the proper seating arrangements. While there are many possible seating arrangements, there are a few rules that you should know. Where are the host and the hostess seated? Once that is established, you can ensure that the guests of honor are seated in the right place. If it is a round table, you do not have to worry too much. It becomes more complicated when you have a rectangular table—banquets have terribly long tables. The most common way to seat guests at a rectangular table is to assume that the host and hostess are not seated together. The hostess is often seated opposite the host. The guests of honor, suppose they are male and female—are reversed in terms of sex, but they are always seated on the right hand side of the host and hostess. The host will have on his right hand side the female guest of honor. The hostess will have on her right hand side the male guest of honor. So, you have to be very careful in your treatment of the most important guest. There is one firm rule that pertains to a head of state or a monarch. He or she is always the most important person. It does not matter who else is present, the head of state or monarch is always the most important guest, and therefore is seated to the right of the hostess.

You may have a situation where there is a second guest of honor. He or she is seated on the other side, the left side, of the host or hostess.

After that, you go by the hierarchy of the guests, moving away from the host or hostess. Always remember male/female, male/female. That is always the rule.

You may run into a problem in a set up like this because sometimes you may discover that you have two ladies or two men sitting next to each other. But there's nothing you can do about it in the case of this type of table arrangement. Make sure host and hostess sit opposite of each other, followed by the most important guests, the next most important guests, and so on. The guest of honor is always on the right hand side of the host or hostess.

Be aware that when you have a set up for eight people, you will always have two males or two females sitting next to each other. You will find that you can always arrange it in such a way that it works.

There is another general rule. The hostess and the female guest of honor are supposed to face the crowd, the doors and the focus of activity. You do it when you go to a restaurant with a lady, you're supposed to seat the lady in such a way that she can see what's going on. What you see is not as important. You're supposed to concentrate on her.

"Gentleman's" behavior is disappearing nowadays, whether it's in a restaurant or at home. We don't pay much attention anymore, or show respect to our table partners, not even when a woman enters. In your profession, it would be excellent manners to rise whenever a lady enters the room and is seated. Sometimes it is very difficult. You do not always have the space or the leg room. But it is a common courtesy to get up when a lady is being seated and, of course, to help her with her chair.

The least you can do is elevate yourself slightly off the chair, come up a little bit, so she will see it, then sit down. You do not see it anymore, but it's very nice to do and ladies appreciate it. You also do this with other guests, even male guests. You are supposed to get up, certainly, when it is somebody who is older than you or when you're talking in terms of hierarchy, somebody of the same or higher rank.

You will also have to be familiar with serving. There are two different ways. The American way is the way of efficiency. You can usually spot the difference immediately between Europeans and Americans. And it has mostly to do with the flow. In America, it is common to serve from the left and to remove from the right of the guest. In Europe, you both serve and remove from the right hand side. Thus, the American way is to have the flow from left to right. You serve on the left and you take off from the right. It does not really matter what way is chosen, as long as there is consistency. In one situation, however, it is always necessary to serve from the left. This is when serving from a platter. Because most people are right-handed. If a platter is presented to you from the left hand side, you can use your right hand to remove it.

Every course of the meal requires certain cutlery. Once you are through with that course, the flatware is supposed to be taken away. Of course, today you rarely encounter this approach. The cutlery that is at your table setting is exactly what you're going to need. Now, in restaurants they often set up for every possibility. They are supposed to take off what you will not need. For instance, a good restaurant always has a fish knife, a fish fork, etc. When you do not order fish, they are supposed to take that away before they serve you. After you place your order, they are supposed to come and take it away, unless you indicate otherwise. Used cutlery is always removed after each course.

A lot depends upon what you are going to eat. The most important rule to remember is that everything is placed in the sequence of use. Therefore, the sequence of the menu is important. This applies both to the glassware and to the silverware.

On the right hand side is a soup spoon because you are likely to start with soup or bouillon. However, in a situation where something else is served first—it's very common to have oysters for example, you will see your oyster fork adjacent to the soup spoon. The next utensil can be a fish knife. Again, in a good setting there is always a fish knife available, although this can be taken away. Closest to the plate on the right is your meat knife.

Forks are always on the left hand side of the plate. Be careful with the salad fork, because in a formal dinner sequence a salad is often served as one of the last things on the menu. Again, you have to know what is being served if you are responsible for checking table arrangements, table settings, etc. Make sure you know the menu and set up accordingly by sequence.

Butter knives are getting to be old-fashioned, but in case you have a table setting with butter knives, and bread plates it's always placed on the left of the silverware with the butter knife on top of the plate with the cutting edge toward the side of the table. Always remember that knives always point with the sharp edge of the blade to the inside, toward the plate, never away.

As for glassware, it's again a matter of what's being served. You may have a glass of sherry, or vermouth before the first course requiring a small sherry glass. Next to that is always the glass for the white wine, in case you have fish for instance. Next is the goblet for red wine. The smaller wine glass is always for white wine, and the larger glass is always for red wine. Then there is the water glass, or water goblet. It is common to have one more, the champagne glass which is to be found behind the water glass.

Have you ever been in a restaurant where everybody is finished? You see stuff all over the table, napkins thrown everywhere, on the floor and on the chairs. It looks terrible. The ground rule is you always use your napkin. You have it on your knees, not in your shirt. It's always on your knees, always on your lap. After you have finished your meal, fold the napkin up and put it next to your plate on the table. Do not hang it over the edge of your chair or do not throw it on the floor. Just fold it up and leave it on the table. The restaurant owner will enjoy it because his place looks much better, and you have left the impression that you care.

One question that's often asked is how do you eat soup? Well, you eat it with a spoon. However, when it is thin it is not bad manners to drink your soup, but not out of a plate. When you have a cup or a small bowl, it is appropriate to lift it to your mouth with your hands and to drink it. When it's a thin soup or a bouillon, it can spatter. So, it's acceptable to drink your soup from the cup, but not if it's a thick one. Scoop your soup away from you. Do not tilt soup bowls, just leave whatever is left at the bottom of the bowl. Only drink soup from a cup or from a bowl with handles. Never take your bread and rub it all around your plate.

The stem of a wine glass is there for the glass to sit on and for your hands to hold onto it. Never hold the glass around the glass top. Fingerprints are greasy and unsanitary. If serving, always grasp the stem. You do not have to hold your little finger up. It was a custom many years ago, but you do not have to do it today.

Another important point when you are serving, You always leave the glass on the table—be very aware of this—without touching it, without moving it. However, you may run into situations where it's simply impossible to abide by this rule. The solution is simple. Move the glass or cup to a spot on the table where you can pour without spilling or splashing. But never, never lift cups or glasses off the table for serving.

A table should never be cluttered. As soon as you do not need certain plates or glasses anymore, they are taken away. Normally you will not have many glasses or plates on your table other than those you start out with. After that, they are removed. When you serve champagne or any other wine during a reception or a party occasion, you serve off the table or off a tray. People take it off themselves. That's the most appropriate way to do it. The one who serves will usually present a tray, so the one who takes it, grasps the stem.

Realize one thing—that it's up to the host and hostess to determine what they want to do. Now we are talking about common rules, and not necessarily the only way to do it. Consistency during a certain occasion is important. Never go from this to that. At a dinner party, you should start out with a light fortified wine, like a sherry, certainly not a creme sherry, just a dry sherry—usually served with a soup. Some people prefer to have vermouth, usually a white vermouth instead of a sherry. Champagne comes normally at the end. Therefore, the champagne glass should be farthest away.

In Europe, it's very customary to serve a sherry as an apertif, instead of serving it with bouillon or soup. Here in the United States, you will start with cocktails. Normally sherry goes with the soup. There's one thing that you may find in the table setting, a little deep finger bowl. At certain conservative parties, you may still find the finger bowl. Now, the question is always what is the finger bowl for?

Here is a true story. In Holland, Queen Wilhelmina was invited to the annual Cattleman's Association banquet in the northern part of the country. Cattle in the northern part of the Netherlands are very important. A beautiful banquet had been prepared for her. Her entire entourage came with her. And they had set up the tables with finger bowls. Most of the cattlemen did not know what they were for; they thought they were just bowls of water. So one drank it. And somebody else drank it, too. At a certain point, the Queen noticed what was happening. She was a very smart lady, and an excellent queen. She looked around and saw that all her people were laughing and grinning. It was embarrassing the hosts. So she lifted her finger bowl and drank it, too. This is a true story. This really happened. She was a great queen.

You can toast through the entire meal. That is correct. The person may respond after everybody has toasted him by lifting his glass and making a thank you gesture.

You should always tip. Realize that even when you do not get the service you deserve, the server may not be at fault. Something might have happened in the kitchen, it can be extremely busy, or they may have broken a case of wine glasses, and therefore everything is late. That is not necessarily the server's fault. In order not to cause embarrassment to your principal in particular, and also to show your own sophistication, you tip.

It is appropriate to talk to the supervisor or the manager if you are not satisfied. Do not leave one penny on the table to express how bad the service was. You still tip. If you are extremely happy with the service, you tip more. It is customary to leave 15% of the total, or more. If the service is exceptional, it is not necessary to tip the wine steward and the maitre'd. The maitre'd in a class restaurant should make enough salary anyway not to have to depend on tips. It is inappropriate to distribute tips yourself. Give one amount and the staff can distribute it any way they want.

One thing that you can do if you are grateful, yet rushed, leave an envelope with the name of the maitre'd on it on the table, preferably hidden. Do not just throw it on the table and leave it, especially if you go to a class restaurant and your bill is a few hundred dollars. In most European countries now, the gratuity is always included. A standard 15% tip is included everywhere you go in Europe. If you want to give the people a little more, you can do that.

You do not have to buy good help by way of gratuities. What if people are downright rude to you at times? Still, you do not want to lose face, regardless of what they do. So, you tip anyway but you aim your remarks at the management. That is the only proper way to solve it. Do not do it by not giving tips. You are the one who is more sophisticated.

Photo by Candi Kobetz

FORMAL DINING

The small fork to the right of the soup spoon is for oysters, followed by the soup spoon. Then if fish is served, the outer fork and outer knife are used, followed by meat using the center fork and knife. The inner fork and knife are used for salad and cheese. (The server should remove silverware when specific items will not be served.) Above the soup spoon is a sherry glass which will accompany the soup. To the left of the sherry glass is a white wine glass to be served with the fish and then a red wine glass for the meat course. The water goblet is the last glass behind which is a champagne glass used with the dessert.

EXECUTIVE PROTECTION INSTITUTE— located in Clarke County, Virginia

WEAPONRY TRAINING involves expertise in skill and knowledge, emphasizing the weapon as a "last resort" solution.

PERSONAL PROTECTION SPECIALISTS experience varied training (clockwise from below): in explosives, classroom exams, defensive driving, and physical protection.

PROVIDING EXECUTIVE PROTECTION requires attention to detail (clockwise from above): in field training, car searches, and property security surveys.

PERSONAL PROTECTION SPECIALISTS have to update techniques and procedures that allow their principal ease of movement with protection.

PROVIDING EXECUTIVE PROTECTION essentially means allowing the principal to experience freedom of movement throughout the world without harm. Professional training is necessary to deal with protection in crowds, at airports, on yachts, and during outdoor recreation.

EXECUTIVE PROTECTION INSTITUTE holds many of its training movements at historic places such as Jordan Hollow Farm Inn, Stanley, Virginia (above), and Blandy Farm in Boyce, Virginia (bottom, opposite page). The remaining photographs were taken during training sessions at Gettysburg National Military Park in Pennsylvania, and in the Shenandoah Valley.

EXECUTIVE PROTECTION INSTITUTE is located in the magnificent Shenandoah Valley, surrounded by the beautiful Blue Ridge Mountains of Virginia. The mountains and the Valley are also the location of many training scenarios.

For further information on professional security training programs, contact:
EXECUTIVE PROTECTION INSTITUTE
Arcadia Manor — Route 2 — Box 3645
Berryville, Virginia 22611
(703) 955-1128 (24-hour Desk)

PART IV

Defensive Measures

THIRTEEN

Defensive Driving Techniques

by Anthony J. Scotti

EVERY MORNING EXECUTIVES ENCOUNTER the most dangerous part of their day, the drive to work. Statistics show that anywhere from 60 to 85% of all kidnappings and assassinations happen while the victim is in a vehicle and en-route from the home or office. These numbers confirm the fact that when an executive is in his car, terrorists can easily pick the time and location of the attack. Although state-of-the-art equipment is readily available to protect the executive in his office and in his home, twice a day he must travel to and from work, and during this time he is afforded only limited protection by his car. Transportation is the weak link in the security chain. A successful vehicle ambush requires certain tactics, and these tactics are clearly described in Carlos Marighella's book, *The Mini-Manual of the Urban Guerrilla*. Marighella is considered to be the father of modern urban terrorism. They are:

1. Surprise
2. Better knowledge of the terrain
3. Greater mobility and speed than the enemy.
4. Total command of the situation.

For a vehicle ambush to be successful the attackers must have all four ingredients working for them. Understanding the tactics of the enemy is the first defense against them. By developing specific countermeasures, a protection team can take away one or all four of these tactics. Then the attempt will fail or, more than likely, it will never take place.

Marighella's book describes the importance of knowing the terrain.

1. "The urban guerrilla's best ally is the terrain and because this is so, he must know it like the palm of his hand."

2. "To have the terrain as an ally means to know how to use with intelligence; its unevenness, its high and low points, its turns and its irregularities."

3. "Our experience is that the ideal urban guerrilla is one who operates in his own city and knows thoroughly its streets, neighborhoods, transit problems and other peculiarities."

Most vehicle ambushes occur near the home or place of business because it is easy for the terrorist to select a TIME and LOCATION near the home or business. Therefore, if an ambush does occur there is a good chance that the driver knows the area as well as the terrorists. A mental note should be made of where the high risk or "danger zones" are, defining a "danger zone" as a location where one's time of arrival or departure is very predictable. Just put yourself in the terrorists' position—and say to yourself—"If I were the bad guy, where would I conduct the ambush?" A basic definition of a "danger zone" is:

1. A location near the home—most dangerous—or business that cannot possibly be avoided. The executive may live on a one-way street, or in an area where there is only one trunk road into the area.

2. Narrow or one-way streets where it would be impossible to maneuver the car.

3. An area where the car is going very slowly and would be easy to stop—such as on a very twisting road.

4. Blind spots in the road, such as a crest of a hill or blind corners.

The list above is food for thought. You can develop your own list and, depending on the level of threat, you should identify "danger zones" near the homes of the people you are concerned about.

Once a "danger zone" is designated, the next important issue is finding a safe haven, a location where the driver can find safety in an emergency.

Areas such as:

1. Police Stations.
2. Fire Stations.
3. Hospitals.
4. Large Shopping centers.
5. Military Bases.

It is essential to know how to access these safe havens. In the event of an ambush, there is no time to stop and ask for directions. A definite evasive action plan should be drawn up with fixed destinations where the driver will go in the event of trouble. Once that is done, the driver should drive each route to make 100% sure that he knows how to get to each safe haven. Putting aside the threat of terrorism for a moment, all drivers should know where the hospitals are along their routes of travel. In the event that his principal has a heart attack or any other medical emergency, the driver must know the location of the nearest hospital, fire and police station. The phone numbers of these safe havens should either be memorized or easily accessible. Also, knowledge of a hospital location is not enough by itself. The driver should know in advance how to get to the emergency room.

Among the tactical advantages needed for a successful ambush, as defined by Marighella, are MOBILITY, SPEED and DECISION.

MOBILITY AND SPEED

Marighella's book describes the importance of mobility and speed. "To insure mobility and speed the police cannot match, the urban guerrilla needs the follow prerequisites:

1. Mechanization.
2. Knowledge of the terrain.
3. A rupture or suspension of the enemy's lines of communication and transport.
4. Light arms."

The vehicle, whether it is company or private, must have some degree of maneuverability, reasonable acceleration capabilities and a good communication system.

Speed and maneuverability are easy to achieve by purchasing optional equipment. Most new cars can be purchased with some sort of improved handling package. However, if you want handling, you must give up the quality of ride. A car is a compromise.

Maintenance of the car is the key issue, not the initial purchase.

No machine will work if it's not maintained, hence the need for a good maintenance program. With executive vehicles, the man in charge of driving the car should also be in charge of maintaining the car. He should have the authority to oversee maintenance. If a man can be entrusted with the task of driving the CEO, then he should also determine when the car needs maintenance. And the car should undergo scheduled maintenance—not a "fix it when it breaks" program.

Mobility also means the ability to call for help. A good working communications system must be available. At a bare minimum car phones should be installed in vehicles. If the level of threat is high, or car phones are not practical, then a radio system may be necessary. As important as the type of communication system is its proper use. Everybody involved should know how to recognize and respond to any emergency.

DECISION

The last ingredient for a successful ambush is "decision." Again, from Marighella's book—"It is not enough for the urban guerrilla to have in his favor surprise, speed, and knowledge of the terrain. He must also demonstrate his command of any situation and a capacity for decision, without which all other advantages will prove useless."

Once the ambush starts the terrorists rely heavily on the driver taking no action. Saying that you must take an evasive action in the event of an ambush is easy. But to take an evasive action, you must have time and time means an extra 5 to 10 seconds. If you need 15 seconds to wake up, all the training in the world won't help. Therefore, how quickly you recognize the ambush is a key issue.

How do you know if an ambush is about to happen? Although it is impossible to cover every situation, we can lay down guidelines that will help. A rough idea of when and where ambushes happen can be established.

Statistics indicate that the majority of ambushes occur near home or work and occur in the morning hours. Since the attackers must stop your car, they create a situation that requires you to stop. Therefore, you have to be suspicious of any unusual situations that will compel you to *stop the car,* especially if it's in the *morning* on your *way to work.*

Any time of the day or evening, if a situation is forcing you to make an unscheduled stop—you should immediately ask yourself the the following questions:
1. Am I on a scheduled trip?
2. Is it widely known that I will be at this location at this time?
3. As you are stopping, look into the rear view mirror. Is there activity behind you?
4. Does it look like you are about to be boxed in?
5. Look all around you. Is there activity?

BE SUSPICIOUS OF EVERYBODY AND EVERYTHING?

What do you do in a situation where a police officer is asking you to stop? The first question to ask yourself is, "Have I done anything to get a ticket?" A good loud speaker system in the car would help a great deal. They're inexpensive to install, and they allow you to converse with someone outside the car without unlocking the door or opening the windows. You can also maintain a reasonable distance while conducting the conversation.

In countries outside the United States, it is a good idea to make sure that all drivers know:

- What is the design of the local police uniform?
- What kind of weapon do they carry?
- Is the officer's cruiser or motorcycle nearby?
- If it is—is it the proper model and color?
- If it is not nearby—how did he get there?
- Is it normal to have a foot patrol in that area? This is a lot to think about, but if the threat warrants it—it is essential.

VEHICLE AMBUSH AND THE TACTIC OF SURPRISE

A successful vehicle ambush, or any ambush for that matter, requires planning and with such planning, a defined set of tactics emerges. Again, these tactics are clearly described by Carlos Marighella.

THE ELEMENT OF SURPRISE

Surprise is the key to a successful ambush of any type. Reducing the element of surprise is extremely important. Marighella's book focuses on this technique. The ability to carry out a surprise attack is based on some essential prerequisites:

1. "We know the situation of the enemy we are going to attack, usually by means of precise information and meticulous observation while the enemy does not know he is going to be attacked and knows nothing about the attacker.

2. We determine the hour and the place of the attack, fix its duration and establish its objectives. The enemy remains ignorant of all this."

When the tactics for surprise are analyzed, a definite pattern develops. A successful vehicle ambush develops over time and actually occurs in stages. While not every vehicle ambush happens this way, the element of surprise requires effective planning and from this planning comes a series of steps. These steps are as follows:

1. TARGET SELECTION: In the preliminary stages more than one target is selected. Attackers will, through meticulous surveillance of driving habits, gather information about the driving lifestyle of the victim. Once the information is gathered, they will focus on the individual who, while in a vehicle, is the most vulnerable.

2. RISK ASSESSMENT: Terrorists will make a *risk versus success* assessment. If they feel one target is easier than another, they will focus their efforts on that person as he offers the least risk and the highest possible success rate. Terrorists must rely on the victim's complete unawareness of what's going on.

3. SURVEILLANCE: Surveillance may take weeks—possibly months. The victim's movements will be analyzed and patterns of habit established. Surveillance will continue until the attackers can predict, with reasonable accuracy, the best time and place for a successful ambush.

SURVEILLANCE AWARENESS: The keys to an effective awareness program are:

1. The need to observe all the victim's vehicle movements.

2. In order to know the victim's movements, his vehicle is kept under constant surveillance. If he is a creature of habit, the job is made much easier.

Changing your time of departure plus your driving routes is an absolute necessity. Unfortunately, it is often impossible to alter time schedules by any great amount.

Executives are demanding. They do not get to be executives by arriving at work late—promptness is a hard habit to break. As mentioned before, changing routes is desirable, but often this cannot be accomplished, due to the location of the home. In most locations the driver has the choice to go either left or right. It is no surprise that a majority of abductions take place in the morning near the home. In fact, an amazing statistic is that most kidnappings occur between the victim's home and his place of work. The ambush will happen either just after the victim has left his residence or within several blocks of his home.

This pattern of abduction near the home is not coincidental. It is simply too hard to change routes near the home so a terrorist group finds it easy to fix the time and location for their ambush.

Being unpredictable is the best line of defense. The location of the potential target must be difficult to pinpoint; however, many people are not ready to accept this element of unpredictability because it could develop into a major change of lifestyle. This is a decision only the executive can make. It is at this surveillance stage that an "early warning system" must be developed.

EARLY WARNING & ROUTE PLANNING

Early Warning System: An "early warning system" requires that a close watch be kept for any abnormal activity near the home and office. It is important to point out that it does not require much effort to be security conscious. In fact, most people are much more security conscious than they may realize.

When someone leaves their home in the morning, they could probably write a couple of pages of notes concerning the activities around their home such as; types of vehicles in the neighborhood, children going to school, and even sightings of new faces. In fact, most people can tell whether they are late or early by what they see when they leave their homes. As a result, important questions regarding potential danger can be raised. Suppose there is a strange car parked across the street or perhaps the phone company must be working early this morning because they have a van parked near by. Or, while driving down the street, unfamiliar people are spotted in the area, an unfamiliar car, or a vehicle that just does not belong in the neighborhood.

Most VIP's live in affluent areas—which usually dictates the general type of vehicle that will be present in the area. What usually happens is that a mental picture of what should be there and what should not be there registers. When an object or a person comes into the picture that doesn't belong, a signal is received that causes a question to be raised "What is it or he doing here?"

If you feel the threat is high, then a small tape recorder can be used by the driver to register any unusual activity. From that a log or uncomplicated reporting system can be developed. In the event that drivers are changed, an important information bank is available. A new driver can tap this resource, or if a regular driver is not sure that he has seen the same thing twice, he can check back to make certain. The key to defeating surveillance is that when a troubling signal is received, do something about it!!

What Is Do Something? A system must be in place so that if and when you receive such a signal, you can ask someone the same question he is asking himself and receive an answer.

This vital information must get back to the driver as quickly as possible. The driver should not be made to feel that he is paranoid. In fact, he should be told he is doing a good job. A good way of doing that is to get the information back to him as soon as possible. What follows can be the best advice you can give a driver.

"It is better to suffer a little embarrassment in the event you are wrong than to suffer the consequences if you are right!"

The key to an effective surveillance awareness program is alertness. The philosophy that should be paramount is once—happenstance, twice—coincidence, and three times—enemy action. Sir Geoffrey Jackson, who was kidnapped by terrorists, describes his awareness of their surveillance in this manner:

"When, after a relatively quiet life, nocturnal calls begin to proliferate, when one's hitherto pleasantly solidarity walks along beaches and sand dunes and in pine forests begin to bristle with horizon-marching silhouettes and sudden encounters with the young in unlikely trio formation, when one's golf game—not only one's own—regularly begins to be interrupted by casual young spectators on remote fairways, where for the third time one's path is crossed by professional violence literally at one's door step—by this time the least perceptive of mortals begins to grasp that, however much the world around him may be changing, his own private world is changing still more."

The above is an eloquent description of surveillance and awareness of a changing environment. The level of awareness must be raised to a point where:

1. Strange vehicles parked near the residence or place of employment are noticed and reported to authorities.

2. People standing, walking, or sitting in cars near the residence or place of employment must be noticed and reported.

3. An individual can recognize that he is being followed. If he feels that he is being followed, he can simply drive around the block and confirm that the suspected vehicle is still there.

An important point is to keep track of any unusual sightings. A small tape recorder can be used to register any unusual activities. From the tape, a log can be made describing the strange vehicles.

1. Make
2. Model
3. Year
4. Color
5. License Number
6. General Condition
7. Number of People in Vehicle

If possible, obtain a description of the people involved, such as:

1. Male/female
2. Age
3. Size
4. Hair color/style
5. Ethnic background

Remember a reporting system such as the one described above is mandatory if chauffeurs are used and drivers are changed often. If the log indicates that a certain pattern is developing, then this pattern should be brought to the attention of the local authorities. Any information discovered must get back to the driver quickly.

Devices: As the number of car thefts go up each year, so does the number of devices designed to prevent them. No single catalog contains every device and new ones are appearing all the time. Many companies make similar devices. They are advertised in many publications, and most are available at large retail stores and at stores specializing in auto parts. Most experts contend that the most effective deterrent is a combination of devices, such as an alarm system and a mechanism that disables some major operational system of the car.

None of these devices will make it impossible to steal your car. What you are trying to do is deter the thief by making it as time consuming as possible for him to get in the car, start it, and drive away. Every extra minute he has to spend at this task increases his risk. The effectiveness of your countermeasures is determined by how long it takes him to get around them. If you make that length of time long enough, chances are he'll move on, since there are plenty of less protected cars to choose from.

ANTI-ENTRY DEVICES

1. Door Locks—Until recently, most interior door lock buttons had a flared head to give you something to hold on to as you pulled up or pushed down. A thief will straighten out a coat hanger, bend a loop in the end, slide it between the window and the frame, and hook the loop over the flared head. Replacement buttons are available that taper inward at the top, offering nothing for the loop to hook on to.

2. Internal Hood Locks—These are cable-type devices that extend through the firewall of the car and up to the hood latch mechanism, where they operate a dead-bolt setup that immobilizes the hood release. The cable can be run through an armored shield and operated by a manual pull-switch under the dashboard. Some models also include a feature that grounds out the ignition, rendering it inoperative.

The ultimate anti-entry safeguard would be to weld clasps on the doors, hood, and trunk, and then use four hardened steel padlocks. However, this would make a car a little unsightly.

DISABLING DEVICES

1. Fuel Shutoff—This can be done in two ways. First, you can place a manual valve—a faucet of sorts—on the under hood fuel line. The second way, for cars equipped with electric fuel pumps, is to wire a switch into the pump circuit and hide it under the dash. When the fuel is shut off, the car will start but run for only a few seconds, until it has exhausted the fuel in the carburetor float bowl. If a thief finally gets in your car and starts it, he only gets a block away before it stops and won't start again. He will probably abandon the car quickly.

2. Battery Disconnect—This is a knife-type or rotary switch spliced into the battery cable. Flip the switch and the car has no electrical power. To get the car started, the thief has to get the hood open and find the switch, which is time consuming. He could push the car, but it is unlikely.

3. Brake System Lock—This varies considerably from car to car, but it is basically a method of locking all four brakes by locking up the master hydraulic cylinder in the engine compartment. Even if the thief gets in and gets the car started, it won't go anywhere. He may ruin the clutch, but the car stays put.

4. Pedal Clamp—It consists of two bars, hinged together at one end, that clamps across the clutch and brake pedals and lock shut. It has extensions welded on the back side that prevent the pedal from being depressed. If the thief can't get the car in gear and the brakes don't work, he'll probably lose interest.

5. Steering Wheel Bar—This takes two forms. One is a cane-shaped steel rod that hooks around the steering wheel and goes down to the brake pedal. Another hooked-shaped piece goes around the pedal and locks onto the rod. The second type locks around the face of the steering wheel and extends well past the edge of the rim. The purpose of both of these devices is to make the steering inoperative. If the thief takes your car anyway, he should be easy to find, since he can only go in a straight line.

6. Steering Column Band—This consists of two curved wide bands of metal, hinged at one end, that lock around the steering column, making the ignition switch inaccessible. If the car has a locking column, it means the thief has to take time to go under the dash and disconnect the linkage.

ALARM SYSTEMS

1. Switch Alarms—This is a basic system which requires that switches be placed on the doors, hood, and trunk. When the system is activated (usually by a key switch mounted in a fender) and one of these is opened, the alarm sounds. Some systems sound the car's horn and flash the lights. Some have their own noise-making devices ranging from bells to sirens. Most have a pre-set time limit after which the system resets itself. This is to prevent the battery from being drained.

2. Electrical Drain Alarm—This is a system that senses any electrical drain on the battery, from the energizing of the starting circuit down to the interior light coming on, or the brake lights flashing, or even the radio being turned on. It is set to a sensitivity level to accommodate the continuous operation of the dashboard clock, but the presence of any stronger current will set off a variety of alarms. Better systems usually feature a secondary device that deactivates the ignition when the alarm goes off.

3. Motion-Detector Alarm—A mercury switch inside the system control box adjusts itself to the level of the car when the system is activated. If the attitude of the car changes, as when someone sits in the driver's seat, the alarm goes off.

4. Pager-Type Alarm—This is actually a feature added to many types of alarm systems. When the alarm goes off, besides setting off a bell or siren, a pocket-pager device also signals the car owner. The effective range varies with the system and some claim to cover a mile and a half.

5. Coded Start Systems—This system comes in several different forms, but basically it's an electrical switch that requires a coded input to release it. Some are operated by a sequence of push buttons, others by a special card with a magnetic strip. They are coupled to an alarm that sounds if the proper input is not entered. They can also ground out the ignition. Top-of-the-line systems respond automatically whenever you step out of the car and close the door by rolling up the electric windows, closing the sunroof and locking the doors.

6. Garage Alarm—If you park your car in a garage, an additional safeguard would be to put some sort of alarm system on the doors and windows of the building. Systems range from simple switches to radar, motion and noise detectors, which are hooked up to a noise-making device. This protects the car and your tools as well. Dummy closed-circuit television cameras add another dimension to your efforts.

There are always ways of stealing a car that don't involve sneaking around in the dark. The concept might be called "purchase theft." It occurs when you buy or sell a car and the transaction is somehow bogus.

Tsar Alexander II — March 1, 1880 (from the book *Assassin*):

The royal party, moving swiftly, suddenly turned into the quay. First came the Tsar's two-horse sleigh. Alexander sat alone. An orderly sat next to the driver. Behind came three more sleighs filled with security officials. One hundred and fifty yards down the quay, Rysakov stepped forward and tossed his bomb under the legs of the Tsar's horses. It was 2:15 PM. One Cossack was mortally wounded, as was a passing delivery boy. The windows of the royal sleigh were shattered, the floor and back smashed, and the Tsar dazed, but with only a small cut on his hand. Colonel Dvorhitsky, district chief of police, rushed up and urged the Tsar to get into his sleigh. Alexander agreed, but wandered over to look at the site of the explosion. The Cossack and the boy still lay on the ground. The delay had been only five minutes. Alexander turned and began walking toward Dvorzhitsky's carriage. He passed near a man leaning on an iron railing holding a parcel—Grinevitsky. The second bomb-thrower turned and hurled his parcel at the Tsar's feet. There was a second roar, another cloud of blue smoke; this time the street was littered with the wounded and dying. The Tsar crouched in a pool of his own blood. The Tsar was driven swiftly to the palace, his sleigh leaving a trail of blood behind. By the time medical aid could be summoned, it was too late. He rallied briefly, was given Holy Communion and then, at 3:40 PM he died.

Moral of Story: "If something happens, get the man and get out of there. Don't give anyone a second chance."

Antonio da Empoli, Drawing A— On February 22, 1986, four members of the Red Brigade wounded a top official from the Italian government. **As he was being driven to work** by his bodyguard/chauffeur, Antonio Da Empoli, an economic aide, was shot twice in the leg and once in the hand. The shooting occurred as Empoli **stepped out of his vehicle to buy the morning newspaper. He bought the newspaper at a newsstand near his home every morning.** As the attackers rushed towards Empoli, his driver/bodyguard shouted to Empoli to duck and get under a nearby parked car. He sped forward towards the terrorists, jumped out of the car and returned fire. He killed one of the terrorists, a 28-year old woman wearing a bulletproof vest. She was shot in the neck. The other two attackers fled on motorbikes.

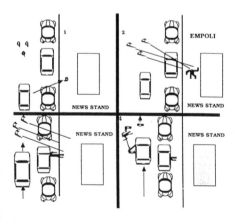

Empoli Incident Diagram—Drawing A

Orvile Gunduz, Drawing B—Orvile Gunduz was the Turkish consulate general in Boston. After his place of business was bombed, he received a warning from an Armenian terrorist group that "they were going to assassinate him next." **As he drove home from work,** he had to drive by a construction area where traffic proceeded very slowly. A single terrorist was waiting for him at one particular corner. **On May 4, 1982 in Somerville, Mass.,** as he turned this corner, the terrorist fired a nine millimeter handgun into the driver's window, killing Gunduz. The car rolled to a stop up against a fence. The terrorist then took a .357 Magnum and fired a shot in the ear of Gunduz. He dropped the .357 Magnum, walked calmly down a hill and stepped into a waiting car. There is a donut shop at the bottom of this hill. Video cameras recorded the terrorist in question sitting in the shop calmly having a cup of coffee and occasionally looking at his watch. The terrorist had Gunduz's schedule down so pat that he knew exactly when Gunduz would drive by that precise spot on the road.

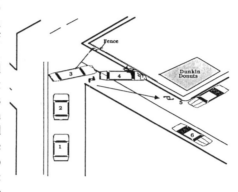

Gunduz Shooting Diagram—Drawing B

ARMORED CARS

Do your executives need an armored car? This is a hard question which can only be answered by you. If something has prompted you to think about armored cars—then you need one.

LEVEL OF PROTECTION

According to Underwriter's Laboratories, the standardized levels of protection are:

Level I—Medium power arms: .22 pistol, .38 and .38 special.
Level II—.357 magnum, 9mm carb.
Level III—same as above, plus .44 magnum, 12 gauge, .30 carbine.
Level IV—same as above, plus 30.06 military ball.

Reading the UL's standardized system it appears that in order to establish the degree of protection needed, one must know the type of weapons that may be used in an attack, and the method of attack (firing from a distance versus close range.)

To help with this rather important decision we look at a recent study conducted by Risks International, Inc. This study shows that 30 percent of all kidnap teams use automatic weapons. Many other studies show that the attack will often be at close range. Combining this data we can conclude that the level of protection should be Level IV or higher. It is in this stage of the purchase where the armorer can be of great assistance because he knows the levels of protection that are suitable in different areas of the world. If he has not constructed a car for that part of the world, you should not be his first customer, and any information he imparts to you should be backed up by your own intelligence network.

TYPE OF VEHICLE

The type of vehicle must blend in with the existing cars in a particular country. You should not have someone driving a red Mustang when he is the only man with a Mustang in the country. Also, there should be ample room in the car for four people. Therefore, the car selected should:

1. Blend into the vehicle environment.
2. Be a four door and allow enough comfort and ease of entering.
3. Have a power unit, engine size and gear ratio that will allow for reasonable acceleration.

VEHICLE DESIGN

The armored vehicle can be designed to:

1. Absorb the attack, take repeated hits, return fire, and call for help.
2. Absorb the initial fire and break the ambush.
3. A combination of both of the above.

Please understand that the first design option is extremely expensive, and that a book could be written about its pros and cons. Armored vehicle design #1 should be used for the threat of assassination with the cost directly proportional to how long you would like to sit there and absorb fire. Cars armored to maximum ballistic levels are very expensive, costing well into the six figure range.

To absorb the initial burst and then drive out of the ambush a car requires two separate capabilities:

1. The car is armored in a manner so that it can absorb initial fire.
2. The car is maneuverable.

Armoring: The doors, windows, and rear of the passenger seat must be armored to the maximum threat level. If grenades are a threat, the roof and floor must be armored. If this is necessary then obviously the price of the vehicle goes up. The engine compartment is always armored, but you want to look into armoring the firewall of the car, the battery, engine compartment, radiator and fuel tank on a unit by unit basis. Discuss this modular approach with the armorer. Armoring these compartments creates problems that are too complicated to cover in the amount of space we have.

The types of material range from steel and aluminum to super-lightweight fiberglass. Heavyweight armor allows you to button up and wait for help. The whole issue is a moot point because most corporations are not willing to spend $150,000 plus for a heavyweight armored car.

This leaves us with lightweight armor and the attainment of a performance level that allows a driver to break an ambush. First we have to define "lightweight". The state-of-the-art appears to be adding 700 to 1000 pounds to the original weight of the car. The key is not the 700 to 1000 pounds of additional weight, but the original weight of the car.

If the car is a Lincoln Town Coupe, for example, it might weight 4,843 pounds. By adding 800 pounds of armor you are increasing the weight by 16.5%. Change to a car that weighs 3,200 pounds, and add the same 800 pounds. You are increasing the weight by 25%—a dramatic difference and a significant modification.

In breaking an ambush, the acceleration and handling capability of the vehicle are very important. If the increase in weight is 25%, the acceleration of the vehicle will decrease by 25%; assuming a standard engine or gear box. The following chart will give you an idea of the percentage increase between various car weights and armor weights.

ARMOR WEIGHT

Vehicle Weight	600	700	800	900	1000	1100
3000 lbs.	20.0%	23.3%	26.6%	30.0%	33.3%	36.6%
3500 lbs.	17.1	20.0	22.8	25.7	28.6	31.4
4000 lbs.	15.0	17.5	20.0	22.5	25.0	27.5
4500 lbs.	13.3	15.5	17.7	20.0	22.2	24.4
5000 lbs.	12.0	14.0	14.0	18.0	20.0	22.0

Manufacturing process: The following requirements must be met when armoring a car:

1. Any retention of panel requires the use of high tensile captive bolts. This design prevents the bolts from becoming projectiles.

2. Ballistic seals ensure that incoming projectiles or missiles cannot penetrate the vehicle at unusual angles.

3. Fabrication techniques are critical. Certain materials can reduce the inherent ballistic properties. Care must be exercised in welding, overlap construction, and general format.

4. Sealants used to prevent moisture from entering the layers of armor must be sufficiently resistant to contain edge stress. Particular care must be given to hinges and locks.

Basic equipment:

1. Power steering/brakes
2. Air conditioning
3. Automatic transmission
4. Automatic door locks

Additional equipment (optional):

1. **Steering**—a heavy-duty steering pump. If it is essential for quick steering maneuvers, because steering maneuvers are needed, the steering fluid can foam and cause loss of steering.

2. **Communications**—The occupants of the vehicle should be able to communicate instantly with someone at the home or place of business. The higher the threat, the more elaborate the communications. What is equally as important as the hardware purchased is how it is used. The procedure on how and when to use communications equipment must be made clear to all involved.

3. **Mirrors**—Good rear and side-view mirrors should be installed on the car so the driver does not have to move his head to look to the rear. They should be flat and used often.

4. **Covert Antennas**—If you have a communication system in your car, you don't want everyone to know about it. Antennas can fit into the skin of the car so they cannot be detected.

5. **Horn**—A loud horn or speaker system can alert passers-by and it may scare your attackers into calling off the assault.

6. **Public Address System**—The driver and occupants should be able to talk to someone outside the car without opening the doors. Also, the driver does not have to drive up to someone to talk to him; they can stay a safe distance away and communicate. It can also be used to hear what the people outside the car are talking about.

7. Tires—Be careful about foam tires. The foam can liquefy and the tires can go flat. Plastic liners are the best, but they are expensive.

8. Optics—Be sure there is little or no distortion through the windshield. When purchasing a car, the ambient temperature of the environment is important. If the window is not designed properly, it can distort the view rather badly. The old bullet-resistant glass is quite ineffective against high-powered weapons and repeated hits.

9. Engine Protection—Depends on where the executive lives. In an urban environment, you need to get only a short distance away from an ambush to be safe. An engine will keep going without water for a sufficient amount of time to get clear of the ambush. But in rural settings, where the driver may need to drive 50 miles before he can stop, it may be smart to armor the radiator.

10. Chassis—If the car is sufficiently armored, there should be some modifications made to the chassis. If the gas tank is protected by armor, the rear frame definitely needs modification.

11. Tool Kit—A tool kit is necessary in the trunk of the car. The tool kit can be used to free oneself from the inside of the trunk in the event that an abductor puts you there.

12. Testing—When driving a car, make sure it can stop in a reasonable distance. Find a hill, stop on the hill and test the car's ability to accelerate up the hill. If the car struggles to make it up the hill, it's not worth the price.

BRIEF OUTLINE

1. Comparison shop. Don't talk to only one armorer.

2. Don't be his first customer in a specific area of the world.

3. Ask for recommendations. Don't accept the answer "They're confidential." If he can't trust you, who can he trust.

4. What is the percentage increase in vehicular weight after armor is installed? If it approaches 25%, the performance of the vehicle will be severely limited.

5. Be very careful about the optics. Ask how much distortion will occur in the windshield. There should be very little.

6. Ask what his quality control procedures are. The ratio of quality control workers to the assemblers is important. The more quality control workers, the better.

Driving:

1. Avoid driving close behind other vehicles, especially service trucks, and be aware of activities and road conditions two to three blocks ahead. If there is a situation which requires you to stop, don't drive up to the incident—hold back and see what develops or take an alternate route.

2. In so far as possible, travel only on busy, well traveled thoroughfares, staying away from isolated back country roads. Know where the dangerous areas in the city are located and avoid them.

3. On multiple lane highways, drive towards the center of the road. This makes it more difficult for your car to be forced to the curb or attacked from the driver's side—the most common direction of the attack.

4. When traveling in an automobile, keep all doors locked. Keep the windows closed or opened only a small crack.

5. When abroad, avoid cars or actions that identify you as an American or as someone wealthy or important. Use locally-produced cars of a popular color, if possible.

6. Before you drive off, look around to see if there are any occupied cars parked nearby. If there are, watch to see if any follow you.

7. Check periodically to see if you are being followed. If you think you are, make a note of the chase car's license number, make and model. Note its occupant's description. Give this to your security director or the civil authorities. In high-risk situations, use your radio or radio telephone to notify authorities. If you do not have such a communication device, proceed at once to the nearest designated safe haven.

8. Be extremely leery of any type of roadblock or holdup in traffic. Stop well back of any type of obstruction and observe it carefully. If you are suspicious, make a quick turn and a hasty retreat.

9. Don't stop while driving. Kidnappers stage accidents or plant beautiful girls on the roadside with flat tires as bait. Don't let any of these tricks fool you.

10. You are in danger both going to and coming from the airport. In most cases, airline security measures do not protect you until you are inside the terminal. Therefore, the precautions we have previously outlined are important.

Vehicle:

1. Keep the ignition key separate and never leave the trunk key with parking or service attendants. If at all possible, never leave the car keys with anyone. In a recent kidnapping, the terrorists walked up to the car and opened it with their own key.

2. Park cars off the street at night.

3. Lock unattended cars, no matter how short the time.

4. Before you get into your car, walk around it and check it for signs of illegal entry and for anyone hiding behind the back seat.

5. Park your car in a locked garage or protected area.

6. Don't identify executive parking areas as such. Private parking spaces should be identified by number rather than by name. If possible, the parking spaces should be randomly changed.

7. Parking areas should be well lighted and patrolled by members of your security force.

8. Always keep your gas tank at least half full and use a locking gas cap. Check you fuel level before you drive anywhere.

9. All vehicles should be equipped with hood and gas tank locks to hinder the quick attachment and concealment of bombs.

10. Gasoline should be provided through a company controlled facility or purchased on a random basis from local stations.

11. Equip cars with a loud siren or some other audible device for activation in case of attack.

FOURTEEN

Emergency Medical Care

by C. Steven Ruble

THE DAY BEGINS AS USUAL with Mr. Principal going to his office. The route of travel has been covered at the morning briefing along with Mr. Principal's scheduled activities for that day. The cars and radios have been checked out. All weapons are loaded and ready for any possible trouble that might occur.

It is 9:00 A.M. and Mr. Principal is becoming more upset by the minute as his first meeting is starting right now and here he is stuck in traffic. At 9:15, Mr. Principal tells you that he feels tightness in his chest and begins to breath rapidly. Still stuck in traffic, you pick up the cellular phone only to learn you are not in a service area. A trucker next to you asks if he can help and calls for assistance on his citizens band radio. He lets you know that help is on the way, but it will be delayed due to the traffic back-up.

Mr. Principal informs you that he wants you to do something. He says the pain is getting worse and that he left his nitro pills in his bedroom.

You remember that there is a first aid bag in the trunk of the car, even an oxygen kit. Opening the trunk you find Mr. Principal wasn't the only one who had forgotten something this morning. How you wished now that you had taken time to attend a CPR course and stayed awake during the first aid lectures at the protective service classes that you had attended.

Mr. Principal, now unconscious, is in as much danger of death as if assaulted by a human attacker with any weapon that could kill. This time the attacker is his own heart. If it was a human attacker, you would know what to do, but now what?

If you begin to break the story apart, you will find certain key mistakes that often occur when a professional protective specialist faces a medical emergency.

This chapter will examine these mistakes and offer possible solutions so that this type of event will never happen to you.

The areas to be covered will be as follows:

I. Being Prepared For Today.

II. Basics of Sickness & Trauma Emergencies and Care.

III. Fighting Time and Triage.

IV. Recommended Equipment and Emergency Care Courses.

I. BEING PREPARED FOR TODAY.

The imaginary protective specialist in the story believed he had checked out all the "important" equipment and relevant information. He thought that he was adequately prepared for events on this day. However, he found out too late that he was not.

Emergency medical equipment that can be found in your vehicles should be checked every day, and kept clean. Equipment stored at a business location or personal residence needs to be checked each week. All items must be present. The types of equipment to be utilized will be discussed later in the chapter including a personal kit that can fit in a coat pocket.

A question that should have been asked of Mr. Principal when he was first picked up that morning would have been, "Do you have your medications?" This information would come from a medical history card. All persons that you are responsible for protecting as well as members of your team should have medical history cards filled out and maintained up to date. This card contains such vital information as the following:

1. Name of patient.
2. Age of patient and date of birth.
3. Doctor's name and phone number.
4. Medical history.
5. Medications presently being taken.
6. Allergies.

These information cards should be kept both in a stationary location and immediately available with you while in transit.

Questions concerning Mr. Principal's nitro pills and his other medications—taken throughout the day—should have been asked at the morning briefing. Thus, a deadly mistake would have been corrected.

Another scenario where medical cards play a critical role involved a diabetic patient who takes insulin. He must eat in conjunction with taking his medication. Failure to eat normally results in a diabetic getting weak, and if no corrective actions are taken, lapse into unconsciousness and may die. For this reason, you should always carry sugar packets or a sugar solution if you are dealing with a known diabetic. Should the patient suddenly become weak, you can add some sugar to a soft drink or juice and have the person drink it. Should the person become unconscious, the sugar can be placed under the tongue to be absorbed. In this case, you are trying to restore the balance level of sugar that the brain requires to a level somewhere near normal.

The following questions should be posed to your client in the morning to avoid any problems:

1. Have you taken your medication today?
2. Have you eaten?

If you are assigned to a known diabetic, arriving on duty with a doughnut, orange juice, packets of sugar, and his favorite newspaper will help you to avoid a potential problem. When asked the above-mentioned questions, if he answers "yes" to question 1 and "no" to question 2 then offer him juice with sugar, the doughnut, and paper and remind him that you are just doing your job,—protecting him from all attackers including himself. Should the answer to both questions be "yes" then you offer him the paper and enjoy the well-deserved snack yourself or toss them out and save your waistline.

Essential questions that you must be prepared to answer on each and every day without fail are as follows:

1. Do I need to get additional medications? Where can they be found? Do I need to make special arrangements to maintain them? Remember, insulin needs to be refrigerated. Don't lose time by not having medications when needed.

2. Where are the nearest medical facilities? What are their capabilities? Don't waste time getting lost going to a medical facility. Have a map ready with central and alternative locations clearly marked. Make sure that the facility can handle your emergency needs. Always try to find the closest "Trauma Center"—not just any hospital. There are distinct differences in these two types of facilities. Overkill is the name of the game when it comes to comprehensive care of the sick and injured.

3. Is there a need to arrange alternative means of transportation to reach the medical facility? Don't try to drive when flying may be the way to go due to distance, traffic conditions, or weather factors. Recognize this need, it saves precious time. Think in minutes of response time. Five minutes or less can make a crucial difference in a medical emergency.

The final question that needs to be asked is one of the most important of all. I have the equipment and the information to react to an emergency but do I have the training to properly utilize my resources and avoid wasting time?

Time is truly the invisible enemy that must be contended with in any medical emergency. Being properly prepared is the first defense against wasting time. The second defense is knowing the basics of all sickness and injury treatment.

II. BASICS OF SICKNESS AND TRAUMA EMERGENCIES AND CARE

This chapter alone will not properly prepare you in terms of the wide range of proper procedures or responses to all forms of medical emergencies. The following information will cover certain basic principles of medical care. Remember, you may find yourself acting as the first responder or lifesaver on the scene. For this reason, some form of standardized emergency medical training is recommended. Attending lectures is not enough. Hands on training is essential because it gives you a chance to apply your new skills.

The first and most important principle to remember in emergency treatment of the sick and injured patient is forget the idea that help will reach you quickly. In many cases, the delay can exceed twenty or thirty minutes, so you will have to be self-sufficient until help arrives. This response time factor should justify the expense of attending an emergency care course in your yearly budget.

The next basic principle to memorize is the meaning of the following letters of the alphabet:

A—Airway—The means to get oxygen into the body.

B—Breathing—The action of getting the oxygen in.

C—Circulation—The pumping of the blood that carries the oxygen to where it is needed.

B—Bleeding/Blood—The loss of the fluid that carries the oxygen that is needed by the body to survive.

If you look upon the human body in the form of a machine that is broken down into three main working phases that rely on each other for survival, you will begin to understand the importance of knowing the ABCB terminology.

The three phases of the machine are as follows:

1. The "energy phase"—commonly known as the Respiratory Phase. It is this part of the machine that the letters A and B fit in. Oxygen in the air serves as the energy for the machine. The energy comes in via the **Airways,**—the nose and mouth—and it is drawn into the lungs through piping. It is like electricity that enters a machine through the power cord and reaches the part that needs the energy to work. Through **Breathing** this energy level is maintained at an acceptable level to keep a person conscious and alert. Should anything block or slow this phase down, then the energy level diminishes. Like a machine, the ability to produce work will diminish as a result. Work in the human body is the ability to remain conscious and alert, and, the ability to function. A question that arises from this phase is, "If the oxygen coming into the body is being used, then how does mouth to mouth resuscitation work to save someone else?" The answer is that when you breathe in air it contains 21% oxygen. Your body only uses 5% and gives back 16% when breathing out. Therefore, enough energy is in your exhalation to keep someone else's machine going.

2. The **"pumping phase"**—best known as the Circulatory Phase. It is here that the letters **C** and the **second B** fit into the working of the machine. The Circulation portion of the pumping phase is broken into the pump and the pipes. **Circulation** occurs when the machine pumps blood into the lungs. It carries oxygen or energy and simultaneously returns used blood, which lacks oxygen, back to the pump to go through the whole cycle again. It is the Blood that actually carries the oxygen. This is why **Bleeding** is part of the four letters to remember. The more blood that is lost means that less fluid is available to carry oxygen or energy to the vital parts of the machine. You have to stop bleeding in the injured patient as soon as possible or death will result. If the pump fails, commonly called a heart attack, CPR allows the trained rescuer to keep the pump working by depressing the chest and forcing the heart to function. Blood then enters the pump when the pressure is removed from the chest. The heart itself requires a constant flow of blood.

It is important to remember that this phase of the machine relates closely with the Respiratory Phase in that CPR stands for Cardio (Heart) Pulmonary (Breathing) Resuscitation.*

If you fail to maintain an open Airway and if you do not assist Breathing with mouth to mouth or mouth to mask resuscitation, the energy will have no way to enter the body, get to the lungs and be picked up by the Circulation to keep the pump and the rest of the body functioning. Failure to breathe for the victim will result in the heart pumping out oxygen-depleted fluid. The energy needed to survive will simply not be there.

Remember, chest compressions should NEVER be performed on a person with a pulse! A person can stop breathing and still retain a pulse, such as in the case of drug overdose or spinal injuries. In these cases it will only be necessary to breathe for the victim.

3. The **"computer phase"**—This phase is commonly called the Nervous system. This phase is responsible for the input of information, linking the energy phase, the pumping phase and the remainder of the body, analyzing what is needed from these sources, and then sending out the information to see that these needs are fulfilled to the best of the total system's abilities.

---

*CPR is a course that is taught by the American Heart Association and should be attended on a yearly basis to perform the lifesaving technique in a safe manner. Through this course the student is trained to perform one person CPR as well as learning the Heimlich maneuver which is utilized to attempt to save a choking victim.

This phase is made up of the brain (computer), spinal cord (main information transport line) and the nerves throughout the body. This phase depends on both the energy (oxygen) that is delivered by the other systems to survive, and on sugar. Depletion of the levels of either sugar or oxygen will result in the slowing of the computer's ability to react and in extreme cases, it can result in a complete shutdown. Thus, CPR is the manual method to bring the body's computer system back on line.

These three phases interact within the machine that we know as the body. To aid in your understanding of how these phases are affected by sickness/injury/emergency and the proper responses that can keep the machine functioning until a repairman (doctor, medic, nurse, etc.) can arrive to attempt needed repairs, here are some scenarios that may occur during the daily life of a personal protective specialist.

1. The most likely cause of Mr. Principal's cardiac problem is that his heart has decided to repay him for all his abuse over its life time.

Pain results when the pump is not receiving enough energy to work properly. This cuts down on the pump's ability to supply the computer system with adequate energy. In turn, the computer system slows down which leads to the pumping system not getting the proper commands to operate at the level needed and so it begins to malfunction. As Mr. Principal gets more excited, he is placing more demands on the phases of the machine that are already unable to to meet normal demands, thus the problem will worsen without your intervention to correct the problem to the best of your ability.

There are two solutions to the problem that must be considered: Reduce the workload or increase the energy level.

First, the workload can be reduced by having Mr. Principal calm down and remain in a reclined or resting position. Second, increasing the energy level can be accomplished by two means. Mr. Principal takes nitro pills. This medication works by opening up the pipes that carry the blood to the pump thus allowing more blood and therefore more oxygen to get through. In the case where nitro medication is utilized, the pill goes under the tongue. It is not taken with water and swallowed. Care should be taken that the person receiving the nitro pill be sitting or laying down as the person may pass out. This is caused by the pill taking effect, opening up the pipes to allow more blood to flow. This added flow can result in a sudden drop of pressure, which in turn impacts upon the computer system. If the person is standing, gravity will work against getting blood to the computer and he could suddenly collapse. An oxygen system (if it had been available) would have increased the amount of oxygen that was being taken in by the energy system to be used by the pumping system to keep the nervous system on line. That is why it is a good idea to carry a portable oxygen tank. However, oxygen has to be administered carefully as too much oxygen can be dangerous to people suffering from severe chronic pulmonary lung diseases. The danger comes from the brain now using an oxygen level to tell the respiratory system how often to breath instead of a carbon dioxide level as in a healthy person. If you were to administer large percentages of oxygen rapidly to this person, you will be telling the system to go slower and slower and finally stop. It is for this reason that the safest oxygen system to carry is one that delivers oxygen through a continuous flow of 4 to 5 liters through a nasal tube or mask. The system to avoid is the push button or forced flow system as too much oxygen will be given and this system may also totally block a partial obstructed airway by blowing the obstruction further into the lower airway.

Failure to react to the signs of a machine having problems means that the phases of the machine will grow weaker and may fail all together or at different points of time. That is why it is vital to constantly monitor the sick or injured person and to confirm that he is breathing, has a pulse, and is still able to speak with you. Be sure he knows where he is. Breathing lets you know that the machine is getting the energy to survive. The pulse which should be taken first at the carotid artery will inform you of whether the pumping system is functioning.** To speak to the person and ask questions lets you know if the computer system is still on line and functioning normally.*** Also, through the persons ability to answer, you know he is able to breath well enough and his airway is open as it takes air passing over your vocal cords to make sounds.

2. While on a detail with two other special agents assigned to protect the client, a brick comes out of the crowd of demonstrators and hits your client in the head. He falls to the ground unconscious. He lands on his face and appears to have blood coming from his nose. The police move in and secure the crowd and inform you that they have called for an ambulance with an approximate time of arrival at the scene of fifteen minutes. What should your main concerns be for your client's care?

The first concern should always be to follow the ABCB rule. The blood coming from the nose could block the airway and lead to problems with the energy phase due to the rapid reduction in the amount of oxygen flowing into the system.

Whenever there is head trauma, there is often lots of bleeding and neck trauma as well. This trauma would directly affect the computer phase of the machine and due to swelling, lack of oxygen, or actual lacerations or tears to the brain or spinal column, there could be partial or total loss of consciousness, even paralysis which could lead to failure of the respiratory system.

Due to possible neck injuries, although rapid transport is desirable, care must be taken to immobilize the neck and back. Use your hands to maintain neck stabilization. Stabilizing the neck requires that you avoid moving the head. To stabilize the back, any hard surface such as a door or piece of plywood will work to reduce possible additional injury to the computer system. If you have to roll somebody over, attempt to roll the head, neck and spine as one unit. You will need extra help to accomplish this delicate task.

If there is oxygen available utilize it. You will find that in almost every situation that the addition of oxygen (energy) will be favorable for the patient. Restrictions on emergency oxygen applications, if present, should be part of your principal's medical history.

3. While defending a client from an attacker with a knife you are cut on the upper leg. The bleeding is heavy from the wound. The attacker has been subdued and you begin to take care of yourself. What is your chief concern?

**The carotid pulse is found on either side of the throat best found by placing two fingers in the middle of the throat—stay away from the windpipe—and sliding them back towards the base of the ear slowly. Be gentle and do not reach across the person's throat, you could obstruct his breathing. Never use the thumb to take a pulse. This could result in feeling your own pulse and not the patient's.

***Remember to make the questions that you ask to gauge the computer function abilities simple, such as "What year is it?" "What is your name?" If the right answers are given, get more in depth with "What happened?"-type questions. Do not play trivial pursuit.

Your chief concern in this case will be the loss of blood. The body has approximately six quarts of blood. A loss of ten percent or more will begin to cause the pumping phase to go into shock and to weaken noticeably. Therefore, the bleeding must be stopped as soon as possible for it is the red stuff pouring out that carries the oxygen throughout the body to keep the machine alive.

The best means to stop blood loss is direct pressure, and elevating the wound above the level of the heart. Taking a clean dry bandage or, if no bandage is available, just your bare hand and place it over the wound and apply pressure.* Should blood come through the bandage that you have applied, **DO NOT REMOVE THE BANDAGE.** Add more on top and add pressure.** If this fails to slow the flow you can go above the site of the wound and place pressure around the extremity but not to the point of cutting off a pulse below that site.***

Finally, should these steps fail to ease the flow, a tourniquet can be applied to cut off all blood flow below the tourniquet site. A tourniquet is the LAST resort because if it is left on for too long there can be permanent damage to the site below the tourniquet, even loss of the limb.

The theory behind the direct pressure method and the pressure above the site of the injury is simply the fact that your applied pressure must be greater than the pressure the body is exerting through the wound. Just like turning the water on in a hose that has a leak in the rubber lining. You could grab onto the leak which may stop almost all of the flow or there may be so much pressure fighting your efforts that no results are seen. This would be direct pressure. If you go above the site of the break and squeeze the hose the pressure at the break will be lowered and thus less fluid will spray out at the damaged site.

The best means will always be the direct pressure to the wound and, if needed a constrictive band above the injured site which will only permit partial blood flow.

The best way to determine if the band is too tight is look at the nail beds of the fingers or toes. If you press firmly on the nail bed you will see that it will turn white and then if there is blood flow the area will pink back up again. Should this return of color fail to appear, your constrictive band may actually be a tourniquet. It needs to have pressure released until blood flow can occur. Don't lose a limb due to this mistake being overlooked.

4. There was a gunshot and you notice that your client has one more hole in his body than he did when you first picked him up this morning. There is blood coming from his chest on the right side and he is having trouble breathing. The problem seems to be more noticeable when he is inhaling. He is beginning to breathe faster. Which phase of the machine is in the most danger of failing?

---

*A dry dressing or bandage is preferred because water will not allow the blood to clot as the blood dries.

**There is clotting occurring against the dressing or bandages even though blood may come through the first bandage that is applied. Should you remove this dressing from the wound before total bleeding has stopped, the clotting that had occurred will be destroyed and the bleeding will continue. It is for this reason that you should never remove a dressing once applied to a wound except in one case which will be discussed in the next example.

***The tourniquet once properly applied stops all blood flow to the area below the application site. This means that no energy is getting to that part of the machine and that could result in that part of the machine being permanently damaged. This is why a tourniquet is the last resort that would be used to stop a bleeding wound.

The answer is the energy phase provided that the heart and larger arteries were not involved. The respiratory system is the main concern because of the damage that the wound has caused to normal chest and lung action.

When we inhale, the chest muscles, chest cavity, and the diaphragm, which is a large muscle located just below the rib cage, work together as a unit to draw in an adequate amount of oxygen.

To properly inhale, the chest muscles stretch outward and the diaphragm pulls downward on the total chest cavity which creates negative pressure within the body like a vacuum. Less pressure is present than the atmosphere. Thus, the air is drawn into the system.

This total system is enclosed by the skin of the body. It does not function properly if any leaks to the outside allow air in or out. In this example, someone has now created a leak that needs to be fixed, the vacuum is broken.

When an opening occurs to the chest cavity from the outside, one or two wounds may result. It is important to always remember to look for an exit wound when dealing with gunshot victims as the second wound is usually much larger than the entrance wound.

If the wound has only entered the chest cavity, but it has not injured the lung, air could leak into the chest cavity and/or blood. In this case the best treatment is to cover the wound with an air tight dressing.*

The second type of wound would not only involve the skin portion of the chest wall, but also the lung itself. Now there is air coming into the chest through the chest wall as well as leaking into the chest from the hole in the lung. This air and/or blood is now beginning to take up the space that the chest cavity normally has to expand to allow the lungs to properly fill. Therefore, the injured lung is being compressed into an exhalation mode by the air and/or blood that is now where it should not be.

Just as in the previous case, there is a need to stop the air that is leaking into the chest wall through the wound. Use an air tight dressing. There is nothing that you can do to stop the air that is leaking from the punctured lung. Now is the one time that you may remove a dressing.

This victim needs to be watched closely because of your actions. You might lose the victim if you fail to recognize a problem that can arise from the air that continues to leak from the damaged lung.

As the air fills the chest cavity from the lung, more pressure is being applied and this prevents the lung from filling. This pressure will increase if the built-up air is not vented. It will begin to move the damaged lung over toward the uninjured lung. Because the heart lies between the two lungs, the circulatory/pump system may be in trouble too. What can you do to aid in relieving this build up of pressure?

There are two things that can be done. First, place the injured person as much as possible onto their injured side. This will utilize gravity to keep the injured lung from compressing onto the heart and the remaining good lung. Second, remove the air tight bandage from the chest wall wound when the injured person is exhaling. This will aid the person and unblock a relief valve. During exhalation, the chest cavity has the most internal pressure to force air out in a normal status as stated earlier. In an injured state,

---

*One of the best means to gain an air tight seal by using your hand while wearing a plastic glove. Should depressurization be necessary, simply lift your hand. The process can be completed and the resealing can take place with minimal movement and equipment.

there is the additional pressure present in the injured chest cavity. Upon exhalation the bandage will be lifted and air and/or blood will be heard and seen escaping from the wound site. On the next inhalation you should see the person breathe slightly deeper. At this time the dressing over the chest wall wound should be resealed. The patient should be monitored to avoid over-pressurization. If it occurs, repeat the same procedure.

In all cases of chest trauma, the airway must be watched closely as the victim may bleed from the lung and up into the air passages. The patient may have to be positioned to assist drainage through gravity if no mechanical form of suction is available.

All chest trauma should receive massive doses of oxygen if it is available. Surgery must be performed immediately, so move to the nearest trauma center at once.

When dealing with a person having trauma to the chest, if the person continues to worsen after you start to treat all wounds that you have found, remember to look for more. All wounds must be covered to maintain the air tight seal that the respiratory/energy system needs to continue to function.

5. There has been an explosion. When the dust clears you notice your partner now has a piece of wood sticking out of his upper leg. There is some bleeding around the piece of wood and he states that his foot below the wound feels numb. Should you remove the piece of wood? What needs to be checked below the injured site?

The answer to the first question is that you never remove an impaled object. The object may be acting as a plug in a dam. In this case, the piece of wood may have passed through the femoral artery which carries all of the oxygenated blood to the lower leg. Bleeding from the femoral artery could be difficult to control and failing to do so could result in severe shock leading to death.

The piece of wood needs to be stabilized in place and transport the person to the nearest hospital that can handle the emergency.

The second question surrounds the need to check to see if the extremity below the site of the injury is receiving oxygen rich blood. This would result in the need to check the toe nail beds as mentioned earlier.

6. You have been called to the bedroom of your client. His wife explains that she is having trouble awakening her husband and that he seems to be unable to speak clearly. She also informs you that he had complained of a headache before going to sleep last night. What has happened to your client and what can you do to help him?

Remember, the leading cause of pain when there are no signs of injury is that part of the body being deprived of an adequate supply of oxygen. In this case, a headache last night, sluggish response, lack of alertness and incoherent speech would lead you to think that the problem lies in the area of the nervous/computer system not obtaining the supply of oxygen it needs to function, especially if there is no sign of injury. Your principal has probably suffered a stroke, although this diagnosis may be incorrect.

The best treatment in this case is very similar to that of a heart attack. Talk to the person, letting them know that you will help them. This will relieve some of the stress that they will be feeling and lower the demand for oxygen so that the injured area will benefit from the supply on hand. In some cases, the stroke patient may become somewhat combative and this condition needs to be controlled to preserve the oxygen supply.

The next step will be the administration of supplemental oxygen to enrich the oxygen that the person is breathing.

Some common causes of strokes are fatty deposits that build up in the artery leading to one part of the brain. This creates a smaller opening for the blood to go through. This problem can become severe if a blood clot breaks free somewhere else in the body and becomes lodged in this location. The second cause of stroke relates to a worn area of an artery which breaks and blood fails to reach the section of brain requiring this supply or the stroke could be as a result of trauma past or present.

7. There is a fire in your clients home and he is burned when his night clothes catch on fire. What is the proper treatment to give him? Can he go to just any hospital?

In the case of a person receiving a burn, the best treatment at first is to cool the burn site and then apply a dry sterile dressing as soon as possible. A dry dressing is preferred because the burn patient is very vulnerable to infections. Moist dressings create two problems. First, they create the perfect breeding ground for bacterial infections, and then moisture could cool to the point of causing hypothermia (low body temperature).The leading cause of death among burn patients is infection.

The answer to the second question is that if the person has been burnt to the point where there is blistering or charring, 2nd and 3rd degree burns, they should be seen at a trauma center preferably one with burn treatment capabilities as well.

There are different levels of burns. These levels are determined by the depth of the burn into the skin layers. The percentage of body area burnt, along with the known level of burn, determine the severity of the burn.

Burns can be created from different sources that will require special attention to other areas besides the wound.

In the case of an electrical burn, you must remember the danger connected with the source of the injury. If you touch the person and he is still in contact with the source of electricity, you will become victim number two. The power source must be shut down before attempting to do anything for this person. Once the power is off this person is then treated as any other burn patient with one exception. The electrical burn patient will present the same wounds as that of a gunshot where there is an entrance wound and an exit wound. This is created by the electrical source going through the body which is mostly water to a grounded source.

One other area of concern for the electricity induced burn patient is that of heart problems as a result of the electrical current passing near or through the heart which can result in heart beat irregularities or sudden cardiac arrest.

In all cases of burns, should the hands, feet, genital area, and/or face be involved, these burns should be considered serious. The hands and feet due to the disabling effects that the burn has to normal recovery. The genital area due to the high risk of infection and facial burns due to the impact on the respiratory system which will be in danger due to swelling, blocking the airway, or hot gases damaging sensitive internal tissues.

8. You are called into the home of your client by the maid who leads you to the client's three-year-old son who is unconscious on the bathroom floor. You notice a silvery substance on his fingers and lips and both sites appear to be red and burned. What are you faced with? Should you attempt to make this child vomit?

You know that you are dealing with a poisoning. In this case all the signs are there, but whenever you find an unconscious child you would be wise to always smell his breath and check his fingers and hands for the possible cause of the problem.

Never make a person vomit who has swallowed a corrosive or a petroleum-based product. A simple rule to remember is "If it burns going down, it will burn twice as bad coming up." As this person is unconscious, you would never want him to vomit. This could cause him to lose his airway.

The best treatment is to always know the closest poison control center's phone number. While traveling, keep national or local "800" numbers on hand. They will ask you for the following information:

1. What was taken?
2. How much was taken?
3. Were other medications or alcohol involved?
4. When was it taken?
5. What have you done so far?

When all of these questions have been answered, they will advise you of the proper solution. In all cases the person should be taken to the hospital. It is also advised that the substance taken be brought along as well.

9. You have just returned your client to his home from a hectic day of meetings. When you open the door to his limo you see that he is jerking rapidly in the seat and you notice a spilled medication bottle on the floor. Upon checking the bottle you see the name of the medication is Dilantin. What is this client's problem? What caused him to have this problem? What can you do?

This person is having a seizure. The computer phase of the system is malfunctioning and telling all body parts to move. This condition can come from a variety of sources such as the following:

1. Heat related—Seen in small children and infants, when a high fever results in seizure activities. In this case, the best treatment is cooling the child with a wet rag and fanning him with your hand. The child should also be taken to the hospital.

2. Trauma related—Normally seen in head trauma or trauma to the spinal cord. The best treatment in these cases is to administer oxygen and transport to a trauma center as soon as possible.

3. Disease related—This could be as a result of cancer or more commonly, epilepsy. The drug Dilantin is usually given to try and stop such seizure activity. The leading cause of most epileptic seizures is simply that the person either forgets to take the medication or feels he does not need it today. The best treatment for this patient is to give him oxygen and attempt to place a bite stick (to be discussed later) in his mouth to keep him from biting his tongue. As in all of the above cases, the emergency medical system should be brought into play.

In all cases of seizure, the leading cause of death is due to lack of oxygen. This is caused by the rapid use of the normal amount of oxygen. When the entire body is jerking about, the body's muscles are demanding an additional supply.

10. The garden party was going well and there wasn't a cloud in the sky. Mr. Principal was mixing with all the right people and you had aided him in avoiding those whom he liked to avoid. Suddenly you hear Mr. Principal yell and grab the back of his neck just below his shirt collar. You immediately run to his aid to protect him from any added attack. Upon your arrival you find that the assault was committed by a bee that had found Mr. Principal's cologne too sweet to pass up.* Mr. Principal says he will be fine and that no insect is going to stop him from getting the votes he needs to get that big merger through. Five minutes have passed, you notice that Mr. Principal is sweating and seems to be trying to loosen his tie and clearing or trying to clear his throat. What is happening to Mr. Principal and what should you do?

---

*More people are killed by insect stings each year than snake bites.

The answer is that Mr. Principal is having an allergic reaction to the bee sting. The part of the machine that is being attacked is the nervous/computer system.

The attempt to clear the throat is caused by the shutting down of the respirator/energy system due to a constricted airway. The throat is closing due to the messages being received from the computer system that has been affected by the bee's venom.

In a very short time Mr. Principal may stop breathing. Mouth-to-mouth may be called for. You should give him oxygen if available, as his energy system is in need of help. Get him to the hospital as soon as possible as this is a true emergency. He is in need of medication to stop the effects of the allergic reaction.

This concludes the examples to show how the energy, pumping, and computer phases of the body are effected by different forms of sickness and trauma emergencies. Of course, this is only a small fraction of the possible situations that you may be confronted with in your daily activities as a personal protection specialist. If you just apply the simple approach of understanding what phase of the body is being affected and think about what you can do to correct the problem you can spell the difference between life and death. The key is to recognize, understand, and correct the problem, and to eliminate the loss of time that cannot be replaced.

FIGHTING TIME AND TRIAGE.

Time is the biggest factor in emergency incidents. The body will tell you how much time it has left by the way it shuts down less important functions of the machine.

Such functions as getting blood to the hands and feet will slow as the need to get the blood to the computer and pumping systems takes priority. It is due to this reaction that a pulse taken at the wrist may not be present but there would be a pulse at the carotid artery in the neck. Levels of consciousness go down as the computer doesn't want to waste energy on keeping the eyes open and the thought processes functioning normally when the pumping and the energy phases needs its full attention.

The body is now giving you signs that time is running out. It is up to you to determine what the problem is and to slow or stop this time loss through your care.

Time can be saved by learning to evaluate how the systems of the body are doing and how well the body is functioning. This can be done through questioning the person to evaluate the computer system. Take a pulse at the wrist and then the carotid in the neck to gauge the effectiveness of the pumping system. Watch the person breathe to see if it is normal. The one area that is always checked in cases of injury is the body itself. If the person is conscious and can follow commands, have him carry out certain requests that will allow you to see if every part of the body is acting in a normal manner. Should you have a question as to what is normal, you have a learning aid nearby. Look at yourself and compare.

For example, if you wanted to see if the person has injured his chest, ask him or her to take a deep breath and expand their chest. If there is a problem, there will be pain, obvious facial expressions, and vocal complaints of pain. Injured people also indicate the site of the injury through "self splinting."

Self-splinting occurs as the person uses his own body to ease the pain of movement. A person who has pain when breathing deeply will not breathe deeply. If there are broken ribs, the person will hold onto their side to ease the pain. If their arm is broken, they will normally use the other hand and arm to support it. Nobody with a broken arm holds it up and waves it about to indicate which arm is injured.

Should the person be unconscious, then you must physically check the person from head to toe looking for problems. In performing this form of check it is extremely important not to miss any part of the body, so a set pattern of checking should be utilized. The most common area that is forgotten is the side that you do not see or the back when the person is laying face up.

This check must be done with enough pressure to feel any deformity and may even cause the person to make a facial expression of discomfort when a problem is found. For this reason, you should visualize the person's face so as not to miss any signs of pain that you may create. Use your own body as a means to compare what is normal or abnormal. Remember, you are dealing with an injured human being, not a robot. Comfort and reassure the patient. You reduce anxiety and this reduces stress on the patient's system in turn. Try to act calm and to keep the attention of your patient. Do not give him anything to drink as this could cause vomiting. Try to keep him still so as to reduce the energy demand.

A pulse should be taken for fifteen seconds, multiply by four to to get a rate for a minute. The same would apply for a respiration count. This should be done before and after the total body is checked.

If the person is not your principal, you should try to get as much information from him as possible. It keeps the patient alert and thinking. He can give you information such as what happened, allergies, and his medical history. Remember to write all this information down as well as the time of your pulse and respiration count and what you found in your head to toe check. This will be the type of information that the paramedic or doctor will request.

To say "I think his pulse was 100," to a trained care provider means "I didn't take the time to take it." For this reason they will take it again. In the case of allergies, it is extremely important to have this information ready. This will aid rescuers in their selection of appropriate medications.

Your prompt decision to treat the cause of the problem will save time. If you see rapid bleeding, you need to stop it quickly. The decision to stay where you are and wait for help to arrive or get enroute to the nearest hospital without delay, is by no means easy to make.

The type of situation will normally dictate what your reaction will be. A person having severe chest pain with a history of heart attacks shouldn't wait a half an hour for help to arrive. He needs more that just air and basic care to survive.

Call for help by dialing the correct emergency number. Be properly prepared. Give your route of travel to the hospital so you can meet the ambulance enroute. A fracture to an arm with a good pulse below the break could wait for help to arrive unlike the above situation.

Remember that your own safety should be of the upmost importance. All of the above statements are meant to save the injured person's time, but if you fail to recognize a hazard to yourself while attempting to care for the injured person, you now compound the problem. You have started a second clock ticking toward losing more time.

Who will you save and who will you leave alone when you are dealing with a group of injured people? The term that is used to describe this problem is "triage" which means "to sort."

This is one area that is usually found to be the most difficult to accept. No one likes to give up on anything especially when the item is someone else's life.

There are many rules of thumb to determine who is critically injured and who is not. The most logical approach I have ever witnessed can be attributed to a state trooper that I had the luck to meet on my first accident scene.

This officer arrived at the scene of an auto crash involving twelve injured people at the same time I did. He told me help was on the way and that he would let me know who was the most serious to look at first. The injured people were all Spanish and, as I didn't speak a word of Spanish, I wasn't looking forward to trying to ask each one where they hurt the most or figuring out who was the worst one injured.

As I started to examine the first of my many patients, the trooper stopped me and told me to stay by him for a moment. He then said something in Spanish and ten of the injured people began to get up off the ground and walk up to the police car. I asked him what he had just said to these folks. He replied that he had told them that I was a doctor and that anyone who would like me to check them out, I would do so if they would come up to his car. He then looked at the two remaining people who did not move and told me that I had better check them out first. They obviously were hurt the worst. He was right and I had learned my first lesson about triage which is, let those that can help themselves do so.

If you take the time to try and splint a fracture or stop a wound from bleeding by holding pressure on it yourself, instead of instructing the injured person to do so, you may save just one or two, whereas by letting them help themselves you could have moved on and aided others.

Accountability is another important item to be remembered in triage incidents. Try and get the correct number of persons before the incident occurred. Be sure that when all the victims have been taken to the hospitals that the same number of people are accounted for.

Someone has to take charge and maintain control as best as possible. Tell other rescuers who and where you are and then don't move from that spot. You become the command post. Think ahead and think logistics; things like loading zones, and helicopter landing zones. If the scene is large, break it down into smaller sections and assign a leader to each section. Keep less injured victims—the walking wounded—together, don't allow them to wander around. They can always be put aboard the first available bus. Remember, your team can locate and treat many people, whereas you alone can treat but a small few.

There are many factors and events that can affect triage incidents. If you are faced with the possibility of a large number of injuries occurring in your area of protection it would benefit you to attend a course on the subject of triage.

IV. RECOMMENDED EQUIPMENT AND EMERGENCY CARE COURSES.

Just as there are different firearms to suit the situations confronted in your daily activities, there are different levels of equipment that you can carry.

The bare minimum that the professional personal protection specialist should carry is a small and relatively cheap personal kit that consists of the following items including their uses:

1. A large plastic sandwich bag that has a sealing mechanism. This item is used to store the remaining list of items as well as act as a large air tight dressing.

2. One pair of plastic gloves. Used to protect the rescuer from possible communicable disease and once placed on hands, tends to make the hands into an excellent air tight dressing.

3. A pocket mask with one way valve. This item is used when doing mouth-to-mask resuscitations which helps to avoid transference of communicable diseases and, if there is a oxygen hook-up valve with oxygen available, a means to give a higher flow of energy to the body.

4. Three to four packets of sugar in original wrappers. These packets can be added to orange juice to assist the diabetic patient who forgot to eat after taking his insulin and is going into insulin shock. In all cases of diabetic patients sugar that you give will not do additional harm. Original wrappers should be maintained and do not put sugar into other containers.

5. Tongue depressors or plastic bite sticks. A bite stick is for the seizure patient. Use once and throw away. You can buy tongue depressors or plastic bite sticks that are ready-made.

6. Four pieces of strong cloth cut approximately six inches wide by two feet long. These are used to splint fractures through the technique of "body splinting." As an example you would tie the good leg to a broken leg with a rolled up coat between the legs to fill in any voids or spaces. This will act as a splint when a patient is to be moved while lying on a stretcher or board.

Larger emergency kits can be made up or purchased ready-made to cover a vast array of injuries, they come equipped with everything from Band-Aids to sterile burn sheets.

Splints are easily found. Just look around you and see what can be broken to proper size. A folding metal backboard is nice to have, but again, use what is around you. A door or board works just as well.

Oxygen systems are an excellent item to carry but they are expensive and usually too heavy to carry around all day. Should you look into a system and you carry it from place to place, remember that pressurized cylinders may require special handling procedures and permits, as well as periodic inspections of valves, oxygen lines and pressurization. A pair of Military Anti-Shock Trousers round out this suggested list of items. These can be used to slow the onset of shock due to blood loss. They can also be used for splinting or applying direct pressure to a bleeding wound. These trousers are expensive and special training as necessary, but they can really make a difference when they are needed. As for bandages and dressings, although the purchased kinds are nice, remember that any clean cloth will do.

To learn to use these emergency tools properly, you should attend at least the following courses:

1. American Heart Association CPR Course—Course Duration: one day (eight hours), Contact for course information: American Heart Assoc. This course teaches manual life saving methods to assist in respiratory and cardiac emergencies as well as choking emergencies. You should attend on a yearly basis.

2. Some form of emergency care course that involves both lecture and hands on training. As an example, the course called Emergency First Line Care. It has been utilized by the U.S. State Department to train new agents. Due to schedule demands of the personal protection specialist, the course is presented in a three-day format involving material that is designed to give the student a basic understanding of situations that can be faced on a daily basis. For more information contact the Executive Protection Institute.

To close, remember that your own safety comes first! Don't make their emergency your emergency, be prepared!

FIFTEEN

Techniques and Principles of Protection: Close Range

by Steve Rhodes and Pat Rice

A CLOSE-RANGE ATTACK on a principal by an assailant, armed or unarmed, is difficult to counter. The circumstances, including location, the method and direction of attack, number and skill of protective personnel, relative position of all persons, the assailant's skill and mental state, etc., combine to create a unique situation. Because each situation is different, no single technique can be guaranteed to be completely effective in all situations. However, there are techniques and methods that are quite effective in most situations. They are widely applicable because they are based on broad principles and have general methods of application.

OBJECTIVE

Obviously, it is not possible to teach an entire martial art in one brief chapter or lesson, nor is it possible to teach specific sets of techniques that will always work. But it is possible to present a few general techniques that are simple and easy to learn and that are immediately accessible to people regardless of their previous experience or ability level. It is better to learn broad principles that allow you to react in a variety of ways to whatever situation presents itself rather than to try to learn specific techniques that may or may not work.

The basic concepts in this unit come directly from the teachings of Taijiquan, one of the oldest martial arts in existence. These concepts include "understand your own position," "take advantage of the center," "move efficiently," and "be aware of your own weaknesses." Although many Taijiquan teachers do not concentrate on martial application, its principles are often referred to as the "root" of all martial arts. The techniques included in this unit come from a variety of martial disciplines such as Chin'na, Aikido, Jujitsu, and others and have been simplified for easy learning and effective usage.

If you seek further instruction, find a reputable martial arts or self-defense instructor. Be suspicious of anyone who promises you a "foolproof" set of techniques even after years of training. (If only one technique would always work, why don't we all know that one technique already?) Almost all self-defense courses are designed to protect oneself rather than another person. Third-party protection requires a slightly different set of skills and different mental preparation.

Reaction skills can be learned and it is important for you to practice what you learn. A training partner can help your skill level advance very quickly. Practice each step independently and then all steps in sequence. Repeat the movements until they feel comfortable to you and you are able to perform them automatically, quickly, and smoothly. Your partner should not be overly cooperative but should give a realistic reaction to your attempts. Practice seriously to hone and sharpen your skills. Studies show that mental concentration combined with repetitive movement is far superior to repetitive movement alone.

Before practicing, you should spend a few minutes warming up the muscles and tendons of the body, stretching major ligaments and joints to prevent injury when you work out. Pay special attention to the neck, waist, wrists, and shoulders, and be careful of knees and ankles. Include neck rolls, arm swings, waist twists, knee bends, ankle rolls, leg stretches, and various other common martial arts stretches.

ASSUMPTIONS

For this type of training, certain assumptions have been made. The first is that you are a well-trained, intelligent, alert, and somewhat calm agent protecting your principal. The second is that the attack made is serious, that is, if not intercepted, it will harm the principal, and it should be treated as life-threatening. When an attack occurs, there is little time in the situation to analyze anything. You must react appropriately, and your reaction must be immediate and automatic.

THE ONE, TWO, THREE METHOD

The steps of the method taught here are numbered because they have a hierarchy of importance. The first step is the most essential, the second step adds control, and the third step, while not absolutely necessary, adds insurance that the assailant will not be able to resume the attack. If the first step is not done well, the subsequent steps will be very difficult or even impossible to implement.

Step One: Deflect

Deflecting the attack, Step One, is the most important part of defense.

The most critical element of the attack is its direction. The most effective counter is to change that direction, as quickly and efficiently as possible, before it reaches its target.

Your choices of where to re-direct the line of attack are limited only by the surroundings and circumstances. A change to any direction—up, down, to either side—will keep the attack from reaching its target. It is not necessary to deflect a great distance. Often the crucial difference is only a few inches.

Most people think of using their hand to grab or move the weapon. You can also use your arm, shoulder, leg, foot, or whole body to deflect. Move as much as necessary and as efficiently as possible. Don't be stuck mentally on deflecting the weapon itself. Depending on the relative positions of all persons, it may be more efficient to redirect the assailant's entire body or even to move the principal rather than the weapon or the assailant.

However, if you take time to analyze where or how to deflect, or what to deflect with, it will be too late. It is interesting to note that most preconstructed methods of deflecting are time consuming to perform. Your response must be 99% reaction and 1% premeditated movement. You must practice, both physically and mentally, until your response is automatic. You must rely on your trained ability and your desire to protect in order to make your reactions quick and sure. Success depends on speed. The deflection does not have to be smooth or pretty, it just needs to be effective. At the very least, you will have bought time.

Important points for "Deflection":

- Get as much body as possible into play
- Deflect as directly as possible with no wasted movements
- Make your deflection as much reflex as possible
- Don't try to think of what to do next until the deflect is successful
- Leave the fancy stuff for the Hollywood stunt workers

Step Two: Adhere

"Adhere" is the next important step after you have accomplished "Deflect". Steps One and Two are separate stages for an important reason: adhering requires some thought, and the time it takes to think may be the critical time lapse for deflecting. If you take even a fraction of a second too long to deflect, you may be too late to protect. Make deflection the first step and a separate step; once you have deflected, you have given yourself an instant to institute Step Two: Adhere, and to analyze.

The assailant is still very single-minded and will continue trying to attack. All the energy goes into the weapon or the hand, and he or she will re-aim the weapon if possible. Don't let the assailant get back to a position of attack. Ensure that the direction of the attack remains changed by adhering to the attack.

Adhere to whatever part of the assailant you have deflected. Grasp the assailant's weapon, if possible. Since his or her mind is concentrated on the weapon, this is your optimum point of control. The next best points of control are adhering to the hand, the wrist, the arm, or the body.

Use your hand or fingers to grip. Two hands are better than one. However, you can also adhere by using a combination of arms, body, legs, or other objects to trap the weapon or the assailant.

Adhering requires some thought. You must know whether the deflection was successful and whether and where you should adhere. You can take into account some other factors such as how the assailant and the principal are now positioned, the surroundings, and the crowd. You have an instant to re-assess the present seriousness of the attack and determine how much force you need to use in protecting.

Step Three: The Ground?

If you have accomplished Steps One and Two, "Deflect" and "Adhere," then Step Three: "The Ground" will be possible. The training for this step is not commonly taught, but the concept follows logically after the first two steps. It ensures that the assailant cannot recover control of the attack.

"The Ground" means taking what you have adhered to and putting it on the ground or floor. If you have deflected and adhered to the weapon, hand, or arm in steps one and two, step three will be relatively easy to accomplish. If your attachment was made elsewhere, you can still continue with step three but it may take more strength or force.

Although only a second or two has elapsed since the deflect, you should be able to analyze the situation and determine how much force is necessary before completing step three. Unless you have been able to determine that little or no threat remains to the principal, carry out step three with a great deal of force. A minimum amount of force drops the assailant to the ground gently while maintaining control of the weapon and the assailant. A maximum force causes the assailant's body to rotate in the air without a controlled landing and could result in serious injury to the head, neck, or spine.

When taking the assailant to the ground, get your own body low, either by bending your knees or by dropping your whole body to the ground. Concentrate on putting the opponent's weapon or hand on the ground; the rest of the body must follow. Then use pressure of your arm, knee, or body to pin it to the ground.

Refinements of Step Three

Although the "One, Two, Three" Method is sufficient in itself, there are additional techniques for further refinement of Step Three. These sub-techniques deal with maintaining further control of the situation by controlling the stability of the assailant's body. At the same time, you must keep control of your own body.

STABILITY

In order to implement the sub-techniques in the final stage, it is helpful to understand the stability of the human body. Stability—the ability to remain upright—is affected by the body's center of gravity (which varies with a person's height, weight, and posture), by stance, by balance point, and by movement. It is also affected by other subtle factors such as flexibility, tension, weight distribution, body alignment, and even by mental attitude. The area of balance is the space with which the body can remain upright. If you can force the assailant outside of the optimal area of balance, that person will lose stability and then it is easy to cause him or her to fall. Try to maintain your own area of balance for maximum control.

The stance, or base, is formed when we stand with feet apart. The shape of the base changes as we move. An upright two-legged stance supplies great reach and maneuverability. However, the base is narrow, and it is easy to overreach the balance point, because the center of gravity is no longer over the feet. Standing with the feet further apart increases the base and therefore, makes it somewhat easier for the balance point to remain within the base, and stability is slightly increased. However, when the base increases in one direction, it shrinks in the other. A stance is strong only in the direction of the stance and is weak in all other directions. In Figures 1, 2, 3, and 4 below, the direction of stability is indicated with a solid line, the direction of instability with a dotted line. The shadowed area indicates the shape of the base.

Test these stances with a partner. One partner assumes a stance and the other finds the strong and weak directions by pulling or pushing enough to cause the other to lose balance and take a step.

Concentrate first on stance and position. Consider both your own stance and that of the assailant in order to understand how best to take advantage of your stability and the opponent's instability. In addition, the relative body positions (the distance between your center point and the assailant's center point) are very important in controlling both your own balance and that of the assailant. Once you have understood the stances and their effects on each person's area of balance, you can employ several techniques to disarm and/or temporarily immobilize an assailant.

"THE GROUND" SUB-TECHNIQUES

The first sub-technique of Step Three is to place the weapon or person on the ground outside the assailant's area of balance. Even if the assailant tries to recover that

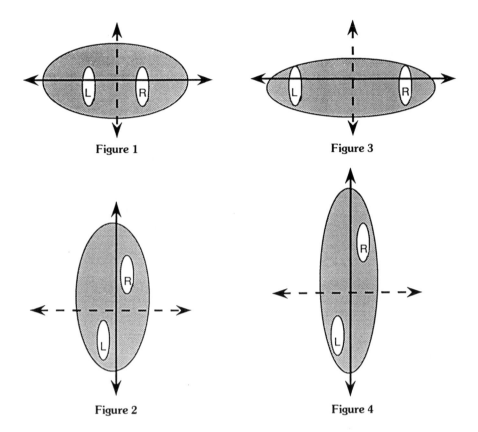

Figure 1

Figure 3

Figure 2

Figure 4

Figure 1: A typical side stance with feet parallel and body facing straight ahead. Figure 2: A typical front stance, with one foot in front of the other. The stance may be weighted on the front foot or back foot or may be evenly weighted.

Figure 3: A lower side stance. Figure 4: A lower front stance. The lower stances increase the length of the base and the strength of the stance, but the width is decreased, and the directions of instability remain the same.

balance, you can move again to change the relative positions and take advantage of the weaknesses of his or her stance. The second sub-technique is to place the weapon or person on the ground outside the opponent's area of balance but within your own area of balance. You will have maximum control of the situation if you are not struggling for your own stability.

A third sub-technique has to do with controlling the other person's body by means of pressure and leverage against joints. You can get the upper hand in an aggressive fashion by keeping the assailant off balance. Once you have attached to the assailant, you can jerk, twist, or bend limbs to manipulate the body. Going against the natural direction of movement causes joints to lock and forces the body to move. Pain techniques may or may not be involved and may or may not be effective, but using the opponent's own limbs to apply leverage causes the body to follow the direction you dictate. Elbows and knees (hinge joints) are vulnerable to damage if stressed in any direction other than the natural direction. The shoulders (ball and socket joints) and the wrists (sliding joints) are damaged if taken to the extreme, or when put into a binding or jammed position. Elbows, wrists, and knees can easily be stressed and damaged as a takedown is executed, leaving the assailant helpless or at least more preoccupied with his or her own safety than with continuing the attack. More detailed explanations and techniques are more difficult to learn and to apply than the previous techniques, and you should implement them only if you have successfully achieved Steps One and Two.

Considerable effort in terms of practice and physical conditioning is necessary to perfect the sub-techniques of "The Ground" skills. A patient and willing partner is indispensable. Go slowly, gradually increasing speed as you become more adept at the moves. Think of more than one alternative to each situation during your practice sessions.

Once the assailant is on the ground, take further measures to maintain control or to disarm him or her. Do not attempt to disarm someone unless you have prepared yourself, physically, and mentally, for any subsequent measures of control required.

FLEXIBILITY OF THE MIND

Choreographed sequences and personal "favorite" or "best" moves are great for training, but in real situations, not everything happens as planned. You must be flexible not only in your body, but also in your mind. Don't miss good techniques by being determined to make a certain technique work.

SUMMARY

- During an attack, you must react instantaneously.
- The One, Two, Three Method
  —First, deflect effectively
  —After deflection, adhere
  —Control the assailant by taking the person and/or the weapon to the ground
  —Control further by going outside the assailant's area of balance
- Rely on instincts, speed, agility, and position
- Learn a variety of techniques
- Practice your reaction skills
- Be mentally flexible

PART V

Additional Concerns

SIXTEEN

Legal Considerations in the Use of Force

by Dr. Arthur B. Fulton

ONE OF THE HAZARDS FACED by personal protection specialists engaged in executive protection work is the real possibility that the personal protection specialist, as a "protector", may have to use force to protect his or her executive/principal. It is, in fact, the very essence of executive protection—protect the executive. It is one of the primary objectives of the protective mission.

If and when it becomes necessary for a personal protection specialist to use force, physical or even deadly force, a number of questions immediately arise:

1. When can one use force?
2. How much force is justified?
3. What liabilities are incurred when one does use force?
4. Is anyone else made liable when one uses force?
5. What governmental regulations exist that restrict the possession, carrying and use of lethal weapons?

The underlying problem in all of these questions is LIABILITY, civil and/or criminal. When force is used, it invariably results in some form of an assault and/or battery or, if lethal force is used, a homicide or attempted homicide. Any one of these results raises the possibility of LIABILITY.

I. AMERICAN LEGAL SYSTEM

The American legal system has two types of law—criminal and civil. The use of force may give rise to either a criminal (public) wrong or a civil (private) wrong, *or both*. These wrongs, public or private, give rise to a criminal and/or a civil remedy. This remedy can be sought in the court of the proper jurisdiction of any of the 51 separate legal systems that exist in the United States.[1]

Criminal Law

The commission of a crime, a public wrong, represents a breach of duty against society. This duty is defined in some prior statutory prohibition. We are a society of order and to insure order there must be rules (dos and don'ts) that must be followed by society. Since there are rules, there must be sanctions to punish rulebreakers. Without sanctions the rules become meaningless and the order which society is seeking collapses. In order to insure the proper functioning of sanctions, society also has enforcers who bring the rulebreaker before its sanction system. The American system of "rules" is the criminal or penal code of the federal and state governments. The "sanctions" are the penalties imposed by court systems and the "enforcers" are the various branches and levels of law enforcement throughout the country.

Inasmuch as American society has imposed these rules or duties on itself, a violation thereof constitutes a breach of one's duty to society. Accordingly, legal action against the rulebreaker is brought by society (e.g. Commonwealth of Virginia v. Johnny Lawbreaker) by its representative, the prosecutor.

The remedy for violating the rules of society is some form of punishment—a fine, imprisonment, or both, or, in some jurisdictions, execution for capital crimes. To impose this remedy it is necessary for society to:

a. show that a statute existed making the particular act criminal
b. prove every element of the crime "beyond a reasonable doubt"
c. establish that the accused had the capacity to form a criminal intent (mens rea)[2]

Civil Law

A civil or private wrong is a breach of duty against another individual. The theory behind this breach is that the causing of harm, injury or loss to another is the basis for legal action against the actor to recover damages. This remedy for the private wrong is sought personally by the injured party in the appropriate jurisdiction against the person alleged to have breached his/her duty to the injured party (e.g. John Jones v. Tom Smith). The most common form of legal action for private wrongs in our society is for breach of contract or in tort.

The civil remedy for breaching private duties is not to punish the acting party but to place the injured party in the same position as if the harm had not occurred. Since this is not physically possible, the civil remedy is normally accomplished by awarding money damages to the injured party making him/her economically whole.[3] In order for the injured party to qualify for this remedy he/she must prove "by a preponderance of the evidence" that the acting party was responsible for the harm.[4] If the latter cannot prove a defense to the charge, he/she will be civilly liable in money damages. NOTE: the burden of proof in a civil case ("preponderance of the evidence") is not as stringent as the burden of proof imposed on society in a criminal case ("beyond a reasonable doubt").

In the field of executive protection, where the potential for the use of force is ever present, the most likely form of private wrong that a personal protection specialist may commit is a tort.

II. TORTS

"Tort." The word comes from the Latin torquere, to twist. It is a private wrong or injury in which the acting party owed a duty (not to injure) to the injured party, the duty was breached, and injury resulted.[5] Torts are divided into three types: (1) intentional wrongdoing in which the acting party deliberately or intentionally causes injury to another; (2) negligence in which the injury to another was accidental or unintentional; and (3) strict liability in which the acting party may be liable without fault for injury to another due to the hazardous or dangerous nature of the act.[6]

Although personal protection specialists engaged in executive protection could find themselves civilly liable for their actions in negligence or strict liability, the probable tort they may commit in protecting a principal is the intentional one of assault and/or battery. Although these two are frequently used together and often occur together, they are in fact two separate torts.

An assault is an *attempt* or a *threat* to inflict immediate physical injury. It is the conduct of the actor that is essential, not necessarily his/her intent. The question is this: "Was the action sufficient to place the injured party in fear or apprehension of immediate physical injury?" If the answer is "yes," an assault has occurred even though there was no actual touching.

A battery is nothing more than a consummated assault or the willful use of force or violence upon the person of another. Since it is "willful," intent in a battery is essential. There can be an assault without a battery, and a battery without an assault. Furthermore, the assault/battery can be the basis of a criminal charge in addition to a civil suit in tort.[7] Other potential intention-type torts for which a security officer may be civilly liable include false imprisonment, infliction of emotional or mental distress, malicious prosecution, defamation and invasion of privacy.[8]

III. USE OF FORCE

Non-Lethal Force

The use of non-lethal force is the basic assault/battery. Whenever a security officer willfully uses force on another he commits one or both of these torts.

Example: Fearless Fosdik, a security officer in executive protection, is accompanying his principal, corporate executive Dadee Worbuks, on a walk down the streets of New York City. Suddenly, Nastee Nedd, a disgruntled former employee of Worbuks, lunges toward Worbuks. Finding Fosdik in his way, Nastee strikes Fosdik and grabs his coat lapels in an effort to move him out of the way. Fosdik strikes Nastee in the face with his fist, grabs Nastee's arm and twists it behind his back breaking his wrist.

Has Fosdik committed the tort of assault and or battery? Absolutely! Fosdik breached his duty not to intentionally injure another and an injury has resulted. Can Fosdik be sued in civil court for this tort? Absolutely! Will Fosdik be liable to Nastee for money damages? Not on these facts! Why? Fosdik has a legal defense that justifies his assault/battery on Nastee. This is the defense of "self-defense." It is a legal excuse for the use of force—the resisting of an attack on one's person. It justifies a willful act (the tort) done in the reasonable belief of immediate danger and, if an injury results from the act done in self-defense, that person *cannot* be punished criminally nor held responsible for civil damages.[9]

Under the defense of self-defense, the law permits one to use *such force as is necessary* so long as it *is not disproportionate* to the nature and extent of the threat.[10] This right of self-defense, however, is good only if the defendant claiming same was not the aggressor and did not use abusive or provoking language. In determining if the force used is reasonable (i.e. not disproportionate) the court will look not only at whether or not the threat was apparent, but also at such secondary facts as age, size, strength, reputation, martial skill, use of weapons, etc.

Would Nastee Nedd in the above example be criminally liable as well as liable in a civil suit by Fosdik for the tort he (Nastee) committed against Fosdik? Certainly!

Deadly (Lethal) Force

Inasmuch as many personal protection specialists employed in executive protection carry weapons, a natural question is: "When can deadly force be used?"

The law says one can use deadly force ONLY if that individual or someone in his/her presence is faced with an *actual* or *reasonably apparent danger* of losing his/her life or of suffering serious bodily injury. One is not required to "retreat to the wall," and force can be met with commensurate force.[11] As in the non-lethal force situation the legal defense for using deadly force is "self-defense," with the same caveats—the party claiming the defense cannot be the attacker and the attack must be unprovoked. The test for determining if a "reasonably apparent danger" exists to support a self-defense claim is the test of "good faith"—what was the situation as it reasonably appeared at the time.

Defense of Another

The law grants to one who is defending a second party the same "self-defense rights" that the second party would have had in defending him or herself.[12] Consequently, a personal protection specialist who uses force against a third party in defense of his/her principal (second party), acquires the legal self-defense rights available to the principal. On the other hand, the personal protection specialist *cannot* acquire any more rights than those available to the principal being defended.

Example: Fearless Fosdik, our security officer, is traveling with his principal, Dadee Worbuks, on a business trip to Baltimore. During the evening Worbuks decides to experience the exotic nightlife of East Baltimore Street and Fosdik naturally accompanies him on this sojourn. In a rather ratty bar Worbuks makes a pass at a blonde girlfriend of a drunken sailor. When the sailor tells Worbuks to "butt out," Worbuks curses the sailor and then punches him on the nose. The sailor commences to beat on Worbuks and our big executive protector Fosdik enters the fray. Fosdik pulls the sailor off Worbuks and knocks him to the floor. The sailor strikes his head on the bar rail opening a gash in his skull that takes 24 stitches to close.

Has Fosdik committed an assault/battery tort against the sailor? Yes! Is he liable to the sailor for money damages in a civil suit? Yes! What happened to Fosdik's legal defense of self-defense? It did not exist! Inasmuch as Fosdik was not the one being attacked by the sailor he did not have his own personal right of self-defense. If Fosdik had a defense at all it was one acquired from Worbuks, his principal whom he was defending. But Worbuks, having instigated the altercation lost his right to claim self-defense in a civil suit in tort against him or in a possible criminal action. Since Fosdik, who used force against the sailor (third party) in defense of Worbuks (second party), can have no more defense rights than the second party—Fosdik had none. Is Worbuks also liable to the sailor? Yes (See below.)

IV. LIABILITY

The use of force by a personal protection specialist gives rise to a liability potential that can be criminal, civil, or both. Just because a personal protection specialist is doing his executive protection duty when he/she uses force on another, does not give the specialist any immunity from possible criminal prosecution or a civil lawsuit. This is true even if the personal protection specialist is a sworn peace officer. In fact, the sworn officer has a greater potential of liability than the private officer. Both can, of course, be charged criminally by local authorities for various degrees of assault/battery or homicide. Both also can be sued in civil court by the injured party for the tort committed. In addition to these normal potential sources of liability a sworn police officer is further subject to liability based on Constitutional restrictions imposed on governments and their agents.

These additional liabilities include a Federal criminal charge for violating an individual's civil rights,[13] a civil suit in Federal court for depriving an individual of their Constitutional rights[14] and, of course, sworn officers are subject to possible administrative action by their own department.

V. RELATIONSHIP WITH PRINCIPAL

A personal protection specialist's relationship with his protected executive-principal can lead to the principal being liable for torts committed by them. It is often referred to as "vicarious liability"—substitute one for another; or *"respondeat superior"*—let the master answer.[15] The legal relationship that exists between someone engaged in executive protection and the principal or executive he is protecting is one of "agency". By law, an "agency" is created when one party (the Principal), expressly or implicitly, authorizes a second party (the Agent) to act for him in transacting business with or in dealing with a third party.[16]

Agency Law grew out of the old master-servant relationship and today is often classified as employment or employer-employee law. The purpose of Agency Law, however, is to determine *who is liable* in a civil action when an Agent, acting on behalf of his/her Principal, makes a contract with or commits a tort against a third party.[17]

The agency relationship can be visualized in this diagram:

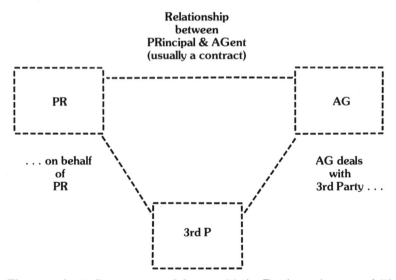

**Relationship
between
PRincipal & AGent
(usually a contract)**

PR

AG

. . . on behalf
of
PR

AG deals
with
3rd Party . . .

3rd P

There are basically two types of Agents: (1) the Employee-Agent, and (2) the Independent Contractor-Agent. Simply stated, the law differentiates between these two types of Agents by examining the factual relationship that exists between them and their Principals with emphasis on the degree of *control* exercised by the Principal.[18]

If the Principal *controls* the Agent as to the (1) objective of their work (*what* is to be done) and also as to the (2) means to achieve that objective (*how* it is to be done), the court will find that the Agent is an Employee-Agent. If the Principal, however, only *controls* the Agent as to the (1) objective of the work, while the means to achieve that objective is the province of the Agent, the court will find that the Agent is an Independent Contractor-Agent.[19]

Inasmuch as one of the purposes of Agency Law is to determine just who is liable when an Agent commits a tort against a third party, the distinction between an Employee-Agent and an Independent Contractor-Agent becomes extremely important.

If, in a civil tort suit, the court determines that the Agent is an Employee-Agent, then the Principal *is liable* in money damages for the injury to a third party. This Principal liability has one additional and logical requirement in that the Agent must have been acting within the scope of his/her employment when the tort occurred.

On the other hand, if the Agent is determined by the court to be an Independent Contractor-Agent, the general rule is that the Principal *is not liable* for torts committed by his/her Agent.[20]

Due to the potentially confrontational nature of the dealings with a third party by an Agent who is a security officer, the courts in recent years have been prone to relax or bypass this distinction when the tort committed by the Agent is *intentional*. In other words, courts today are finding Principals liable for *intentional torts* committed by their security officer Agents *even if* the legal relationship between them is that of Independent Contractor-Agent.[21] The apparent rationale is that the Principal, knowing of the potential confrontational duties of security officers, *should have* exercised proper control over them. These holdings have been in cases involving security officers (as Agents) working for retail stores (as Principals) when the third parties are invitees, i.e., customers, and the Agents are working on the store premises (shoplifting-type cases). Nevertheless, it is an emerging precedent that could possibly be extended to executive protection situations particularly if the third party turns out to be an innocent party.

Note that this erosion of the Principal/Independent Contractor-Agent relationship extends *only* to *intentional torts* and does not extend to the tort of negligence committed by the Independent Contractor-Agent.

Note also that in these cases the Agent, who committed the tort against the third party, continues to be liable to the third party even if his/her Principal is found to be liable. After all it was in fact the Agent who actually committed the tort and caused the injury or harm to the third party. A security officer cannot escape personal liability for a tort just because he was an Agent working for a Principal.

Consequently, the use of force by a security officer in executive protection not only makes the officer potentially liable in a civil tort suit but it can also make his Principal (executive) potentially liable. If the tort also constitutes a crime, only the security officer (Agent) is prosecutable since the executive (Principal) is not liable for crimes committed by an Agent unless they were done under a Principal's instruction. The rationale here is that a crime committed by an Agent is outside the scope of his/her employment.

VI. FIREARMS REGULATIONS

Firearms represent the ultimate force that can be utilized by a security officer in the performance of his/her mission, be it executive protection or otherwise. It is persuasive, effective and quite often terminal. Like the use of any force it may subject the acting party and possibly others to potential liability of a criminal and/or civil nature. But one who chooses to carry a weapon on his/her person is also subject to a myriad of conflicting and contradictory regulations promulgated by all levels of government. As one moves from one governmental jurisdiction to another these regulations can become hazardous to navigate and, for a security officer, extremely embarrassing if violated. These regulations are applicable to all who are within the jurisdiction where they are in force with some limited exceptions such as sworn police officers, military personnel, etc.

In the United States today there are in excess of 20,000 gun control laws, the great bulk of which are aimed at the carrying of a concealed weapon. These numerous regulations of firearms fall into one or more of four general categories, to wit:

I. Marketing—regulations imposed on manufacturers, importers and retailer (e.g., taxes, forms, records, etc.)

II. Registration—to enroll or record with various officials the possession or ownership of a weapon (basically a form of permissive licensing since almost anyone can register)

III. Restrictive Licensing—limit or restrict the licensing of weapons only to those who have a legitimate purpose for having the weapon (as defined by statute)

IV. Prohibition—a complete ban on weapon ownership (or certain type of weapons) by private citizens

History

The regulation and control of weapons is not a new phenomenon in today's society. As far back as 1328 in England the Statute of Northampton prohibited citizens from going in public places or around elected officials while armed. The earliest recorded weapon regulation in North America was passed by the Province of Massachusetts in 1692 and prohibited the carrying of weapons in public. During the 19th century, many states, counties and cities adopted regulations directed at the carrying of concealed weapons. The purpose behind these statutes was not the safety of the general public, but good old American fair play. In 1958 a New York court in upholding New York's 1881 concealed gun law stated:

> At the time . . . concealment . . . statutes were enacted the open carrying of weapons on a person was not prohibited. The purpose of concealed weapons statutes was to prevent men in sudden quarrel or in the commission of a crime from drawing concealed weapons and using them without prior notice to their victims that they were armed. The person assailed or attacked would behave one way if he knew his assailant was armed and perhaps another way if he could safely presume that he was unarmed.[22]

The next form of firearms regulation to appear in the United States was a New York State statute in 1911 commonly referred to as the "Sullivan Law" (Sec. 1897 of New York Penal Code). This regulation was aimed not at the concealed carrying of a weapon but at the *right of purchase*. It requires a private citizen in New York who desires to purchase a handgun to first obtain a license to purchase and possess the weapon. The problem with the law was that it could not regulate those who moved into New York State with a weapon purchased elsewhere nor could it prevent citizens of New York from purchasing a weapon in another state.

Federal Regulations

There are no Federal licensing-type laws on the purchase, possession, ownership or the carrying of firearms. There have been, however, numerous efforts in this century by members of the U.S. Congress to either ban or regulate firearms and most such efforts have failed. Set forth below is a summary of the various Federal firearms regulations that have been passed.

1919—Revenue Act of 1918: imposed a 10% manufacturer excise tax on firearms as a part of the revenue act or World War I. This act, revoked at the end of the war, did establish the precedent for Federal firearms regulations under the Constitutionally granted taxing power of the U.S. Congress and the placing of regulatory responsibility in the U.S. Treasury Department.

1927—A U.S. Postal Law prohibited the shipping of concealable firearms to private citizens via the U.S. mail. The regulation was aimed at the weapons mail order business that was undermining state and local regulations.

1934—National Firearms Act: This act was aimed at so-called "gangster weapons" and required:

1. registration of gangster-type weapons (defined as machine guns; sawed off shotguns (18"); sawed off rifles (16"); and weapons with silencers
2. imposed a transfer tax of $200 on all gangster-type weapons
3. required serial numbers on all firearms manufactured in the U.S.
4. required a Federal license for all manufacturers, importers and dealers who engaged in the interstate shipment of firearms

1938—Federal Firearms Act: This act, aimed at preventing the sale of firearms to known criminals, included the following provisions:

1. prohibited sale to convicted felons and fugitives (basically ineffective since it required a declaration by the buyer at the time of purchase that—"I am not . . .")
2. required licensed dealers to maintain records of firearms transactions for six (6) years
3. restricted the interstate shipment of firearms to Federal licensed dealers
4. made it illegal to transfer interstate any weapon on which the serial number was obliterated, removed or altered

1968—Gun Control Act of 1968[23]: This is the current Federal regulation of firearms in which the 1934 and 1938 acts (above) have been consolidated. It was passed basically as a reaction to the Kennedy/King assassinations and includes these *provisions:*

1. increased the Federal license fee for interstate dealers, manufacturers and importers
2. required all dealers to use a standard form for all weapon transactions
3. added cannons/bazookas to the list of "gangster-type weapons"
4. prohibited the import of surplus military firearms and so-called "Saturday Night Specials" (Note: it did not prohibit the importing of parts and assembly thereof in the U.S.)
5. prohibited the interstate retailing of all firearms providing for contiguous state agreements in certain situations (Note: this prohibition was amended in May 1986 by McClure-Volkmer Bill which relaxed the regulation on the interstate retailing and shipping of long barrel weapons such as rifle and shotguns)
6. prohibited the sale of firearms to minors; mental defectives; drug addicts; felons;

or fugitives (as in the 1938 act it only requires the purchaser to make a declaration that he is not ineligible). Enforcement of this current act is the responsibility of the Bureau of Alcohol, Tobacco and Firearms of the U. S. Treasury Department

State Regulations

The great majority of firearms regulations in the United States are found at the local level—state, county and city. These local regulations are primarily aimed at the handgun, particularly the carrying thereof. There is today, however, increasing public and law enforcement pressure on legislative bodies to regulate and even prohibit in the private sector assault and combat-type weapons. These weapons are available in a semi-automatic mode and are often easily converted to automatic fire. They have become the weapon of preference in the drug underworld, frequently placing law enforcement in the unenviable position of being outgunned in confrontations.

There are basically seven types of local firearm regulations:[24]

1. Waiting Period—a minority of states and the District of Columbia (D.C.) require a waiting period between the purchase of and the actual delivery of the weapon. The periods range from 48 hours to 15 days.

2. Purchase Requirements—approximately half of the states and D.C. have varied requirements which must be met in order to purchase a handgun. These include simply filing an application; a criminal history check; review by local police; taking a firearms training course; and obtaining a permit to purchase. The latter are usually based on a finding that the purchaser is authorized to possess or carry the weapon. Illinois and Massachusetts have this requirement and they issue a Firearms Identification Card which must be carried on the person.

3. Registration—over half the states and D.C. have a formal registration requirement for handguns which makes it a violation to possess a handgun without a valid registration certificate.

4. Dealer Requirements—a vast majority of the states and D.C. require dealers to have a state license (in addition to a Federal license) and maintain certain records of transactions.

5. Saturday Night Specials—at least four states (Hawaii, Illinois, Minnesota and South Carolina) prohibit the purchase and ownership of so-called "Saturday Night Special" handguns. The legal test for determining if a weapon is a Saturday Night Special is the temperature at which the weapon will melt. The norm is 800 degrees Fahrenheit although Minnesota's standard is 1000 degrees.

6. Mandatory Minimum Sentences—well over half the states have some form of mandatory minimum sentences for the use of a firearm in the commission of a crime. It normally involves an added sentence to that of the crime or the denial of probation or parole.

At least three states (New York, Maryland and Massachusetts) have a mandatory sentence requirement for carrying in public an unlicensed handgun. The Massachusetts law (Bentley-Fox Act of 1974) is by far the most severe in that it carries a one year minimum sentence and prohibits the judge from suspending sentence or granting probation.

7. License or Permit to Carry—a vast majority of the states and D.C. require a license or permit to carry a concealed weapon in public. The requirements to obtain the license vary from state to state. A minority of states also require a license to carry a handgun openly, cowboy style.

A recent licensing requirement in several states is of particular interest to security officers. This is a requirement that anyone who carries a weapon while providing a security service must complete a minimum number of hours of firearm's training and in some instances pass a physical and psychological evaluation. The Lethal Weapon Training Act of Pennsylvania is an example of this requirement. It requires 40 hours of firearms training plus the evaluations and applies not only to private security officers but also to sworn police officers who work as security officers when off-duty.

In addition to these basic types of state firearm regulations many counties and cities have additional regulations that are normally stricter. For example, a New York state permit to carry a concealed weapon issued in any county outside the five boroughs of New York City is not good in New York City.

If one does not qualify as a sworn police officer within a jurisdiction he/she must comply with the purchasing, registering and licensing requirements of his/her state and local jurisdiction. Furthermore, sworn police officers who leave their jurisdiction become private citizens in the new jurisdiction and must comply with regulations although it is customary (but not required) to extend them official courtesy when they are on law enforcement business.

Transporting Weapons

The general licensing laws relative to carrying a concealed weapon are applicable not only to carrying the weapon on one's person but also to carrying it in a vehicle where it is readily accessible. If one is traveling in a jurisdiction where one does not have a license to carry, the *best* (but not necessarily the legal) method to transport the weapon is unloaded, broken down if possible, cased and locked in the trunk of the vehicle. Note that most states provide an exception or special regulations for attendance at weapons shows and shooting matches.

Other areas of importance to security officers engaged in executive protection are national parks which may be visited by a vacationing executive. Firearms are prohibited in national parks but they may be transported within the park by notifying the ranger and carrying them unloaded, cased, broken down if possible and out of sight.[25]

Foreign Travel

Due to severe and restrictive firearms regulations in foreign countries, particularly in Europe, **do not even take your weapon** without prior permission and certification from each country you plan to visit regardless of your length of stay.

Canada prohibits absolutely the bringing of automatic weapons into the country, requires a permit in advance to bring a handgun into the country AND YOU *WILL NOT* GET IT, but Canada will permit the bringing of long guns (for hunting) into the country.[26]

Mexico permits the bringing of weapons into the country for hunting only and a prior permit is required.[27]

Considerations

In view of the numerous regulations and restrictions on the carrying and transporting of weapons, particularly handguns, a personal protection specialist who plans to travel outside of his own jurisdiction must plan in advance if he intends to take his weapon. His or her first consideration should be: "Do I really need to take my weapon with me?" If the answer is affirmative, then careful advance planning is required to obtain the necessary foreign licenses and appropriate plans must be made to safely secure the weapon whenever or wherever it is carried.

Due to the different regulations in different states, it is suggested that anyone traveling with their weapon should carry the following documents:

a) home jurisdiction permit

b) certification of firearms training

c) proof of ownership describing weapon and serial number

d) set of one's own fingerprints and photograph

VII. FIREARMS ABOARD AIRCRAFT

The transportation of firearms on commercial airlines departing or arriving at an airport in the United States, territories, etc., is covered by the Federal Aviation Act of 1958 as amended by the Air Transport Security Act of 1974.[28] This act makes it illegal for anyone to have on or about his person where it is accessible on any commercial aircraft a firearm, dangerous or deadly weapon, explosive or incendiary device. This restriction applies while aboard the aircraft or while attempting to board the aircraft.

The act also makes it illegal to place or attempt to place on board an aircraft a loaded firearm or explosive/incendiary device in baggage or property where it is not accessible to passengers in flight.

The act then provides two exemptions to these restrictions relative to firearms:

1. Law enforcement officers of state or municipality and officers and employees of the Federal Government who are authorized or required to carry arms in their official capacity.

2. Persons transporting *unloaded* firearms in baggage or property not accessible to passengers in flight provided such weapons are declared to the air carrier.

Based on the FAA regulation about declaring weapons there may be some doubts as to whether the passenger is criminally liable for violating the Federal Aviation and Air Transport Security Acts if he/she fails to disclose to the air carrier the presence of an unloaded weapon in checked baggage. Even if the passenger is not criminally liable under the aviation acts he or she is criminally liable for violating a section of the Federal Gun Control Act of 1968[30] which makes it unlawful to knowingly deliver or cause to be delivered to any common contract carrier for transportation or shipment in interstate commerce any package or container in which there is a firearm or ammunition without notice to the carrier. An air carrier is a common contract carrier. This latter act does exempt licensed dealers, manufacturers and collectors.

Other Commercial Transportation

Bus—Greyhound and Trailway regulations prohibit the carrying of a handgun on a bus, checking same in baggage or transporting as a package.

Rail—Amtrak regulations require that all firearms be broken down, encased and the firing pin removed.[31]

ENDNOTES

I. American Legal System

[1] *Law for Business*, 3d Ed., A. J. Barnes, T. M. Dworkin, E. L. Richards, Irwin, 1987. p. 11

[2] *Criminal Law*, S. T. Reid, MacMillan, 1989, p. 68, 45

[3] *Private Security and the Law*, C. P. Nemeth, Anderson, 1989, p. 111

[4] *Law for Business*, op. cit., p. 50

II. Torts
[5] Black's Law Dictionary, 4th Ed., 1951, p. 1660

[6] *Law for Business,* op. cit., p. 50, 64, 75; and *Private Security and the Law,* op. cit., p. 114

[7] *Legal Aspects of Private Security,* 3d pr., A. J. Bilek, J. C. Klotter, R. K. Federal, Anderson, 1984, p. 159

[8] *Private Security and the Law,* op. cit., p. 112

III. Use of Force
[9] Black's Law Dictionary, op. cit., p. 1525

[10] *Legal Aspects of Private Security,* op. cit., p. 145

[11] *Legal Aspects etc.,* op. cit., p. 147

[12] *Legal Aspects etc.,* op. cit., p. 147

IV. Liability
[13] Title 18 U. S. Code 241

[14] Title 42 U. S. Code Annotated 1983

V. Relationship with Principal
[15] Black's Law Dictionary, op. cit., p. 1475

[16] *Law for Business,* op. cit., p. 339

[17] *Law for Business,* op. cit., p. 338

[18] *Law for Business,* op. cit., p. 364-65

[19] *Law for Business,* op. cit., p. 364-56

[20] *Law for Business,* op. cit., p. 365

[21] *Noble v. Sears-Roebuck,* 33 Cal. App. 3d 654 (1973); *U.S. Shoe v. Jones,* 255 S. E. 2d 73 (1979); *Capo v. Vincent Guard Service,* 400 So. 2d 1148 (1981); *Safeway Stores v. Kelley,* 448 A. 2d 856 (1982)

VI. Firearms Regulations
[22] *People v. Raso,* 170 NYS 2d 245 (1958)

[23] Public Law 90-618, Title 18 U.S. Code 921-928

[24] *Gun Control: A Look at the Various State and Federal Laws,* Wisconsin Legislative Reference Bureau, Madison, 1979, p. 5-7

[25] *Transporting Personal Firearms, A Guide to Firearms Regulations,* J. P. Vince, Sparrow, Boulder City, 1984, p. 7 & 33; and *Interstate Transportation of Personally Owned Firearms,* Institute for Legislative Action, National Rifle Association, Washington, D. C., 1984

[26] *Transporting Personal Firearms etc.,* op. cit., p. 32-33

[27] *Transporting Personal Firearms etc.,* op. cit., p. 33-36

VII. Firearms Aboard Aircraft
[28] Title 49 U. S. Code 1472 (1)

[29] FAA Regulation 14 CFR 121.585 (c)

[30] Title 18 U.S. Code 922 (c)

[31] *Transporting Personal Firearms etc.,* op. cit., p. 8

BIBLIOGRAPHY

Articles

Firearms and Federal Law: The Gun Control Act of 1968, Franklin E. Zimring, The Journal of Legal Studies, Vol. IV(1), The University of Chicago Law School, Chicago, Ill. (Jan. 1975)

Books

Criminal Law, Sue Titus Reid, J.D., Ph.D., MacMillan Publishing Co., New York (1989)

Law for Business, 3d Edition, A. James Barnes, Terry Morehead Dworkin, Eric L. Richards, Irwin, Homewood, Ill. (1987)

Legal Aspects of Private Security, 3d Printing, Arthur J. Bilek, John C. Klotter, R. Keegan, Federal Criminal Justice Studies, Anderson Publishing Co., Cincinnati, Ohio (1984)

Private Security and the Law, Charles P. Nemeth, Anderson Publishing Co., Cincinnati, Ohio (1989)

Booklets

Firearms: State Laws and Published Ordinances, Department of the Treasury, Bureau of Alcohol, Tobacco and Firearms, U.S. Government Printing Office, Washington, D. C. *(1982)*

Transporting Personal Firearms, A Guide to Firearms Regulations, James P. Vince, Sparrow Publishing House, Boulder City, Nev. (1984)

Pamphlets

Compendium of State Laws Governing Handguns, Institute for Legislative Action (ILA), National Rifle Association (NRA), Washington, D.C. (1985)

Federal Firearms Laws, ILA, NRA (no date)

Firearms Statutes in the United States, The U.S. Conference of Mayors, Wisconsin Legislative Reference Bureau (WLRB), Madison, Wis. (1979)

Gun Control: A Look at the Various State and Federal Laws, WLRB (1981)

Interstate Transportation of Personally-Owned Firearms, ILA, NRA (1984)

Summary of Federal Restrictions on Purchase, Sale, Possession and Transportation of Firearms, ILA, NRA (no date)

Treatises and References

Black's Law Dictionary, 4th Edition (1951)
Prosser, Law of Torts (1971)
Restatement 2d of Agency (1958)
Restatement of Torts (1965)

SEVENTEEN

An Executive's Guide to Security Construction Projects

by John J. Strauchs

MORE THAN ANY OTHER TIME in the past, many of America's senior corporate officers are including "security" as an important and integral part of many construction projects. Corporate headquarters—especially executive wings and board rooms—private residences of key executives, and corporate aviation departments, are being given special attention in this regard. This trend is not only continuing, but it appears to be accelerating as America enters into the decade of the 90's. Some of the largest corporations, such as IBM, have gone so far as to include security in internal building codes. One would expect corporate security directors to be included in the process, but CEO's and presidents are occasionally getting themselves involved—without much coaxing. It has become too important to leave these matters exclusively to the security department. For multinational corporations with overseas facilities, "designed" security systems are regarded by many as being mandatory.

These renovation and new construction projects can involve security costs in the tens of thousands, hundreds of thousands for large facilities, and even millions of dollars for "special" security requirements. Such projects are often large enough to warrant retaining architects and engineers, including security engineers. For all but small projects, the past practice of merely buying security equipment and having it installed by a local alarm company is no longer adequate. But, as the projects become more and more technical, and, involve architectural and engineering practices, the key executives are often placed in the difficult position of being asked to make major management or cost decisions in fields alien to them. Even corporate security directors—the personal counselors to CEO's on security matters—are often over their heads. Technology has exploded in the last ten years. For those few who have managed to keep up, most have had fairly limited opportunities to work directly with architectural and engineering firms. The projects simply weren't done that way in the past.

The following, therefore, is intended to be a short "primer" on typical security engineering practices for security construction projects. It lays out what steps are likely to occur, in what sequence, and what to expect from the security engineer at each step in the process. It also identifies, by inference, what questions executives should ask and what decisions they may be asked to make. This chapter will be most informative for personal protection specialists and serve to prepare anyone who may be assigned to manage corporate or personal residence security projects.

Executives should keep in mind that the design and installation of security systems for an executive wing at headquarters, for instance, is important for at least one other reason. The executives will have to live and work in the resulting environment. If they are involved it is more likely that it will be an environment that they feel comfortable in. This chapter is intended to provide a brief overview of the process and to remove some of the "mystery" from "security engineering." By understanding the basic stages of the process, executives can enhance the probability that "what they want is what they get."

PROJECT MANAGEMENT

There are two levels of project management. Clearly, the Corporation is the first tier. Ideally, one representative of the corporation should be designated to manage the project. Often, two persons are needed, depending on how much confidence the company has in its security director. The two persons often are a senior member of the corporate security staff, as well as a mid-level to senior member of the corporate management staff. If the project is large enough, many companies will retain an outside project manager—sometimes termed "construction manager." There are many companies which specialize in providing this type of service.

The other tier is the outside design and construction project staff. Typically, the architectural firm usually leads the management of this tier. All other design team members (generally the engineering companies supporting the project) would report exclusively through the project architect. The other team members may include the following, depending on the size and complexity of the project:
- electrical engineers
- mechanical engineers
- civil and/or structural engineer
- soil engineers
- elevator consultants
- parking consultants
- lighting consultants or engineers
- fire protection and life-safety engineers
- security engineers
- landscape architects
- food service consultants
- and for some projects, very specialized services such as acoustical engineers, historic renovation specialists, communications engineers, and so forth.

Phase One: Basis of Design Report

This is also often called the "concept development phase," as well as, in trade jargon, "security programming" and "preliminary engineering report," or "PER." Regardless of whether the process involves the renovation of an existing facility or the construction of a new facility, the major steps are basically the same. The purpose of the "basis of design report" is to document in concise terms an understanding of the major design assumptions and decisions which have been made, or need to be made. Key executives, security directors, the project architect, all engineering and consulting disciplines, and of course, the security engineer should be involved. The report should present clear statements of previous decisions and future project development issues in such a manner as to permit the key decisions to be clearly identified and resolved. In many ways, this is regarded as the most important phase of the entire project since it establishes most of the design parameters that all further phases will follow.

This is also the phase where non-technical, but sometimes much more important, operational design criteria are introduced. Such consideration could include the recognition of special executive requirements or an understanding of specific approaches which are not acceptable to key officers. The decision, as one example, whether company employees, including senior management, will be required to wear photographic identification badges would be made in this phase. This in turn, may determine which electronic access control system and program is feasible. A decision not to wear badges would exclude certain systems from consideration. Many decisions such as this would need to be made during this phase.

In short, many "corporate culture" issues need to be closely, but delicately, examined during this phase to ensure that there is a consensus of understanding before the tedious and expensive design process actually begins. It is important, therefore, that senior executives are entirely candid and clear when commissioning this work. They should explain in detail what the key goals of the security systems are, and more importantly, what is unacceptable. Further, they should insist that their security engineer be entirely comprehensive and clear in presenting all of their options and alternatives, including explanations of the implications of various decisions they may make. There is no place on the project team for "yes" men.

The executive should ensure that the following tasks are conducted by the security engineer during this phase. The security engineer should:

(1) Interview designated key officers, as well as mid-level managers and personnel to identify goals, objectives, and constraints for the development of security systems and programs for the project.

(2) Review existing plans and documentation of the planned project, if any. If this is a new facility, the security engineer should review the architect's preliminary designs or renderings and the "building program," a document which details space utilization goals and requirements, as well as other key facility operational requirements. The security engineer should also examine the specific site on which the project occurs and should review previous security and criminal incidents for both the company and the community the facility will be situated in.

(3) Review existing security design standards and guidelines, particularly if the corporation has an internal building code or other guidelines.

(4) Conduct an oral presentation of major findings and recommendations to key project staff before the final written report is prepared. As a minimum, the report should include the following topics:

(a) Generic identification of types and classes of security systems and equipment proposed should be provided.

(b) There should be a general description of control and annunciation criteria and design guidelines for the central security console and control center. Included should be a description of integration and future expansion requirements. [This would not apply if off-site contract monitoring of security alarm systems is being considered, but contract monitoring would not be typical for most company headquarters.]

(c) A preliminary employee and visitor access control design scheme intended to streamline traffic flow patterns should be developed. Vehicle access control requirements and visitor processing requirements should also be considered.

(d) There should be an assessment of anticipated future expansion, renovation and/or retrofit requirements, if any, for all security systems.

(e) Design schemes related to guard force reduction and/or efficiency enhancements need to be considered.

(f) Any exotic or unique security requirements should be identified. For example, companies which have had a history of "animal-rights" activist demonstrations would need to address this concern in the design. Companies with a history of bomb threats may, as another example, need to consider the use of shatter-resistant film applied to glazing or the use of safety glass.

(g) In the case of a private executive residence, the executive will need to be candid in very personal terms. Important personal considerations would include whether there are young children, whether a secret vault or safe will be constructed, whether the family would really use "panic" alarm devices, if the family has pets, whether servants can be trusted, and so forth.

(h) A gross estimate should be made of possible security systems construction cost, presenting minimum and maximum ranges.

(i) The products of this phase should include a written report, and often, a "marked-up" set of plans indicating general locations of equipment and illustrating major design concepts.

The company should prepare written review comments about the Basis of Design Report. In fact, it is very important that each phase of the project be thoroughly documented in writing.

Phase Two: Schematic Design (SD) Services

Upon receipt of written phase one comments and acceptance of the report, the security engineer will initiate "schematic design services." At the end of this phase, the design should be approximately 35 percent complete. The purpose of this phase is to develop detailed equipment layout drawings, outlines of written specifications, budget (rough) cost estimates and a collection of representative manufacturers' equipment catalog sheets.

It is important to understand that the security engineer will not be able to start design work until the architect has completed schematic design of the facility—whether it is reconstruction or new construction. As the design concept begins to take shape, it will be easier to visualize how the proposed security systems are intended to function. The new insights made possible by this phase will often reveal either shortcomings in the design or certain design features which are undesirable. This phase is the last opportunity to make major conceptual changes without incurring costs for additional engineering services. After this, the security engineer will be reluctant to make radical changes without charging additional fees, since much of their work would need to be completely redone.

The systems the security engineer is likely to consider include many, but probably not all, of the following:

a. One central (main) annunciation, monitoring and control console, located within the Project site. In addition to monitoring, annunciation and control of the systems listed below under "b" through "l", if required, console features included in the proposed design may be the following:

(1) Remote, automated electro-mechanical door and gate control; control of door and gate operators, if required.

(2) Selected emergency sensor annunciation and controls, such as generator, fan, water flow, and similar items.

(3) Console (panels, turrets, etc.).

(4) Integration of the equipment of others, such as telephone, task lighting, etc..

b. Intrusion detection system (IDS) consisting of interior volumetric (space) detection sensors, glass-break sensors and balanced and/or reed-switch magnetic contact switches, as appropriate.

c. Electronic access control system, to include readers, keypads, controllers, printers and similar related equipment.

d. Closed-circuit television (CCTV) system, to include cameras, housing, mounts, lenses, switches, amplifiers, multiplexers, monitors, controls, and similar related equipment.

e. Security intercommunications system.

f. Electronic guard tour system.

g. Executive personnel emergency or courtesy alarm system.

h. Contraband screening and detection system.

i. Parking/vehicular security control system (roll-down door, motors and controls to be designed by others).

j. Duress/courtesy alarm/communications system; cashier holdup alarms.

k. Conduit and conductors.

l. Security emergency power supplies (connections to building emergency generator/power circuit would be designed by the electrical engineer).

The security engineer will generally not be responsible for equipment and systems not listed above, to include, but not limited to, lighting (other than to define requirements for CCTV), conventional mechanical locking, glazing, public telephone, heating/ventilation/air conditioning (HVAC), generators, facility uninterruptible power supplies (UPS), architectural design of rooms and enclosures housing security systems consoles and equipment, and similar systems and equipment not generally regarded as direct aspects of security requirements. Moreover, their work will usually be limited to low voltage design; high voltage (120 VAC or higher) design would be the work of the electrical engineer.

Again, as in the first phase, the executive should ensure that the company project staff issues a written review report in response to the "SD" submittals. All requests for changes should be clearly and completely detailed.

Phase Three: Design Development (DD) Services

The design development phase is intended to be the first refinement of the schematic design products and an incorporation of the company's review comments. This phase is generally regarded as representing about a 50 to 65 percent completion of the design process. The submittals for this phase should consist of detailed drawings and written specifications, detailed cost estimates, and representative manufacturers' equipment catalog sheets not previously provided. The drawings should now include very detailed layout floor plans, riser diagrams (showing vertical and horizontal wire and conduit distributions), single-line block and/or interconnection diagrams, door schedules, and installation details.

Phase Four: Construction Documents (CD) Services

This phase is also often called the "contract documents phase." Following the approval by the company of the "DD" Submittal and submission of written comments for changes, additions and/or deletions, the security engineer will begin to prepare the construction documents, representing approximately 95 percent completion of design. This phase is nothing more than an almost complete refinement of the DD submittal.

At the conclusion of this Phase, the "CD" submittal should consist of several sets of blue-line or black-line prints of project drawings, one unbound and several bound sets of written specifications, and virtually "final" detailed cost estimates of the final installed costs of all security systems. At this point changes to the design documents should not involve substantive changes of designs and concepts approved under the 65% submittal; and should not represent more than 10 percent changes.

Phase Five: Final Submittal

Upon approval of the "CD" submittal and receipt of final written comments from the company for final corrections, additions and/or deletions, the security engineer will prepare a "final" submittal representing 100 percent completion of design documents. The security engineer should deliver (through the architect) all original drawings, specifications and cost estimates. The security engineer should update the previously submitted set of representative manufacturers' equipment literature, if required by changes.

Phase Six: Bidding Phase

The security engineer should be requested to assist in the preparation of amendments to the construction documents during the bidding phase, to interpret documents, and to correct errors and omissions previously missed. Large, complex projects will almost always have errors and omissions which come up after the completion of design. The security engineer should also be required to participate in the pre-bid conference if one is held. The security engineer should assist in evaluating bids, responding to inquiries from bidders, and attending pre-bid and/or selection interviews.

Phase six is a very important phase which is, too often, neglected by most companies. Regardless of how well the architect and security engineer have done their jobs, turning the construction over to an indifferent or incompetent general contractor will usually guarantee failure of the security systems. Bear in mind that "retrofit" corrections of security systems generally cost three to four times original costs. As the adage goes, "there is never enough time to do it right, but there is always ample time to do it over." Neglecting this phase can be a costly proposition.

Phase Seven: Negotiation Phase

The security engineer should be asked to assist in negotiating a contract with the contractor, or contractors, responsible for security systems procurement, fabrication and installation.

Phase Eight: Construction Period Services

Prior to the start of construction and the ordering of equipment and hardware, the security engineer should be requested to review the contractors initial equipment lists to ensure that it meets the requirements of the specifications. Following that, the security engineer should begin "shop drawing" review services. That is to say, the contractor should prepare his, or her, construction drawings based on the company's contract drawings and written specifications. The security engineer should be required to stamp and sign all shop drawing submittals reviewed. It is important for the sake of avoiding serious errors that the contractor be required to present all submittals for review at one time during each stage of the construction project. If the security engineer is only permitted to review "pieces" of submittals from time to time, there is a great risk that mistakes can be overlooked since they never see the whole construction plan at one time.

The security engineer should be required to respond in writing to all written technical inquiries from the contractor. All telephone communications should also be documented and kept in the project records. All project constructions meetings should be followed up with detailed minutes of the meetings which are circulated to everyone involved in the project.

The security engineer should be requested to visit the site at specific intervals to become generally familiar with the progress and quality of the work of the project and to determine, in general, if the work is proceeding in accordance with the contract documents. One or two unannounced visits are usually a good idea, assuming this does not create "union" problems.

The security engineer should be required to render written recommendations on all claims, disputes and other matters in question between the company and the contractor relating to the execution or progress of the security project or the interpretation of the contract documents. The security engineer should also assist in determining whether to reject work which does not conform to the contract documents or whether special inspection or testing is required. If needed, the security engineer should assist in preparing change orders for this part of the project for the architect's approval. The security engineer, based on observations at the site and on evaluations of the contractor's applications for periodic payment, should also assist in determining the amounts owed to the contractor throughout the project.

Finally, the security engineer should be responsible for the coordination—and, sometime, the conduct—of the post-construction security systems implementation requirements, such as training of company personnel who will operate the system, the preparation of operational manuals, the collection of manufacturers' and/or contractor's warranties, and a maintenance agreement and plan. This should all be thoroughly planned prior to the end of the construction period.

It is important, at this point, if at all possible, that the security engineer conduct a briefing directly for senior executives to explain the operation of any systems they may be involved with. Sometimes, it is equally important to ensure that the executive secretaries and receptionists are also thoroughly trained in the operation of the systems.

Phase Nine: Acceptance Test Monitoring

The security engineer should assist in conducting reviews of the construction to confirm the planned dates of "substantial completion" and final completion. The security engineer should also review the contractor's list of items to be be completed or corrected [termed the "punch list"] and should forward the list to the architect for final disposition. The security engineer should assist in receiving and forwarding to the architect for review, written warranties, and related documents required by the contract documents and assembled by the contractor. The security engineer should "observe" final acceptance testing. As an important aside, insurance requirements generally prevent the security engineer from identifying services during this phase as involving "inspection" or "supervision." The accepted terms usually are "monitor" or "observe."

Phase Ten: Post-Construction Services

The last phase of the project is usually an optional part. If the security systems are complex or if there were problems during the construction phase, it may be necessary to bring back the security engineer to "debug" the system. A high rate of nuisance alarms may be a reason. Another common reason is the discovery of "glitches" in security system software or the need to write new software program components or to modify existing parts. Generally, this work would be negotiated directly with the security engineer; the architect would probably not be involved.

Costs

Many cost estimating firms utilize a square-foot factor to calculate probable costs of project components, including security systems. They apply an "experience" value on a per square foot basis. Generally speaking, square-foot factors do not work when it

	SUMMARY OF THE SECURITY ENGINEERING PROCESS		
PHASE	**DESIGNATION**	**ACTIVITIES**	**COMMENTS**
1	Basis of Design	Security survey, requirements analysis, and development of design concepts	All initial planning and decision-making
2	Schematic Design	Development of outline of specifications, initial equipment layouts, gross cost estimates ("budget" estimates)	Represents approximately 35% of completion of design
3	Design Development	Start of detailed specifications, detailed drawings (riser diagrams, schematics, interconnection diagrams, and installation details), and detailed cost estimates	Represents approximately 50% to 60% of completion of design
4	Contract Documents	Virtual completion of detailed specifications, drawings and cost estimates; assemblage of documents into a bid package	Represents approximately 95% of completion of design
5	Final/Complete Design	Completion of all construction/contract documents	100% complete contract/construction documents
6	Bidding Phase	Release of the bid package to all interested contractors and vendors; responses to questions from contractors about the bid package, intent of the design, and technical questions	This phase is not required for proprietary design and construction projects (if competitive bids are not required)
7	Negotiation Phase	Selection of contractor to be awarded the construction project and negotiation of a final contract	Legal department involvement is usually required
8	Construction Period Services	Review of contractors submittals (such as shop drawings and equipment lists), review of requests for change orders, substitutions, responses to questions about the specifications, and periodic monitoring of construction	
9	Acceptance Test Monitoring	Monitoring of final acceptance tests; approval and acceptance of the security system or requirements for corrections to be made by contractor before the system is re-tested	Subsequent acceptance tests are usually regarded as "additional services" and would involve cost increases
10	Post Construction Services	Assistance in adjusting the system, correcting minor deficiencies, training of operating personnel, preparation of operations and maintenance manuals	This phase is not always required

comes to security systems. For example, very inexpensive items, such as magnetic door contact switches, involve a great deal of labor if there are hundreds to be installed. Other system components, such as computers, can be extremely expensive but involve very little labor cost to install, excluding software development.

Engineering/Consulting Costs

The following "rule-of-thumb" has the potential of being inaccurate, but engineering costs will often be approximately 12 to 18 percent of total construction costs of the planned security systems. The larger the project, the smaller the percentage used; conversely, the smaller the project, the more likely it is that the high range would apply. Further, very highly specialized designs, such as for custom-installation of security devices in executive areas where there is a great deal of expensive woods, marble, glass and brass used, could increase engineering fees to 20 or 25 percent. Installations involving government classified storage facilities, computer-networking, and similar "hi-tech" applications can also drive up design costs.

System Costs

Although square-foot factors do not usually work in estimating probable "installed" security system costs, percentages based on total facility construction costs can sometimes be useful in placing probable costs within high and low ranges. A typical corporate headquarters involving the construction of a new building, for example, could involve "installed" security systems costs ranging from 0.1 to 0.25 per cent of total construction costs. If there are very special or unique security requirements, or if the entire facility is intended to have extensive CCTV surveillance, electronic access control, and similar facility-wide systems, possible cost ranges may be 0.5 to 1.5 per cent. Executive wings and private residences are usually one-of-a-kind designs and percentage factors simple are not accurate.

EIGHTEEN

Terrorism: The Female Dimension

by Deborah M. Galvin

MAN MEETS WOMAN. Man asks woman out to dinner. Man invites woman to his room. Man found dead. It is an old cliche, one of the oldest, yet so often successful. So many men known to be cautious, men who have taken specialized security training, men who are faithful to their wives, men who are religious, are capable of falling into it. Sometimes it is a woman they have just met, the meeting appearing like an accident, only carefully calculated, planned and executed. Other times, the woman is someone the man has known for quite sometime, a mole within the organization, a planted set-up, or a well-placed victim of an outside manipulator used because of her position relative to the target. In all of these cases, the target becomes easier prey, their whereabouts known to those who wish to do him harm, and his weaknesses more carefully analyzed and exposed. It is also possible to fall prey to a disturbed female employee who feels some injustice has been done to her within the work place, real or imaginary. These scenarios are talked about, joked about, and passed off in the minds of many as improbable. "Not something which will happen to me." It makes an interesting cocktail conversation at a party, however its always something that happens to the "other guy." The adage "expect the unexpected" used at North Mountain Pines Training Center in its security and protection courses does include the female terrorist, the female assassin, the female hostage-taker, and the female kidnaper. It includes females who act as decoys, diversions, and directors of these dastardly deadly deeds.

The media has played up these terrorist women as psychopathic, overly aggressive, unreasonable, and more violent than their male counterparts. Yet, in reality, there have been females who fit into this picture along with females who all but portray the opposite. When looking for the female terrorist profile, the authorities may have a difficult time presenting a valid one. Except within a specific case, a valid, reliable profile still does not exist.

The female terrorist may be from any age group, from young adolescent child to grandmother well into her eighties. She has come from all nationalities, from those countries in which women are not allowed to uncover their faces in public and are educated separately from the men to the liberated societies in which women are as free as men to pursue their dreams and goals. They come from societies and cultural backgrounds where there is little, if any, mass media in individual houses to societies in which every house has at least one television set. Some are extremely beautiful, able to compete in and win beauty contests while others are more demure and unattractive.

Indeed, there appears to be no correlation between the level of education, appearance, race, socio-economic status, class, political affiliation, age on entry, marital status, number of children, or religiosity. Some are extremely intelligent, others are dull, some are born leaders with charismatic qualities while others are content to serve in a "do as you are told" capacity. Quite frequently involvement in terrorism is a reaction to a feeling of "powerlessness" and of being in a situation in which the "terrorist" solution appears to be the only choice left. Yet, like the little drummer girl, a number of females (as well as males) become involved quite accidentally, by being at the wrong place at the wrong time, by making one bad decision, by taking one miscalculated step. There are more Ann Murphy's than the public would care to believe.

It is an interesting process of how a "good" girl becomes involved in terrorism, and in someone else's battle for a goal that is not one's own. The case of Patricia Hearst is extremely instructive in this regard. Was she actually kidnaped? Did she play a role in her own abduction as some have theorized? Was she brainwashed when she joined the SLA? What battle was she fighting, independence from her parents or a reaction to being in a bad relationship which didn't work? Or was she convinced that the SLA's ideology was correct, and that the poor would be helped through the free food program? Was she victim or victimizer? Although the Patricia Hearst case appears to be unique, there are a number of other cases which involve women who may have been coerced into acting in a terrorist role. Some who appear aggressive, independent and effective in the role of terrorist, women who espouse their propaganda, actually have been manipulated by another to act in this traditionally non-feminist role. Of these, many are even willing to die for the cause.

Many terrorist women are acting in their own right and have purposely chosen to become involved in the politics and power plays involved in the use of terrorism. These women who independently choose their destiny as "terrorist" may not be more dangerous than those who are manipulated into the role. Indeed, the orchestration and outcome of the action may have little relationship to the process in which a woman becomes involved in terrorism. Success of the terrorist in accomplishing the goal may have more to do with the preparedness of the target. It may be that if a hostage is taken, or the need for negotiation is present, the psychological reasoning for the initial involvement would be useful to the successful outcome of negotiation.

PROTECTION AGAINST THE FEMALE TERRORIST

> "Full security comes from leaving nothing undone."
> *Richard W. Kobetz* and *H.H.A. Cooper*

It is difficult to imagine the ability to protect oneself against the many unknown and known dangers which can challenge the executive's private, personal, familial and property interests. Terrorism attacks the individual's sense of security, preys upon his/her mind in an attempt to wear down the individual and gain advantage in the play for power. Terrorism knows no bounds. The coercive fear created by terrorism provides terrorists with the modality to continue to win in an arena in which the odds are against them. The female terrorist provides the terrorist organization with a continual advantage of the element of surprise. No matter how many lectures security personnel attend, nor how well trained they are and cautious in taking any form of risk, the danger of the female terrorist to the non-professional and professional alike remains a challenge—even to those who have done their homework. One small error can lead to the fatal conclusion so frequently warned against. In the book *Vengeance,* for example, "cautious" Carl, a man who had had many years experience with the Mossad, was caught in the "honey trap". He was found murdered in his hotel room after having dinner with a blond woman. Was she an old friend? Did she kill him or have him set-up? These were the questions his companions asked after it was too late. For the executive, his family and his co-workers, this type of set-up seems too remote, especially for the executive who is skeptical of being victimized in the first place.

How does one protect himself against the female terrorist? This is a society in which females are equal to men, they share the business place, they meet men outside of traditional arrangements, they are free to travel, check into hotels and motels by themselves, telephone and converse with anyone they might wish to, drive cars, pilot aircraft, and even act in the role of personal protection specialist. Despite these freedoms, men and women have both continued to view the female as the "weaker" sex, more passive, less likely statistically and perceptually to become involved in violent crime, especially in terrorist activities. In the 1960's, it was projected that with women's rights, the women would become as involved in crime as much as men. Those who predicted the future saw women as men's equals in every sense. Although women have joined the work force in greater numbers, becoming one-parent child supporters and two member mortgage holders, they still have not matched the numbers of men involved in crime.

Given these factors, it is easy to see how and why many men and women executives and security personnel can and do fall prey to the female terrorist. The pregnant woman carrying a bomb instead of a baby, the girl carrying a bouquet of roses, the older woman dressed like an executive carrying a briefcase, the granny hardly able to walk with her cane and shopping bag, the young innocent woman desiring to go home with the man she just met in a bar for a drink, are all figures of trust, quite non-threatening, rarely a profile of fear. If we are not to trust those images we have established as trustworthy, we are left with the basic fear of waking up in the morning. Fear inappropriately placed can and does lead to precautions which are in and of themselves binding to the degree that the executive is left in a prisoned existence, unable to carry out the goals of his/her business. Overprotection can then be as deadening as underprotection. Life without freedom is hardly a life at all. Thus, it is important to be able to distinguish between real and imaginary dangers, and this distinction is becoming harder and harder to make.

Perhaps the best protection against the female terrorist is the attitude that anything is possible in terrorism. Hard intelligence concerning specific terrorists in any given situation before it occurs is difficult to come by. However, if security precautions designed to prevent attacks are followed equally for women as they are for men, this in and of itself would reduce the possibilities of infiltration or successful attack by females. Understanding the terrorist, the interactions between hostage and terrorist given a difference in sex, and the variations in reactions by security and police personnel to these differences all can aid in the protection of the executive.

DANGEROUS SITUATIONS AND THE FEMALE TERRORIST

One of the basic elements comprising a successful terrorist attack is the location: day, night, summer, winter, raining, clear, public, private, congested, secluded, home turf or foreign land. Much has been written in this area of "crime prevention through environmental design." Yet, terrorism is no ordinary crime and when the perpetrator is a female it alters the basic underlying findings of the research in this area. Crime prevention through environmental design or what Oscar Newman has labeled "defensible space" theories assume that there is less crime in public situations, where there are a number of "public eyes" on the street. In terrorism and for the female terrorist, the public setting can be more appealing than a private one. The public place with the large number of strangers mingling and passing through can be an excellent place to make an initial contact with the target. The public place generates a sense of security with so many eyes looking on, as defensible space theories suggest, crime is less likely in these places. The executive, his family, co-workers and other possible related targets assume that "probably nothing will happen." The female terrorist is likely to meet her prey in a relatively safe location, one in which the target feels falsely comfortable, one in which the target is less likely to suspect that they are being set up. Finally, in public, terrorism can truly achieve its goal, for here with so many people looking on, fear is amplified and the impact is enormous.

If the target has a repetitive schedule, planning for the attack becomes easier. For example, if the target has a regularly scheduled barber or hairdresser appointment, the female terrorist can plan a number of possible attacks: a job at the place of business to be easily in place at the set time, a position at a nearby shop adjacent to the location, a role as customer with an appointment at the same time, to name a few. Whatever the activity involved, it coincides with the target's known whereabouts at that specific time.

The office place is one location that the employee and executive tend to trust as "safe". One does not expect terrorist activity such as the burst of gunfire after the ex-IBM employee burst through the glass windows of the IBM facility in Bethesda, Maryland. The female terrorist can easily obtain a trusted position as secretary, assistant, security guard or office cleaner. In these positions, the female is in a strategic position to unobtrusively enter into the work environment during normal working hours to gain access to personal or property targets. Their presence, and frequently their friend's presence (boyfriend, husband, girlfriend, etc.) is rarely questioned. In certain positions, they would even be able to have large equipment moved into the building, plant bugs or bombs, or sabotage ongoing work. When a bomb went off in the Staten Island women's restroom which was conveniently located next door to the FBI offices, it seems logical that a female perpetrator planted the device.

Truby, in his article on "Female Terrorists," for the IACP, recounted the story of a female terrorist who purposely transmitted a sexual disease to a top executive in a corporation. The female aware that she was infected, transmitted it over a period of three days to be sure that she had accomplished her goal. The executive was embarrassed both at his home and at the office. The terrorist organization was able to make good use of their acquired propaganda tool in making further demands and breaching security. With the introduction of the AIDS virus, the possibilities seem endless as to the danger this disease might cause. Photographs and home videos are always good for blackmail. Locations such as hotel rooms, private homes or apartments, office buildings, or the client's own residence have been used in many of these sexual encounters turned terrorist events in the past. If a terrorist cannot easily assassinate her target, she may be able to politically assassinate them through the use of sex as a moral and ethical question. Likewise, the purposely passing of a virus such as AIDS would also accomplish the same end, and in a more damaging manner. Women in positions of trust are also able to poison their targets more easily by placing chemicals in their food or drink. The possibilities are innumerable. By placing sedatives, depressants, or stimulants in the executive's intake, the female terrorist would be able to control his psychological being, or ruin an important business conference, not to mention the victim's reputation.

A well-known example of the use of sex to lure the target was accomplished by the League of Women, an IRA off-shoot, known as the Cumann na Bann. Three young Irish females invited three British soldiers to an apartment in Belfast, the latter assuming they would receive more than tea. They were right, instead of tea, they were gunned down with submachine guns. This was not an isolated case. The technique has been used more than many would like to admit. Men like to think that they are in a powerful position in terms of the male/female relationship. Although this may be true in a great number of cases, they may be at their weakest point in the boudoir of the wrong woman. Just as women have been known to be more easily manipulated after they have entered into a sexual liaison, men also can become easier prey. Thus, one of the prime locations to beware of is the bedroom. The bedroom can lead to blackmail, espionage, hostage-taking, kidnaping and death.

Banks, nightclubs, discotheques, and hotel lobbies all have been and will continue to be places in which the female terrorist can meet and dazzle her prey. The female does not always work alone here. A young couple, male and female, often appears safer to outsiders. Charles Sobhraj, for example, frequently used female companions to keep his targets off guard, or to drug their drinks. He had his female accomplices assist him in robbing and, at times, murdering his victims. These are also locations where alcohol is served, leaving the potential target in less control of the situation because he/she has been drinking. People who would not be likely to associate and converse in any other situation are given the social right to introduce themselves, carry on personal conversations and reveal parts of themselves which they would be more likely to be on guard about in most other situations.

Under these conditions, the female terrorist is at an advantage. Being of the opposite sex, and thus inferred to be non-threatening and an object to pursue, she is in a position to gather intelligence, ingratiate herself to be given a future contact point or an immediate invitation to some other more private location. She might gain access to the intended target by various means such as a job offer, luncheon engagement, or consulting arrangement. The female's appearance obviously plays a role in some of these encounters, however, all types of women have been successful in this role. Breaking social barriers that were previously impenetrable or so they seemed, opens a Pandora's box as the target becomes instantly vulnerable to a number of possible threats, aggressions and attacks.

Executives frequently employ security personnel to act as personal protection specialists. It is the personal protection specialist's job to be with the executive to fend off any potential threat. Principals, like most people, like to keep their private affairs away from everyone's eyes including their security staff. By seeking privacy, the executive is inviting trouble. If the rendezvous involves a female outside the executive's marriage, the executive could be setting himself up for a possible attempt. The woman, herself may not be the perpetrator, but the mere fact he elects to meet with her without personal security is a dangerous opening for an attack. The location is almost irrelevant, it could be anywhere. It's just not safe to exclude a personal specialist, regardless of the social activity in question.

MALE AS VICTIM OF FEMALE

So much has been written about the female being victimized by the male. Little has been said about the male being victimized by the female. The literature has traditionally labeled the female as a "victim". Von Hentig, Mendelshon, and other victimologists have placed the "female victim" in their typologies. Psychologists, sociologists and feminists have all noted that women have been socialized as the "weaker sex" to be dependent upon men, afraid of success, physically less capable, not taught the rules of the game, and "wounded" by their socialization. Although there are many studies indicating that the female tends to be victimized by her male counterpart in the business place, at home, and in terrorism, less attention has been paid to the male's attachment to female relationships and possible victimizations arising from such attachments.

The male can be vulnerable to the female if he assumes that she is of the weaker sex; more volatile, less powerful and easily manipulated. He assumes, even in the bedroom, that he is in charge. Many feel it is only the older man being taken in by the young, innocent woman; however, women of all ages are capable of victimizing men in the same way.

It is falsely assumed that men are expected to do terrible things, not women. There is still a shock factor involved when a female is involved in an act of terrorism. The female terrorist is seen as an incongruity, and this assumption is universally accepted.

Beyond the initial act of surprise, the male's ego is easily exploited by his need to believe that he is independent and in control of his destiny especially when it comes to his relationship with a woman. "Johnny" knows that "Debbi" grew up with dolls, that "Debbi" thinks "worms are yucky," and that "Debbi" is easily manipulated given the right circumstances. There are still many in the business place who believe that although you must accept a few women into the board room, they can be easily controlled through the use of power. Likewise, females are easily controlled through sex in many cases. Once in a sexual relationship with a woman, the male assumes that they have gained control. Frequently this is the case. This is associated with the underlying sexual theme of subjugation: "the girl being forcefully taken," "the male in the conquering position," the "woman submitting to the man and changing her point of view to fit his." All run counter to the female acting in role of terrorist, victimizing the male executive. Indeed, these images also run counter to the female victimizing the female executive.

Perhaps the usual senses which warn one of danger are subdued when it comes to the female terrorist. Although he might normally suspect something is suspect, the executive shrugs it off. The greater his ego (or hers) gets attached to the ongoing situation whether it be business or personal, the greater is his attachment to disbelief. We are continually reminded of the "after the fact" lines such as "she was always so normal," "she was just like everyone else," "she was a cheerleader in high school," "she attended church and came from a good family." or "she was so pretty, I just didn't think." All reactions to the inevitable, why didn't we read the writing on the wall.

That males are victims of female terrorists more frequently than females, is the same reason why males are more frequently the victims of terrorism in all cases: they tend to be societal symbols of power. The female terrorist marks her victim not because he is a male, but rather that the victims should provide her and her organization the recognition, media attention, and level of fear for which the event was planned.

WOMEN'S ROLES IN SURVEILLANCE

Women have served in all areas of surveillance: choosing the target, selecting the technique (clandestine and overt), collecting the information, maintaining the information in some orderly fashion (database, etc.), and determining how to use the information. The effectiveness of women in these roles has been proven time and again. To accomplish these roles, the female has played in a number of arenas: secretary, office cleaner, database analyst, and security official. Obviously each of these and other job positions would lend themselves to various opportunities to access data, obtain levels of trust, and set-up the target. These women can be quite useful in obtaining schedules, telephone numbers (published and unpublished), family members names and relationships, blackmail information and a wealth of other data useful in planning assassinations, kidnapings, hostage-takings and other forms of terrorist activities including the funding terrorist organizations through extortion, blackmail, fraud, robberies and white collar crime. Their placement within organizations not only is useful in targeting of specific executives of that organization, but also in obtaining access to information leading to potential targets in related organizations and personnel. Depending upon the organization and the woman's location within it, she may obtain entrance to a number of social settings not previously accessible: private parties, media events, international and national travel, friendships with family members, personal ties with close friends, etc.

Women have been used both voluntarily and involuntarily in these positions. Sylvia Ageloff is a good example of a female insider who unknowingly facilitated the introduction and entry of a male assassin. Ageloff, a 27 year old psychologist, met and was lured into a love relationship by Jacques Mornard. Mornard, a Soviet agent, was aware that Ageloff's sister happened to be Trotsky's secretary in Mexico. Prior to this well thought out plan, no on had been able to breach Trotsky's physical or personal security. Mornard was able to gain a trusting familiarity with Trotsky based on his relationship with Sylvia. The assassination, its initial plan, and execution was then all made possible by Mornard's use of Ageloff.

Perhaps one of the best placed voluntary spies was "Tania", if CIA sources are correct in their assumption and assertions concerning her role as an infiltrator. She was an Argentine-born German, working for the Russians when she became Che Guevara's lover. The CIA contends that as a plant, she successfully orchestrated the killing of Guevara. Many claim that she received her money and orders from some source higher than Che. Yet, others still contend that this was disinformation and that Tania was a great revolutionary heroine who died bravely in the Bolivian jungle fighting for the revolution. Perhaps we will never know the true story. It is never easy acknowledging a mole within the organization, especially one who infiltrates as soldier, companion and lover. The higher the position and the more trusted the individual, the greater the embarrassment, especially if sex is involved. As will all intelligence-based operations, what is fact and what is fiction may never be known.

Women have been placed in certain positions to gain access to monetary sources for funding the revolution or terrorist activities. The Black Hebrews used a number of women in travel agencies to fraudulently ticket false names in a scam which resulted in the extortion of thousands of dollars. The numbers and types of other white collar crimes and illegal rackets are innumerable. Stealing data from a wide range of databases is common. This data which can help these organizations to plan and execute more successful operations. Women employed as database consultants have easy access to company's private information and security files from a number of private and governmental sources. Secretaries also have easy access to these files. Office cleaners can clean garbage cans of output which has been discarded, or simply heist information off of desk tops or shelves.

As information gatherers and in planning positions, women quite often work with a man as a couple. The West Germans profile labels the typical spy couple as: professional, childless, and married late in life. As professionals, these individuals are privy to the greatest amount of information from the highest places. Unfortunately for the West Germans, a review of their database came too late to capture Herbert Willner and his wife, Herta-Astrid. Both were found out as spies after their successful escape on vacation to Spain. Herbert Willner was a defense expert with access to high-tech information. His wife was even in a more sensitive spot, she was a secretary in the office of Chancellor Kohl. Another successful Soviet spy couple, Nikolay and Svetlana Ogorodnikov, were apprehended in Los Angeles. Svetlana lured FBI agent Richard W. Miller into an operation under the guise of a love relationship. As part of a couple, each operative is able to gain access to many individuals who assume falsely that a married couple is more trustworthy than a single person. Being married is a socially acceptable role, which shows stability, the willingness to take on responsibility, to act maturely, and hence, to be trusted. Likewise, having couples as members yields many positive results for the terrorist organizations. It is quite dangerous to trust outside women or men who are not part of the organization. It is quite difficult once operational to have love or sexual relationships. Being a couple allows for easier contact. The spying business is lonely and it makes for a more successful longterm use of spy personnel within the organization. The couple need not be married. Jane Alpert obtained much needed information for her male companion, Sam Melville. If it hadn't been for Alpert, Melville could never have been as successful as he was, as Alpert was the "brains" of the two.

One member of a "spy couple" may not be aware of the involvement of the other. Some may be aware of the involvement but easily manipulated into participation. A "church going" CIA clerk from Virginia was manipulated by her boyfriend, Michael Agbouti Soussoudis, into providing information concerning CIA operations in Ghana. Many believe that this lack of discretion led to the death of a CIA informant in Ghana. There are probably more "unknown" cases of this type than we would care to imagine. Females are frequently drawn into "doing awful things for awful men" through the use of sex by a master manipulator.

WOMEN AND WEAPONS

Women should never be underestimated when it comes to weapons. There are women, just as there are men, who wouldn't know the difference between an Uzi or a B-B gun. There are a number of women terrorists who know nothing about guns, weapons of any sort, but whose job it is to be involved in another aspect: writer of propaganda, safe house operator, information gatherer. For those in operational positions, if the women don't have the knowledge of how to handle a weapon before they enter the organization, they have the intelligence to know that they had better learn their weapons, and they do. A gun held by a woman or man, is equally dangerous.

The amount and type of training is all that matters, although the victim rarely knows the history and training of his opponent.

When Lynette "Squeaky" Fromme went to shake the hand of President Ford with her Colt .45 pistol, she may have been intent on killing him or it may have been an act to get the media to focus on her causes; however, she did not have the means to shoot him. There was no chambered bullet, and she was surprised to find that the gun failed to fire.

Although some weapons are more difficult to use than others (even for males), a well-trained terrorist, as the Little Drummer Girl, Hearst and all others have been taught, will know the gun in every way. Both females and males need to practice with the weapon and be comfortable with it. The Colt .45—Squeaky's choice—weighs over two and half pounds unloaded. It is difficult to carry, and even more difficult to conceal. Other possible weapons in a terrorist's arsenal such as a carbine, assault rifle, submachine gun, shotgun or a machine gun are all heavy, and hard to conceal. These weapons are frequently as difficult for men to handle as they are for women. Yet, it has been reported that women guerrillas carry these weapons and others successfully through jungle terrain over mountain roads, and in adverse weather conditions.

The recent sentencing of Marion Monica Sparg for bombing police stations and the political party offices on behalf of the African National Congress in South Africa might be the first for a white woman in that country, but women (black and white) have been involved in terrorist activities in a number of countries for quite some time. Not all women, like Ann Murphy, were unknowing victims of some male terrorist with a planted bomb upon their person. Many women quite voluntarily carry bombs under their dresses pretending to be pregnant, or in baby carriages, grocery carts and book bags. Country and culture also have little bearing upon the use of women in bombing incidents. In April of 1983, Thye Sieu Heong was executed for carrying, with her husband, 9 hand grenades in Malaysia. It was the first time a woman had been executed for such a deed in this small country. In Beirut, young teenaged women have died while delivering car bombs. Whether they do it of their own free will has been an interesting question. Not only do women carry bombs but they are quite apt in making them. We all have heard of the deaths of Cathy Wilerson and Diana Oughton in a New York townhouse while they were making bombs. However, many other women are still gainfully employed in this profession.

Women are involved with both gunrunning and gun dealing. In January of 1984, police had a gun fight with two males and a female in the Bronx, New York, when they were attempting to apprehend them for selling weapons to terrorists. Some of the best weapon dealers in Europe have been reported to be women. Thus, not only are women capable of handling their weapons, they are also capable of dealing them, and knowing the wide range of available sources and types.

NEGOTIATING WITH A FEMALE TERRORIST

Bargaining in any terrorist event is difficult. Bargaining with a female terrorist changes the rules of the game by definition. Tactics will still vary from incident to incident. The negotiation process in any ongoing hostage-taking is complicated. There are a number of variables which vary from case to case: location, time, psychological background of victim and perpetrator, power positions of each party, individual weaknesses, fears, prejudices, and flaws. All of these factors are important in the negotiation. Having a female involved brings the added problems of female psychology to play. Do women know the rules of the game? Are women inherently weaker than men even if it is only culturally assumed? Do they have to react more aggressively to overcompensate? Are they as cool as men? Are they able to give in? Are they dependent upon their male counterparts? The male negotiator frequently has not been trained to deal with female hostage-takers, and if there are female negotiators, they too, may not have had proper training in this regard.

In negotiation, the hostage-taker needs to be in a powerful position if they are going to succeed in their demands. The female walks into the negotiation lacking power, by the mere fact of her sex. One speculation is that the female must then take on an added toughness to overcome this initial lack of force. The Mariam Coyle case has been a classic case to study. Recently released from Irish prison for the joint hostage-taking of a Dutch businessman, Herrema, she chose not to communicate with her hostage. Her male counterpart, Eddie Gallagher and Herrema on the other hand developed an on-going daily communication. If she had not become ill, the negotiations may not have been able to break through her hardened stance, Herrema might not be alive today to plea in behalf of releasing Gallagher.

What type of negotiator should they send in to deal with the female terrorist? Males might symbolize male chauvinism, a power figure, one which would have to be overcome with greater force. Yet, he may also represent a father figure, a person to be trusted. The female negotiator might be a threat or a comrade. These types of decisions have to be made quickly in every event. The need to develop a rapport with the terrorist is important if the negotiation is to be successful. Depending upon the location of the hostage-taking, a trained female negotiator might be hard to find. Further, in most larger cities where females have been included in negotiation training, the female is generally not given any real on-the-job experience. Thus, more frequently than not, the male negotiator is chosen to end a stand-off. More training in this area is needed, we need to understand the dynamics of negotiation with the female terrorist as well as train women negotiators in the fine art of negotiation.

The female terrorist is not a new phenomenon, nor is she one to ignore. She can be as dangerous as her male counterpart. She has been involved in all phases of terrorism, and she should come as no surprise, although she often is for those who are in counterterrorism positions. The next female assassin may be a lot more competent than "Squeaky" Fromme or John W. Hinckley. The Tylenol scare that began in the fall of 1982 and continues to plague a number of cities, lends itself especially well to the female terrorist. AIDS is an especially toxic threat which can be easily spread by a female terrorist. Much of the information available on female terrorists has been distorted, hastily developed and out of focus. Many misleading statements have been made about female terrorists due to the embarrassment they have caused law enforcement and private security officials. Along with certain false assumptions, there are many analyses and projections which did not materialize, or at least not to date. Women were supposed to become involved in terrorism more extensively, their numbers were to increase, and their evolving degree of proficiency was to give rise to special problems of control and containment. This was to be an epidemic. Although these predictions did not come true, and while there do not appear be more or as many women terrorists as men, the female terrorist is still a reality, one which should not be overlooked in any training or operational procedures. Women terrorists are a formidable adversary who are here to stay, understanding them and being prepared for them is not academic.

NINETEEN

Defense Against Terrorist Tactics

by Robert D. Chapman

ALMOST DAILY THE MEDIA REPORTS on the activities of international terrorists, their hijackings, hostage-taking and cold-blooded murders, while Congress talks about military reprisals.

The public becomes alarmed. Overseas travel decreases, tourism suffers and a few dozen terrorists make their causes known and are feared by the Western world.

On the other hand, little is said about the internal or domestic terrorists who are the action arms of national liberation movements which threaten democratic governments everywhere. Unlike international terrorists who live in sanctuaries and strike at targets in third world countries, domestic terrorists live underground in their own countries. They spring from their clandestinity to attack, kill soldiers, policemen and civilians, or kidnap and take their victims to underground dungeons, called "people's jails," in their war to defeat the government. They are Marxist-Lenists and their objective is to oust the government in power and replace it with a communist one in which they, the terrorists, will rule.

Domestic terrorists are leaner and meaner than their international counterparts. After committing a terrorist act, they run back into the underground and protect themselves by intelligence and stealth, and should this fail, by firepower.

They are more difficult to negotiate with for the release of a kidnap victim than international terrorists, because domestic terrorists are not overly concerned with the final outcome, whether the ransom is paid or the victim is killed. In either case they win, they receive the publicity they want and the population is terrorized. The negotiators must meet the terrorists' demands. It's as simple as that. In fact, a hostage is a burden to domestic terrorists. The hostage must be guarded, fed, watered, even attended to medically, all requiring manpower which might be better used elsewhere in terrorist attacks.

In Guatemala, for example, a terrorist force marched a hostage into the jungle and tied him to a tree while they went on a secondary mission. They never came back. They either forgot where they tied the victim or simply did not care and left the victim to die of exposure and starvation.

Domestic terrorists use kidnapping extensively as a tactic during the beginning phases of an insurgency. Once the revolutionary or insurgency situation is created, they turn to murder, bombing, the destruction of power and transportation lines and the economy. An example of such tactical transition took place in El Salvador.

In the late 1970's, I went to El Salvador and other Central American countries on assignment for international underwriters to interview kidnap and ransom policy-holders and assess the deteriorating situation. I found the terrorists, the Farabundo Marti National Liberation Front (FMLN) and its affiliates, were attempting to intensify the insurgency, and I reported back that increased and continuing kidnapping could be expected. The underwriters stopped writing kidnap and ransom insurance in these countries at a saving of millions of dollars. However, by the late 1980's, the terrorists had intensified the revolution. Their military action teams were attacking army outposts; a left of center government was in power; and United States support was waning. Kidnappings had stopped. While a general fear of the situation still prevailed, it was the time to sell kidnap and ransom insurance policies.

Throughout an insurgency, a distinction should be kept in mind between kidnappings by terrorists and kidnappings by common criminals. In an insurgency, criminals become aware of terrorist kidnapping and the large ransoms that are paid, and soon they begin their own kidnap operations. The difference between the two quickly becomes obvious. Terrorists have a support base while criminals do not. Terrorists kidnap a victim and hide him or her in a people's jail in their support structure. They communicate with their headquarters and work out ransom and negotiations plans. It may take a week or two, even three, possibly more, before a ransom demand is received. Not so with criminal kidnappings. Criminals do not have a support structure, and it is not uncommon to receive the ransom demand on the same day as the abduction.

Without a support base, criminals cannot negotiate over a prolonged period. They are willing to compromise and settle for a smaller amount than demanded. In a case in Guatemala, for instance, the criminal kidnappers demanded $2 million, but they settled for $20,000.

Domestic terrorists have greater operational capabilities than their international counterparts. They are native to the country in which they fight. They blend into the environment. They are native to the customs, the mores and the language. They can get close to their victim, put him or her under surveillance and hover over the target, learning vulnerabilities to exploit weaknesses. International terrorists cannot do this. They live in sanctuaries, sometimes thousands of miles from their victim, and when they arrive to attack, they are strangers in the victim's country and their best chance for success is to arrive at the target area quickly and strike suddenly. Otherwise, they might stand out from others and come to the attention of the authorities.

In countries with insurgencies, where governments are mauled by national liberation movements, there is no way to distinguish friend from foe. Only one side wears a uniform and the nameless people in the street could be plainclothes security police or assassins. Because of such environmental blending, domestic terrorists close in on their victims. They penetrate residences, offices, factories, even government installations, including the military, police and security agencies.

Domestic terrorists plan operations carefully in successive steps or phases. They do not want to take chances. With few exceptions, they are young men and women, of middle or even upper social class, university students or graduates who want political power. If successful in the revolution, they will be appointed to high positions in the new government. The prize is so rich there is no wish to take chances to jeopardize the future. So they plan carefully. Their primary steps are: 1) Choosing the victim; 2) Surveillance of the victim's route of travel; 3) Selection of the ambush site; 4) Casing the ambush site; 5) Planning and dry running the operation, escape, and if the operation involves kidnap, negotiation.

Domestic terrorists do not choose their victim by chance. Random selection is too risky. Instead, the victim's are chosen selectively, either by the intended victim's high profile or through information obtained by the penetration of the victim's home or place of employment.

High profile means that the victim lives or conducts himself in a manner that brings him to the terrorists' attention. His name and photograph may appear in newspapers. He may be active in charities or sports and becomes publicly known. One case I recall is a Swiss ambassador in Brazil who drove around the city in a small, classy, red sports car. He drew attention, everyone looked at him, but unfortunately he was also noticed by terrorist leaders and his kidnap was planned by them and carried out.

High profile can also mean working for a high profile company. Terrorists have certain kinds of companies—even specific companies—on their hit lists and they target these companies and their employees with a greater frequency than others.

The types of companies on terrorist hit lists are: 1) Companies which do business with the government in power, particularly with its military, police and security administrations. The list could include many major companies operating internationally on a routine basis and interfacing with foreign governments. 2) Industries such as oil and gas companies, mineral mining and even agriculture. Terrorists propagandize the farmers and workers, saying foreigners exploit the soil, draining the riches which they send to their own countries where they make huge profits which they do not share. For this greed, this exploitation, they tell the people, foreigners are killed and kidnapped. 3) Banks. Foreign banks and their foreign employees are favorite targets. There is little sympathy in Third World countries when bankers are kidnapped. Popular reaction is that banks can afford to pay the ransom. 4) Nuclear and nuclear-related businesses, including construction firms hired to build nuclear power plants.

Several of these targets are worth further discussion. In the United States, early in 1988, the Department of Energy quietly advised U.S. companies of the growing threat of terrorist attacks on vital domestic energy facilities and pressed them to fortify their defenses. The report was prepared for Congress in 1987 but was withheld because of its sensitive nature.

The Energy Department's advice followed 1987 action by the National Liberation Army (ELN) in Colombia, blowing up the front of Occidental Petroleum's headquarters in Bogota, injuring thirteen people and causing $400,000 damage. The ELN specializes in attacks on oil pipe lines and in 1987 made more than twenty attacks on a pipeline that carries oil to the Colombian coast.

The nuclear target also requires comment. Until the end of the 1980's, the Soviet Union and its satellites engaged in huge engineering projects to convert oil-burning power plants to nuclear power. Simultaneously, communist parties, front groups and leftist organizations in Western countries, waged a relentless campaign to prevent construction and operation of nuclear power plants. The obvious conclusion is that the Soviet goal was to keep Western countries dependent upon petroleum and the long supply lines from the Middle East. The anti-nuclear campaign was remarkably successful, particularly in Spain and the United States where construction and operation of nuclear plants came to a halt.

In 1986, in West Germany the police found a deactivated nineteen pound bomb on a railway line used to transport nuclear waste. The bomb was placed on a section of track used by convoys to carry extremely radioactive waste. The police said it was the 70th known attack on nuclear waste transporters in West Germany.

Terrorist penetration operations to obtain information are not the same as police operations. The police recruit agents to infiltrate and work themselves into an organization and report information on members and activities. Terrorist penetration agents are more often acquired by chance rather than recruitment. Their agents are the family, mother, father, aunts, uncles, brothers, sisters, boyfriends, girlfriends or some friend who is employed in the victim's home, office or factory as sources of information. In Third World countries, there is no strong loyalty to governments, institutions or businesses, but family ties are strong, more so than in Western Countries. Family members provide other family members with information they want. It is given even wittingly, knowing the information will be used to kill or kidnap their employer, his wife or children.

From informants terrorists learn the security of the victim's home or office. They receive some idea of the victim's wealth or how much his corporate employer may be willing to pay for his safe return. They learn the victim's habits. They discover his security practices. They uncover his vulnerabilities.

After the terrorists select a victim, they send surveillants to follow him or her from home to office and return. They need to know the route of travel so they can select an ambush point to make the kill or kidnap. However, the surveillance is not the same as a police surveillance. There is no interest in who the victim talks to, the places where he may stop or the papers he may drop off. The only interest is the route he travels.

I know of no case where the victim detected his route surveillance and reported it to the authorities. The reason is because terrorists have a limited objective, wanting to know only the route traveled; the surveillants can stay back, a block or two, in a small car or motorcycle, and follow the victim undetected.

After the route is known, the terrorists leisurely and studiously go over the route and select an ambush site. They look for a place they can surprise the victim, a place the victim comes upon suddenly with no opportunity to back up or run away. A site around a curve, a bend or a corner is preferred.

The next step, casing the ambush site, is crucial in planning a terrorist act. Surveillants station themselves in the ambush site for successive days to observe the victim as he passes. While they may look for unusual signs, for example the victim's alertness, their mission is to record the time the victim passed through the site. They confirm whether he has a routine.

If the victim passes through the ambush site at approximately the same time every day, the terrorists reconnoiter the area surrounding the ambush site to determine whether at that specific time there is a military or police patrol in the area which could come to the victim's rescue. Kidnapping creates noise. Sometimes there is a crashing of cars as the victim tries to flee, or gunfire if the victim resists. Terrorists do not want to chance noise that may bring a nearby military patrol to the ambush site. If there is such a patrol, the terrorists will find another ambush site, or if they cannot, they will drop the victim and find another.

If no patrol is in the area, the terrorists will map the ambush site in detail showing streets, businesses, houses and obstacles. They will deliver the map to their superiors.

With the casing map in hand the terrorist leaders plan the operation. They decide how may people will be needed and the role each will play. In some kidnappings, twenty or more terrorists take part. Many times uniforms and disguises are needed. Terrorists in uniforms as soldiers or policemen catch the victim off guard, bringing his vehicle to a stop. In one case a woman pushed an empty baby carriage into the street in front of the victim's car, causing him to swerve, crash and come to a stop. He was easily abducted and taken away. In another case, terrorists dressed as telephone linemen were the spotters to alert the ambush party of the victim's imminent arrival.

Once the operation plan is completed, the terrorist leaders assign cell members to the specific roles they will perform. They are briefed, and startling as it may seem, the group will go to the action site and dry run the operation. There, each will perform the steps he or she is responsible for during the actual attack. There is good reason for this. As previously stated, terrorists do not take chances, and they do not want to be caught by the authorities in the middle of an ambush operation. They reason that if someone in the area should call the police at the outset of the ambush, it will take the police about three minutes, at minimum, to arrive. By dry running the operation, by practice, the terrorists reduce the time of ambush to one minute or less, a time verified by statistics. In an overwhelming number of cases, a terrorist ambush is completed in one minute or less.

In many cases the people, living or working in an ambush area, later reported to the police that in the day immediately preceding an abduction or assassination, they saw strangers in the area acting suspiciously. However, I know of only one case where such suspicions were reported to the police before the terrorist act took place, and in that instance, the police did not respond.

Much of the planning and dry running is shown in the terrorist execution of General Carol Urzus in Santiago, Chile. At 8:30 in the morning, August 29, 1983, a yellow Chevrolet pickup truck carrying five members of the Movement of the Revolutionary Left (MIR), parked at an intersection in the Las Condes district of the city. One of the terrorists wore a wig and was disguised as a woman.

At 8:40, two terrorists got out of the truck. One took a position in front of a shop on the corner. The one disguised as a woman hid behind a lamp post.

Seconds later a car with General Urzus, his chauffeur and bodyguard drove into the intersection. As if on command, the terrorists laid down a three cornered crossfire. Sixty-two shots hit the vehicle. General Urzus was struck ten times, the chauffeur eleven. The bodyguard tried to reach cover and fight back, but was hit in the street and killed.

Terrorist acts are terrible in themselves, but in the 1980's a new dimension was added by terrorist collaboration with criminals. This is a new twist. 1968 is the date most terrorist movements were organized and for ten or fifteen years terrorist movements stayed away from criminals and refused to become involved in smuggling, narcotics and prostitution. There were two reasons. The lessor one was that terrorists did not want to tarnish the Robin Hood image given them by most of the international media. However, the principal reason was that they did not want to cross operations. Terrorists felt confident that they could assess risks and conduct political terrorism; however, they also felt that if they crossed into criminal activities, it would bring into play a whole new range of elements about which they knew nothing. For example, they knew little of the informants used by the police; they did not know how far a narcotic user could be trusted; and by this lack of knowledge they could jeopardize the terrorist organization and its political objectives.

The change began in 1978. The Palestine Liberation Organization (PLO) took on the assignment to overthrow the Shah of Iran. It was an enormous task, calling for the training of 10,000 Iranian mujahidin and chariks. All the diverse Palestine organizations, many times otherwise at odds with the PLO, came to assist. Because operations extended over Europe, the Middle East and Africa, even with their help it was not enough. The PLO enlisted Palestinian drug smugglers and their clandestine supply lines to move men, arms and ammunition throughout the Mediterranean. The operation was successful and mutually profitable. Terrorist supplies moved through narcotics channels and smugglers moved narcotics along with the guns. If Western European police suspected what was happening, they did not say, and the partnership between terrorist and criminal solidified.

By the end of the 1980's terrorist organizations, such as the National Liberation Army (ELN), the Popular Liberation Army (EPL) and the Revolutionary Armed Forces of Colombia (FARC), gave up many of their former activities to guard the cultivation and shipment of narcotics to the United States. The operation is more profitable and more devastating to their enemy than the occasional kidnapping of an American businessman.

There are defenses to the tactics used by domestic terrorists. In 1971, Daniel Mitrione, an American police advisor assigned to our embassy in Motevideo, was kidnapped and murdered most brutally by Tupamaro terrorists. Fear spread through the diplomatic communities in Latin America and I received the assignment of developing defensive procedures which could be used by men and women stationed abroad in countries of high risk.

Analysis showed terrorists everywhere used the same tactics to murder and kidnap their victims. The same tactics used by the Irish Republican Army (IRA) are used by 19th of April movement (M-19) and the Basque Fatherland and Liberty (ETA). From this my assistants and I built a simple four-step defensive system which could be used effectively by men and women. The four steps are 1) Residence and office security; 2) Personal security; 3) Running away; and 4) Weaponry. The fourth, for safety, I leave to range instructors and practical hands on application.

Residence and office security is the first and easiest step. It is preventative and mechanical and does not require change in living routines. It requires only that a home or office be made as safe as possible, something that is being done today by residents of most large crime-ridden cities. Many times this can be accomplished using common sense, without spending large sums of money.

If there is a wall around the house, as there is in many foreign countries, sprinkle broken glass on top, or string one or two strands of barb wire. If there is no wall have the landlord construct a fence and weave barb wire through the links with a barbed apron on top. Barb wire is inexpensive and a good deterrent.

Cut down the shrubbery in the yard. Eliminate hiding places, places from which intruders can advance toward the house unseen. Install flood lights to illuminate the yard. Burglars do not rob brightly lighted houses; they burglarize dark houses. So too with terrorists. They also do not take chances.

Repair broken windows, doors and locks so intruders will have to break in, make noise and alert the occupant who can either flee or be given a fair chance to fight for his life. Install dead bolts on doors or a sturdy wood bar or a simple iron pipe. Drill and install a 180 degree spyhole in the exterior entrance doors and add a sturdy night chain. Terrorists generally strike residences by night. The bedroom door should be fortified.

Residential security makes it more difficult for terrorists to penetrate the victim's home. It takes more time. They have to be cautious. They have to break down doors, windows, and locks. They have to make noise which alerts the victim to take defensive action.

My recommendation is that if possible have a dog, even a small, scrappy one. It is not the bite but the bark that is important.

Take, for example, the case where the dog barks at 2:00 A.M. The victim wakes. He reasons immediately there is an intruder in the house, in high risk countries possibly a terrorist intent on kidnapping him. By plan the victim rises, makes certain the bedroom deadbolts are securely in place. He may prop a chair against the door. He takes his weapon, a handgun or shotgun, always within easy reach and aims it at the door while he telephones for help as already arranged with the military, police, a guard company or a private militia. Should terrorists force their way into the bedroom, the intended victims with gun aimed is in position to deter them, drive them off and save himself.

If, on the other hand, the victim is awakened by the barking dog, but he does not have a plan and he did not make preparations, the victim wonders what he should do. It is too late. The barking dog provides sixty seconds for the victim to take action and implement his defense plan. If he waits until the dog barks to consider how to save himself, it is too late.

Personal security is difficult. It is the most difficult step because it requires the victim to change his way of living, and acquire a new life style.

By knowing how terrorists plan their action we learned that they do not take chances. An integral part of an ambush is their confidence that no military or police patrols are in the ambush area which can come to the victim's rescue. They learned this by ascertaining the victim's route of travel and the time he passes through the ambush site. Therefore, and it cannot be too strongly stressed, if living in a high risk country, one must vary routes and times of travel.

While the Shah was still in power in Iran, the police raided a mujahidin safehouse where they found over two hundred surveillance reports on possible murder victims— the mujahidin had no other objective but to kill, preferably Americans. The police discovered in every report where the victim, intentionally or coincidentally, changed his route and time of travel, the mujahidin dropped that person from the target list and went on to another. Similar to terrorists everywhere, they did not wish to endanger themselves. They could not be certain they could attack victims without intervention of a rescue force.

The police also discovered that many of the intended victims who changed their route and time of travel did not do so because they were security conscious but because they were people who did not live routine lives. Nevertheless, this finding emphasizes that changing routes and time of travel is one of the best defenses against terrorist action.

Another part of personal defense is to have a plan as to how to react to a terrorist kidnapping attempt. Similar to the incident where the barking dog alerts the victim to kidnapping in a residence, similar plans should be formulated to resist kidnapping attempts while the victim is in his office or place of employment, on the sidewalk or in his car. When an attack is made, a victim does not have time to think what he will do. He has time only to react, to implement his defensive plan. If he has none, it is too late. There are only seconds to react.

However, there are people who do not want to resist. They do not want to risk bodily harm, wounding or death. They prefer to submit to the kidnappers, take their chances and rely on negotiation and the payment of ransom for release. It is not only their right to choose this course, but most times it is a safe course. With kidnapping there is confinement, brutalization, anguish, even physical and mental torture, but most of the time the victim is released. But that option is not open to everyone. If the victim is a police, army or security member, a government official, or possibly even an American, kidnap means torture and death with little likelihood of release. There is either defense and resistance or certain death.

Also, in terrorist situations, as in defense against criminals, it pays to show that one is security conscious and it will not be easy to kidnap him or her as the kidnappers will likely meet resistance. For example, analogous to criminal activities, police records show that rapists attack women who they believe will offer little or no resistance. If by her appearance, they believe she will scream, kick and scratch, they look for another. So too with terrorists. If the intended victim looks like a tough customer who may be carrying a gun and will use it if attacked, they look for easier prey.

In personal defense, toughness is needed. In foreign countries, mainly in the Third World, where domestic servants are common, they must do what they are told to protect the security of the residence. They must not let unauthorized people into the house. They must not accept unknown parcels and packages. If they disobey instructions, they face termination on the spot. They are paid off and sent away. By nature, Americans believe the world loves Americans and that domestic servants and employees are loyal to them and will never betray them, but it is not that way. In the Third World, the people have little or no loyalty to governments, institutions and employers. Loyalty is to the extended family and to the family alone. If a family member asks for information about an employer or admittance into his home, he will likely get it.

Also importantly, in an intensifying revolutionary situation, domestic servants and employees know there is a chance the revolutionaries will be successful. If they are, foreign employers, the Americans and Europeans, will leave, abandoning their residences, offices and employees to the new government, its police and security forces. As the revolution continues, domestic servants and employees do not destroy bridges to what the future may bring. If asked by the revolutionaries for information, there is understandably good reason on their part to provide it. If asked for cooperation, the same reasoning applies.

The only defense is to be wary, trust no one. Personal defense is what it means. You personally must protect yourself and your family. There is no one else.

Running away is a defense. It means that one should not voluntarily seek trouble. If in a high risk country, one sees trouble ahead, stop and go back. If driving and something suspicious or unusual is seen as one nears home or office, stop, go back or turn at another block and go around it. If suddenly brought to a stop in traffic and helplessly struck with a sense of danger emerging, abandon the car and run.

Many times in kidnapping situations, the victim's car is stopped by a road barricade, generally by two terrorist vehicles parked, blocking the road. Barricades of this kind can be broken, relatively easily, by the victim ramming his vehicle into the blocking cars. I recommend learning how to ram; although easily learned, it should be by hands on application under supervision of an instructor. I stress this because to my knowledge I know of only one case where a chauffeur rammed through a terrorist barricade. All other successful ramming cases, and there have been many, were while the victim was driving.

A chauffeur, approaching a road barricade, instantly reasons the terrorists ahead do not want him. They want the employer in the back seat. For the little money he makes for the wife and children he supports, he stops the car and virtually delivers his employer into terrorist hands. Sometimes it is more blatant. In one case the chauffeur stopped his employer's armored car in an intersection and fled, leaving the door open and unlocked. Almost nonchalantly the terrorists were on the spot and calmly abducted the startled employer from his otherwise tank-like car.

People do not want to live in the situations I have described, living in fortresses, changing their routines, and forever being on the alert. But many have to endure this life. For some it is their country, or their home with no other place to go. Husbands may send their wives and children out of the country if finances permit, while he stays to protect the home, the business or the farm. To others, it is their job. They are assigned short term to countries of high risk to protect the business or corporation which employs them. To others in government services; there is no alternative but to take their turn in a country of high risk.

To quote Quarles: "Let the fear of a danger be a spur to prevent it: he that fears not, gives advantage to the danger."

Car bombings—a common terrorist tactic.

TWENTY

A Perspective on Personal Protection

by Dr. Richard W. Kobetz

THERE IS A NEED TO DISCUSS something very near and dear to all of us—ourselves—with an emphasis upon personal protection. Nothing should ever happen for the first time. Unfortunately, it does, and you might possibly be in a situation sometime in which some of the following points being made might be recalled and may be of some assistance. Upon dozens of occasions over the last two decades, people have related to me that this was the case with them. If you are visible, vulnerable and valuable, as all of us are; then obviously, each of us must determine to the best of our own particular ability what kind of risks we will accept.

It is vital with threat assessment to consult professionals for the management of risks and I highlight the word "professionals," in the security field. These thoughts are based upon your travel activities whether you are with the government or whether you own your own company or you are traveling internationally for business or pleasure. You must be aware of not only what affects you personally but your family, your company, your operations, and ultimately, your country.

A threat assessment is useless unless you recognize what it means to you as an individual. That's the only time it can be of value to you. You could follow all sorts of advice to a certain point, but after awhile, you must decide upon certain priorities for yourself.

Good security is not synonymous with convenience. It is, in fact, very inconvenient. Bodyguards, scheduling, security checks, riding in armored vehicles, and the like must become a way of life for people who are placed in a position of high vulnerability. You quickly find that it is not entertaining to constantly be rushed in and out of buildings or forbidden from leaving your hotel room alone to merely obtain some ice or to go down to the lobby to have a quiet drink. Imagine somebody standing outside your door and smiling at you and informing you that you are not leaving your room until your escort arrives. You can rarely appreciate such a command even though it is for your own welfare.

What needs to be emphasized is the need for you to maintain a constant awareness of possible danger. Danger, like illness, is very specific. It strikes individually but carries an impact far beyond the individual. What this danger also represents to your family, your colleagues, and your company must always be taken into account.

This issue of awareness is not always on the high end of everyone's scale. Not only referring to terrorists specifically, criminal activity must be considered as well. Criminals also read the paper, and often imitate the tactics and techniques of terrorists. So ordinary street crimes can make anyone a target.

AREAS OF CONCERN

Three areas need to be covered. **Avoiding danger** through prevention is the primary one. **Surviving** an attack or hostage experience must also be considered, since even a heightened awareness of potential threats can't help you if you are simply at the wrong place at the wrong time. (Discussion on a few basic points will be presented, not long checklists and guidelines which will be hard to remember in such situations.) And lastly, the challenge of **living with yourself,** your family, your friends, and your career if you have survived an ordeal as a kidnap victim or as a hostage.

Avoiding Danger:

Let's consider your personal awareness with respect to walking, driving, or flying into harm's way. In all practicality, this starts when you walk out of your office or residence, or fly to wherever you are going. Awareness is something that has saved the lives of many people. Many of us are often distracted by our own thought processes, personal issues, and business problems. As a result, we don't look around. We are not aware of who is standing where, who is next to a car we are going to, who is standing in a doorway, or who has been observing us. Hundreds of cases indicate that most victims of assassination or kidnapping have been observed in advance, the incident might have been prevented. Afterward, however, people typically comment, "Gee, I never thought about that," or "Gee, I never thought of reporting that," or "I never suspected that fellow who dressed like, looked like, behaved like and walked like a vending machine maintenance person even when there were no vending machines in the area." A frequent ploy of criminals and terrorists, for example, is to masquerade as street crews, repairmen, postal workers and even police officers.

When you are walking around, are you familiar with where you are walking and what is going on around you? When I say walking around, I mean in your office, neighborhood in your own hometown, and even around your own home. Consider a businessman in Honduras who installed a $1 million security system in his home. Because he was a prime target, he recognized the risk. He was alert to potential danger. However, on one occassion a truck pulled up; it looked like a delivery van, similar to many in his country. The driver wore a uniform. What did the maid do? She turned off the system and opened the door to take the package. Out came two more kidnappers from the back of the van to take the businessman away from his million dollar security system. What's the point if people don't understand how security systems work? If you elect to take precautions, follow them thoroughly. If you take residential precautions with an alarm system, dogs, and even have weapons in your home, then take precautions necessary with those particular aspects of protection and do not ignore or abuse them. It will probably save you during times you are off guard. If you are going to protect yourself, your family, or your employees, it does not always amount to purchasing a million dollar security system.

I conducted a training session in Canada for Canadian officials and representatives from seven nations around the world several years ago. One of the gentlemen in attendance had for many years carried a simple wooden wedge with him everywhere he went and it was his habit every evening to put that little wooden wedge under the door of the hotel room or guest room if he was staying at a residence. It was a good habit. This particular night, he was lying down on his bed in a room on the grounds of the Royal Canadian Mounted Police training school. It was a multi-story residential tower. The practical problem was due to begin the next day at high noon. But to include an element of surprise, it started earlier than planned, at 4:00 a.m., with the Ottawa Police Department Tactical Team moving into action. He had been lying back on his bunk thinking about putting that wedge under the door the night before. However, since he was so tired and was on this high floor of the RCMP residential building, he decided to let it go. And who do you think got taken? He wasn't even on the snatch list, but as luck would have it, they opened the door and took him too. Now he carries two wedges. But the point is, one night in his life, fortunately during a training exercise, he didn't follow through. If you have a system, make it a routine system. If you carry a portable alarm or a small "kubotan" or that "persuader" you have been trained to use, then have that in your hand when you suspect danger and be prepared all the time, rather than just 50 percent of the time.

Another example occurred in Paris in 1982. At that time, one of the terrorist groups decided that Americans were prime targets. One American gentleman walked outside of a building and around the block, and saw a man stalking him. He stopped, turned from behind a car, and just stared at the man. The man panicked. Terrorists are not superhuman. The man drew a weapon which was intended to be used to kill this American and began firing from a distance across a Paris street. He emptied the weapon, missed completely every time he fired, and then fled. This American was watching. He was observing everybody. All the newspapers picked it up, and all were completely aware that he followed the proper course of action. Six weeks later, at the same location, another U.S. citizen, deep in thought, went to his car, and started fumbling for the keys. A man walked up behind him, stuck a pistol behind his ear, and pumped three shots into his head, killing him instantly. There had been an attack that had been stopped just six weeks earlier at this same location and many still didn't recognize the necessity of being aware of the fact that Americans were prime targets. I don't know how much closer it could have come, because no one could say, "Well, that happened across the street, in another city, in another state, in another country, to another company, or to another industry and has nothing to do with us." When it gets that close and is still ignored, it shows a terrible lack of awareness.

In more than 75 percent of the attacks on business people, diplomats, military officers and officials a vehicle is involved; either their vehicle is on its way from the home to the office, office to recreation, recreation back to the office, or a meeting. That's why there are so many defensive-offensive driving schools for chauffeurs and drivers. The military has picked this up as a routine training measure for their security personnel. Special operations law enforcement agencies have done this as well and have come to understand the automobile is also a method of escape and can be used as a weapon.

Flying is a concern for the majority of travelers, especially with regard to overseas flights. If the precautionary measures that have been initiated over the last few years, and there have been many, become too elaborate, too expensive, too unreasonable, then personal security procedures are going to be disregarded. But for the past several years, overseas business travelers have been given a great deal of advice with respect to their trips. Some of this advice is not practical from the businessman's perspective at all: always choose a window seat, do not fly first class, do not carry a briefcase or any business papers, no membership cards, identification, liquor, or business magazines in your carry-on luggage, take direct flights only, fly wide-body flights because there are less chances of skyjacking, dress casually, and be friendly with fellow passengers, but not too friendly. All this advice is nice on a checklist. I wish I could give you a Miranda warning card checklist of four or five points that would be an absolute guarantee. Nobody has four or five guaranteed precautions.

These are merely some measures that you may want to consider. But the difficulty of this advice lies in the fact that if you follow the routine of most businessmen, your work pertaining to that business engagement is done on that flight, and you are going to have paperwork with you. You will sometimes be met and immediatley have to attend a meeting and have to be more formally dressed. You're going to decide before you board that airplane on a risk assessment basis: "What's the chance of this plane being taken versus me giving up ten hours of work on a transcontinental flight?" The question is obviously not going to work out in favor of leaving behind or packing-up and baggage checking all your materials. These are all sound measures and I do not wish to debunk them, but I am saying that in many cases they are not practical and, therefore, are not always worthwhile.

Surviving:

Just a few more considerations: One point is that airlines generally do a fine job of screening for weapons and explosives. But there is always a lot of improvement needed. The threat of skyjacking always exists. People say, "Well, how did they get on the aircraft with weapons and explosives?" Countries that support terrorism take them through security in their country, they board them on aircraft, the aircraft goes into a sterile area of another major international airport, they go off that aircraft with their bags and with carry-on luggage, and board whatever aircraft they intend to skyjack. So the procedures concerning screening obviously have to be tightened up considerably in many nations.

If you should happen to be on a flight, either domestic or international, hijacked by somebody who has a fanatical wish to go to Cuba or wherever, I would offer you a few points of advice. Listen carefully to what's being said and follow instructions. Do not argue. This is not a time for arguing. Many of you are people who are used to being in charge. You are men and women who are used to being in total charge of your life, your business, your employees and operations. Now is the time to relax and comply. Somebody with a weapon in their hand or a grenade at their belt is now in charge. This is not time for foolish heroics that could get you killed or injured or anyone else around you killed or injured.

If you are being held in a hostage situation, don't talk to other people if you can avoid it. This can be perceived as plotting or making some plans for an escape. Be very careful about that. I would avoid eye contact with hostage takers unless they are speaking to you. Unless they are speaking directly to you, eye contact has a way of appearing very threatening and could cost you an injury.

Prepare yourself for questioning. As an American citizen, you are going to be interrogated. Think about that very carefully, that if they start talking to you; consider what you are going to say and how you are going to support what you are going to say and how you are going to tell lies if the occasion demands it.

If they are collecting valuables on the aircraft and they are putting these in a bag or are robbing you, do not argue or ask to keep anything because they are going to take it anyway and they really aren't too concerned about how much you value that particular ring, watch, or keepsake.

Now, what about your survival. How are you going to get out of there alive? The only way you will get out is to adopt a psychology of being a winner; you are going to survive and you are going to get out of there alive. If you do not adopt this psychology, you are going to have a problem. Do not view the outcome as "predestined." Do not become obsessed with worry. You must adopt the psychology that you can conquer this and that you can walk away from it a winner.

You must maintain your equilibrium on the basis of being who you are to stay alive. If the purpose of a kidnapping scenario is to keep you alive and intact, then you have a tremendous value to whoever is taking you. It is very difficult to make a judgment with regard to the best plan of resistance. Usually opportunities for escape are fleeting; escape is now or never. It is not a time to intellectualize about possible options. If someone has gotten close to you, moving up to say something, only to produce a weapon, you've lost the edge. You have allowed them to come into your personal space and if you have hesitated that long, then you can be killed or injured while making an attempt to escape. Terrorists are not necessarily going to approach you in a very gentlemanly manner, holding the pistol flat in their palm saying, "This is a kidnapping, you know, nothing personal. Get into the car." It is going to be a very deliberate, specific poke of a weapon in your face. You will be grabbed and thrown wherever they want to throw you. And if you are thinking about an escape, and many people see the opportunity, that would be the time. Doing anything afterwards with respect to resistance would be clearly dangerous. It's best to just give in gracefully if you have lost the edge at that particular moment and go along with it. If you have to **think** about escaping at the moment of encounter, then it is too late to do it. It must be an instinctive reaction.

If you become a kidnap victim or a hostage, you are pretty much on your own and you must become your own best friend even if you haven't been before. You have the intelligence, the drive, and the qualities that made you important enough to become a victim. Use your head. It is too late to worry. The point is that you are going to be going through a lot of self-searching. You must regain your own composure, get control of your emotions, and begin to put your own logical, intellectual, and reasoning processes into play based upon the personalities of those holding you and what their intentions are. Becoming a victim is a frightening thing, but begging or pleading will do you more harm than good. Terrorists have no interest in listening to your troubles. In some cases, they will tape record a plea because it makes excellent ammunition for whatever their demands ultimately are. You can assert your own personal dignity very quietly with firmness. You can regain your own composure, but you must take that deep breath. Think again about who you are, what you represent to yourself, your family, your company, your friends, and your government. Never attempt to do what you know you cannot do. If an opportunity would ever present itself under the circumstances and you know you can never ever harm or kill another human being, then don't do it. Don't make that try unless you have prepared yourself in advance to do something very specific. This is no time to test yourself. Don't even think about doing it.

One businessman was held for several months in a jungle environment in Columbia. He was held and moved several times and at one point, they brought him to a base camp. He created a plan in his mind. Every morning at about 3:30 a.m. he would get up to go to the bathroom and he would wake the guard. The guard would go with him. He did that for six mornings. On the seventh, the guard said "Go yourself." He was just too tired to accompany him. Well, that was the time he made a run for it and had the time to make his move. This was his decision and he planned it. He laid it out. He thought of the consequences and he carried it out. He made it to a government military outpost and was rescued.

If you are in a situation where you are being held continuously and it is coming to a close, this is the most dangerous time. The people who have held you are getting excited. They are nervous. They are frustrated, angry and exhausted. They might overreact. Government forces are coming in, the SWAT team is coming in, police, or the military. Your best bet is to take cover. Do not move. Don't do anything until your rescuers have taken action. They know you are there. They have to do what they have to do. Just lay down and take as much cover as you can. Don't get up and run and shout as to who you are. Rather, lay down and stay there. Stay out of the way as best you can.

Living With Yourself:

Let me deal with overcoming the personal anxiety which follows release in a hostage or kidnap ordeal. You are going to experience a great deal of emotion whether it is crying or laughing. Geting it out of your system is a good idea. Be prepared for a great many odd psychological reactions. They have to be dealt with. You will be debriefed, obviously. People are going to want to know where you were and what happened and who was involved. Officials are going to want to prosecute. But there are some cases where hostages, because of their total dependence on their "jailers," get quite confused. You might actually find yourself sympathizing with the people who were holding you because they didn't kill you. Because they may have treated you fairly. Such a feeling, however, will dissipate. You are going to eventually sit down and rationally say, "Wait a minute. What are we talking about here?" Many times you'll see the media coverage at a scene of an incident and you will see someone saying, "Oh well, they were nice people," or "But these bank robbers really weren't bad at all because we were only in there six or seven hours and they were very polite to us and let us go to the bathroom and fed us."

You will survive and these feelings will fade. Your readjustment, nonetheless, is going to be difficult. Some may feel guilty about why they didn't try to escape. There may even be mental and emotional problems for long periods afterwards with respect to dreams and sleep and family relationships. But the overwhelming majority of victims have worked these problems out very satisfactorily and have gone on with their lives.

Providing your own protection for yourself is a difficult and unpredictable activity. If there is a threat assessment that indicates you are at greater risk than others, then I advise your employment of someone to manage that risk. Someone who is known to be professionally competent and skilled in providing protective services for you and your family and employees. Many people have obtained fame and fortune in their lives as "winners" only to sacrifice it all through becoming a victim or a "loser." One must put aside their objections to interference with their life-style when in fact their life-style can be enhanced and made more pleasurable through proper planning and precautions.

Epilogue

THE CONCERNS OF THOSE who provide personal protection extend into a wide variety of security interests. Through the contributions of our associates we have explored many of these topics and areas. To deal with these topics appropriately would extend this book into an unacceptable voluminous work. My intent at this point of concluding our offerings is to alert serious students to a few of these concerns to illustrate the expansive nature of the work included in preparing to perform professional personal protection services. Some of these topics have had chapters and books written elsewhere while others have yet to be seriously addressed. Perhaps an expansion in a future undertaking might include and deal appropriately with these and even more concerns.

Protecting The Female Client

Introduction

The subject of protecting the female client needs to be considered not only on account of the rising number of female executives, but also because many male executives have spouses and other family members who may fall under the protective realm.

Besides the obvious, and some not so obvious, physical differences, there are mental, emotional and intuitive differences between men and women. The Protection Specialist must be aware of these differences which will necessitate flexibility and variations in protection techniques.

Difficult Protection Situations

Because the male agent cannot go everywhere with the female client, as he can with the male client, some protective situations require ingenuity and spontaneity. Most men are bored with shopping, so the male agent won't look out of place looking and milling around. A variation in observing the client is to position her with mirrrors and windows, either of which will be found in shopping areas. The male agent should familiarize himself with the "female" type shops and departments (i.e., lingerie, housewares and cosmetics) in shopping malls and department stores before accompanying his female client to any of them.

When shopping and waiting outside dressing room areas, watch her feet if the stall has a half door. If there is a full door, have her use the stall closest to the changing area entrance where anyone entering the stall may be observed. The agent should make note of how many articles of clothing the client has to try on and accordingly judge how long she should be in the stall. And, as always, she should call the agent by the wrong name if she is in trouble.

When visiting doctor or dental offices, check the examining room before the client enters noting windows and exits. Know what procedure is to be done and approximately how long it should take. At the beauty salon, know how long it should take the client to have her hair done or to have a manicure.

Behavioral Differences
Women tend to be more personal than men. They are more interested in communication and social interaction, friendlier, warmer and more animated. Women have a deeper interest in building relationships while men tend to be more preoccupied with the practical aspects of life which can be understood through logical deduction rather than emotional feeling.

Men are more challenge-and-conquer oriented. Their strong interest in sports is brought out by this competing for dominance. Hostility is expressed more in men through physical violence while women tend to be more verbally expressive.

The Socialization Process
Why do men and women generally display these behavioral patterns? What we experince in childhood becomes the foundation of our later behavior and personality. Children learn the sexual roles they are "supposed" to play. Studies have shown that mothers tend to hold their daughters closer and talk to them more, while sons get bounced on their father's knee or tossed into the air. The way parents treat their children is rooted in our culture—we treat little boys as explorers and hunters while little girls are treated as caregivers. When these children grow up, they enter a society that is shaped by the same roles they learned as infants. They will carry their training into relationships as well as careers.

Women's Intuition
Contrary to popular belief, "women's intuition" is not something mystical or merely a wives' tale. According to a Stanford University research team led by neuropsychologists McGuinness and Tribran, women do catch subliminal messages faster and more accurately than men. Since this intuition is based on an unconscious mental process, many women are not able to give specific explanations for the way they feel. They simply perceive or "feel" something about a situation or person, while men tend to follow a logical analysis of circumstances or people. So, whether it be a client or another agent with this innate ability, don't ignore it!

The Female Client/Protection Specialist Relationship
Two very important qualities an agent must have are patience and diplomacy—especially when dealing with the female client. As discussed previously, women interact on a personal level—do not misread this to be an "intimate" level. Women are "huggers" and "touchers" which often can be misinterpreted by men as a "come on." Male agents must break the male physiological process and keep the relationship professional. In other words, "don't play where you're paid."

Dealing With Spouses And Children
First and foremost, remember for whom you are working and always keep your eyes open and your mouth shut—do not repeat anything. A very promising career can be quickly shortened by a lonely wife with idle time. Older daughters of clients can also be a pitfall. There can be many obstacles to performing your protective duties, all of

which may be overcome by remembering to remain professional and objective. When dealing with children, know the parents' rules and do not get caught between parent and child. The agent is not there to befriend or entertain anyone, but rather to protect them.*

Corporate Aircraft

Despite the heavy emphasis on security throughout the world of commercial aviation, the term as yet has little significance in corporate aircraft operations. In many instances the practice of security in flight operations among companies that own or lease their own aircraft in North America has been limited to the edict: "Take the corporate name off the aircraft." Corporate security managers may see the need and be prepared to take appropriate action, but top management—the very people whose lives may be at risk—to date have paid little heed.

Corporate air operations personnel are seldom, if ever, assigned line management positions in the organizations that employ them. In many cases they have no more input into corporate security concerns than do the chauffeurs who transport executives in company limousines. While job titles such as "Chief Pilot", "Aircraft Engineer", or "Corporate Aviation Manager" may be impressive and the pay scale attractive, few such employees have any corporate authority extending beyond the cockpits of the aircraft they fly. This limited area of responsibility can expose corporate personnel to unnecessary risk.

The rationale seems to be that pilots are naturally concerned about their own and their passengers' safety and will presumably take whatever precautions are necessary to ensure safe take-off, flight, and landing. Period. True enough, so far as it goes; but commercial airline pilots are not less concerned with such matters, yet everyone agrees that extensive security measures far beyond air safety care are called for to avoid further bombings and hijackings of the kind that have grabbed world headlines in recent times.

A recent Eastern Michigan University study indicates that representatives of corporate aviation departments' fixed base operators and airport personnel hold "a low opinion of security programs that are designed to protect business aviation operation." This is a reinforcement of a principle that is apparent to those who know: "If corporate aircraft security is going to be improved, then the company's pilots *must* work with the company's security people." For the most part they are not doing so and much of what passes for security measures are shallow and "cosmetic" rather than reality-based. Mixed in with the problems of corporate aircraft operational personnel and security personnel who are concerned with executive protection and prevention of loss, are the complex issues of operating in someone else's "ball park."

Only a few corporations have absolute control over their aircraft and flight operations on a proprietary basis. The majority are in rented or leased space and more often than not, share hangar space with other corporations or aircraft owned by private individuals. Even if they operate their own hangars they are still at the mercy of the security or lack of same at any airfields they are utilizing. These airfields, or space allocated at major airports, are busy areas with flight crews and businessmen coming and going with little or no concern for identification or controls. Access is generally open

---

*Material on "Protecting the Female Client" prepared by Linda Richardson, P.P.S., Tucson, Arizona.

to all, with few questions asked. If you "look as if you know where you're going" you will seldom be asked any questions or be denied entry to any space on the field or in any of the hangars.

A conscientious effort of security must begin with the corporation as it impacts on and affects their personnel. Demands should be made upon the operations of the contract facilities to "tighten up." As security measures go up, or are enforced, convenience goes down as perceived by busy corporate executives and employees. A happy medium on the continuum must be found and agreed to, consistent with adequate threat analysis.

As flights continue to increase in the international arena, concerns about drugs and smuggled contraband increase with "zero-tolerance" levels becoming the rule and not the exception. Stowaways and sabotage to aircraft are added to the continuing problem of theft and vandalism by disgruntled employees or other dangerous kooks and criminals. **These problems are preventable with the combination of sound security procedures and sensible utilization of the wide variety of portable and aircraft-installed equipment available on the market today.** Even the intrusion of someone who "just wants to go inside the aircraft and look around" can cause serious problems intentionally or unintentionally. Skyjackings, kidnappings, and extortion attempts on the opposite end of the threat scale require sophisticated training with regard to how a company wishes those involved to respond and how they will improve their chances for survival, if employees become victims.

Awareness and training are the common denominators for corporations to consider in their strategies of preparedness. The whispered concerns of yesterday are becoming the harsh realities of today. It is negligent for corporations not to prepare their employees for what *can* happen—before it actually occurs. While it is not necessary to frighten people with unrealistic concerns it is foolish to ignore the prevalence of violence in our contemporary world.

Common sense approaches through training which deals with awareness, personal responsibility, and cooperative activities can go a long way in making corporate aviation as safe as posisible against possible intrusions and attacks. It is better to have a preplanned, carefully worked out training program based upon a corporate risk assessment by a security professional, than face the inevitable "let's do something" *after* the occurrence of a major incident involving a corporate airplane.

Nothing tragic should ever happen for the first time—but experience indicates it will; and a corporation that denies the need for adequate security measures around flight operations may well some day pay the price of the uninformed and the unprepared. To deny security measures recommended by security managers as not being "cost-effective" is extremely short-sighted and could well open the door to loss of far more costly and precious life—and/or expensive property. It is imperative that corporate aircraft be recognized as corporate assets that are visible and valuable, and therefore vulnerable. Today, more than ever before, there is need for cooperation between corporate security and flight personnel to ensure a safe and secure environment with respect to people and physical assets of the corporation.

It should be the designated responsibility of the manager of flight operations and of aircraft captains to implement and supervise carefully prepared procedures relating to answering questions from strangers, accepting packages for company aircraft transporting executives, hangar security, fuel pit security, bomb threats, and handling of questionable or unusual phone calls.

Included among basic points made with regard to protecting the company plane are the following:

- Aircraft left unattended by company personnel must have their doors secured and should be parked in well lighted areas.

- Preflight security inspection must be alert to the possibility of sabotage.

- Visitors to operation/maintenance areas should be escorted by security or company personnel.

- Any maintenance or cabin service personnel who board the aircraft should be accompanied by a crew member.

- Unauthorized/unbadged or unrecognized persons should be challenged.

- At boarding time, identify every piece of luggage with the particular passenger who owns it and make sure the that person is on board.

- Know precisely who you are carrying on your aircraft. No hitchhikers—ever! Require identification of all persons; and have all carry-on baggage searched (deny boarding forthwith to anyone who refuses a baggage or a person search if the latter is requested).

Aircraft Searching Procedures

The complexities of aircraft design make it unlikely that even the trained searcher will locate any but the most obvious explosive or incendiary device. Thus, detailed searches of large aircraft must be conducted by maintenance and crew personnel who are entirely familiar with the construction and equipment of the plane. In emergency situations where searches must be conducted by public safety personnel, or personal protection specialists, without the aid of the aircraft personnel, the following general procedures should be used.

1. Evacuate the surrounding area and remove all personal property.
2. Check the immediate area around the craft for bombs, wires or evidence of tampering.
3. Tow the aircraft to a safe distance or designated space.
4. Starting on the outside, work toward the plane's interior.
5. Begin searching at the lowest level and work up.
6. Remove freight and baggage and search cargo areas.
7. Check out restrooms and lounges.
8. Be alert for small charges placed to rupture the pressure hull or cut control cables. The control cables usually run underneath the center aisle.
9. Give special attention to refuse disposal containers, check food preparation and service areas.
10. Search large cabin areas in at least two sweeps.
11. Check the flight deck.
12. Simultaneously, search the baggage and freight in a safe area. If passengers are asked to come forward to identify and open the baggage for inspection, it may be possible to quickly focus in upon unclaimed baggage.
13. Be cautious, suspicious and thorough.
14. Report damage observed or caused by search.
15. When aircraft has been cleared, secure it.

Room Search Procedures

With respect to room search procedures, the following steps may apply in searching for explosive, incendiary or eavesdropping devices—as well as the discovery of broken or missing items which should be reported to housekeeping or the appropriate manager. It is also important to remove items which do not belong where they are found. Look under furniture, in drawers and on shelves—be careful and be thorough.

The following technique is based on use of a two-man searching team. There are many minor variations possible in searching a room. The following contains only the basic techniques.

First Team Action—Listening

When the two-man search team enters the room to be searched, they should first move to various parts of the room and stand quietly, with their eyes shut and listen for a clock-work device. Frequently, a clock-work mechanism can be quickly detected without use of special equipment. Even if no clock-work mechanism is detected, the team is now aware of the background noise level within the room itself.

Background noise or transferred sound is always disturbing during the building search. In searching a building, if a ticking sound is heard but cannot be located, one might become unnerved. The ticking sound may come from an unbalanced air conditioner fan several floors away or from a dripping sink down the hall. Sound will transfer through air-conditioning ducts, along water pipes and through walls, etc. One of the worst types of buildings to work in is one that has steam or water heat. This type of building will constantly thump, crack, chatter and tick due to the movement of the steam or hot water through the pipes and the expansion and contraction of the pipes. Background noise may also be outside traffic sounds, rain, wind, etc.

Second Team Action—Division of Room and Selection of Search Height

The man in charge of the room searching team should look around the room and determine how the room is to be divided for searching and to what height the first searching sweep should extend. The first searching sweep will cover all items resting on the floor up to the selected height.

Dividing The Room. You should divide the room into two equal parts or as nearly equal as possible. This equal division should be based on the number and type of objects in the room to be searched, not the size of the room. An imaginary line is then drawn between two objects in the room, i.e., the edge of the window on the north wall to the floor lamp on the south wall.

Selection of First Searching Height. Look at the furniture or objects in the room and determine the average height of the majority of items resting on the floor. In an average room this height usually includes table or desk tops, chair backs, etc. The first searching height usually covers the items in the room up to hip height.

First Room Searching Sweep

After the room has been divided and a searching height has been selected, both men go to one end of the room division line and start from a back-to-back position. This is the starting point, and the same point will be used on each successive searching sweep. Each man now starts searching his way around the room, working toward the other man, checking all items resting on the floor around the wall area of the room. When the two men meet, they will have completed a "wall sweep" and should then work together and check all items in the middle of the room up to the selected hip height. Don't forget to check the floor under the rugs. This first searching sweep should also include those items which may be mounted on or in the walls, such as air-conditioning ducts, baseboard heaters, built-in wall cupboards, etc., if these fixtures are below hip height. The first searching sweep usually consumes the most time and effort. During all searching sweeps, use the electronic or medical stethoscope on walls, furniture items, floors, etc.

Second Room Searching Sweep

The man in charge again looks at the furniture or objects in the room and determines the height of the second searching sweep. This height is usually from the hip to the chin or top of the head. The two men return to the starting point and repeat the searching techniques at the second selected searching height. This sweep usually covers pictures hanging on the walls, built-in bookcases, tall table lamps, etc.

Third Room Searching Sweep

When the second searching sweep is completed, the man in charge again determines the next searching height, usually from the chin or the top of the head up to the ceiling. The third sweep is then made. This sweep usually covers high mounted air-conditioning ducts, hanging light fixtures, etc.

Fourth Room Searching Sweep

If the room has a false or suspended ceiling, the fourth sweep involves investigation of this area. Check flush or ceiling-mounted light fixtures, air-conditioning or ventilation ducts, sound or speaker systems, electrical wiring, structural frame members, etc. Have a sign or marker posted indicating "Search Completed" conspicuously in the area. Use a piece of colored scotch tape across the door and door jam approximately two feet above floor level if the use of signs is not practical.

The room searching technique can be expanded. The same basic technique can be used to search a convention hall or airport terminal.

Restated, to search an area you should:

1. Divide the area and select a search height.
2. Start from the bottom and work up.
3. Start back-to-back and work toward each other.
4. Go around the walls then into the center of the room.

Encourage the use of common sense or logic in searching. If a guest speaker at a convention has been threatened, common sense would indicate searching the speakers platform and microphones first, but always return to the searching technique. Do not rely on random or spot checking of only logical target areas. The bomber may not be a logical person.

Suspicious Object Located

Note: it is imperative that personnel involved in the search be instructed that their mission is only to search for and report suspicious objects, not to move, jar or touch the object or anything attached thereto. The removal/disarming of a bomb must be left to the professionals in explosive ordnance disposal. Remember that bombs and explosives are made to explode, and there are no absolutely safe methods of handling them.

1. Report the location and an accurate description of the object to the appropriate warden. This information is relayed immediately to the control center who will call

police, fire department, and rescue squad. These officers should be met and escorted to the scene.

2. Place sandbags or mattresses, not metal shield plates, around the object. Do not attempt to cover the object.

3. Identify the danger area, and block it off with a clear zone of at least 300 feet—include area below and above the object.

4. Check to see that all doors and windows are open to minimize primary damage from blast and second damage from fragmentation.

5. Evacuate the building.

6. Do not permit re-entry into the buiding until the device has been removed/disarmed, and the building declared safe for re-entry.

(These basic steps are a common sense approach as indicated in the publication: *Bomb Threats And Search Techniques*, Department of the Treasury, Bureau of A.T.F., Washington, D.C.)

Yacht Search Techniques

Due to the wide range of yacht design and the majority of protective personnel being unfamiliar with operations aboard ship; the Captain, crew members and maintenance and service personnel would be more qualified for a proper bomb search aboard a vessel. In anticipation of the possibility of a bomb threat, a search plan should be decided upon through prior discussion with the Captain and diagrams prepared to assist in search procedures. Specific points of vulnerability and access should be discussed and highlighted for immediate search, working through the various areas aboard and employing standard room searching techniques where applicable.

The actual searching techniques might be similar to an aircracft in a sense that the ship may have to be moved away from its present location by tow, due to the proximity of flammables or for other equally valid reasons. The search might commence on the exterior hull and deck areas prior to continuing along to the interior. (Generally speaking, interior areas aboard ship lend themselves easier to alarm systems which can alert personnel to attempted entry.) Searching through the division of the craft into a grid pattern and starting at the lowest level and working up should be considered, with an emphasis on thorough searches of all lockers, compartments and areas behind easily removable covers and plates.

Preparation

With regard to all bomb searching techniques, plan ahead and be prepared for the possibility of a threat.

Put together your own checklists and sketches for your specific vehicles, aircraft and yachts and have the necessary tools and equipment available to conduct your searches. It is inexcusable not to "expect the unexpected."

Fire Safety Concerns

A current positive trend is the increased recognition of fire danger to the principal while in hotel rooms, restaurants and public places. Of course there should always be a fire evacuation plan discussed and current at the residence and office, with appropriate reviews and up-dates. During travel, recreation, meals, attendance at meetings and public functions a portion of time spent on good advance work must consider and concentrate specifically on safety measures for evacuation in the event of smoke or fire.

Hotels

All personal protection personnel must be aware of basic safety measures in effect at hotels to insure their own survival in order to protect their principal. There are tremendous variations domestically and even more so internationally with respect to smoke detectors, sprinkler systems, fire fighting equipment and alarm systems installed in hotels, motels and resorts. Each location must be reviewed in the advance work, or immediately upon arrival if no advance was possible.

- Never use the elevator in the event of fire or smoke.
- Locate at least two exits nearest your room and the principal's room.
- Make certain exit doors are open with no obstruction in corridors or on stairways.
- Always count the doorways and identify features between your rooms and the exits. Smoke can cause confusion in direction and distance.
- Locate fire extinguishers, hoses and alarm systems for possible activation.
- Orient yourself in your own room to find the door in a dark or smoke situation. Know what is outside of the room windows.
- Plan ahead for possible emergencies to decide what your response will be to evacuate your principal.
- Carry your own portable smoke alarms, flashlights and personal equipment as may be needed for evacuation.

Restaurants—Offices—Public Buildings

Always take into consideration where your principal will be or where he will sit with respect to his visits to restaurants, meetings or business and social functions in public buildings. Plan for safe evacuation in the event of fire or other man made or national disasters. Your responsibiility includes an awareness of all safety and security measures employed on the visited premises and constant monitoring of movement within the premises by your principal.

Motorcades

The alignment of vehicles for transporation purposes beyond two or three cars is reserved for formal parade or escort duties including dignitaries, entertainers and heads of state. A principal will generally, in the majority of travel arrangements, utilize a four-door sedan or stretch limousine for himself and close staff, business associates or family. The vehicle should have a trained driver with the team leader occupying the right front seat. One additional car when utilized should contain the luggage and assume a follow-up or tail car position. If another car is to be employed it would serve as the lead or/escort vehicle.

In motorcades or parade formations the circumstances of distance, time, event, personage, and availability of vehicles, motorcycles and personnel will dictate the line-up. Consideration must be given to the first or pilot car being a marked, usually local police vehicle. Some jurisdictions will utilize motorcycle escorts as available, often surrounding the vehicle containing the principal. Unmarked police and security vehicles, with flashing light and/or siren capacity are also employed.

Provisions must be made for adequate vehicles to immediately follow behind the principal's car and transport close staff, officials and family members. Medical personnel, guests and press must also be considered along with baggage and/or special equipment transportation. A marked police car should be in the last position of the line-up.

Weapons

Any concerns about the use of weapons for protection of the principal will be based upon the threat assessment of potential problems to the principal in various locations. In un-trained or improperly trained hands weapons can be dangerous to the principal as well as everyone around him. If members of the protective detail are to be armed the choice of weapon is generally a personal decision. More pistols than revolvers are the preference even when handguns are purchased and issued to the protective agents. Concerns of concealment and accessibility are important in training and safety considerations. Suitable quality holsters, purses, special purpose bags and cases are currently available in a wide variety.

There is no one specific handgun or caliber that is the absolute answer for all possible defensive measures. Since a revolver or pistol is an extreme "last resort" decision, and only then employed under severe life saving guidelines, the appro-priateness of training as to when and how to use the weapon is essential. A handgun caliber must be suitable and adequate in defensive tactics with good shot placement to stop someone from continuing their lethal attack upon the principal and/or the personal protection agent. Recently there has been a wide variety of ammunition made available for this purpose as well as other specific use if one is engaged in defensive or offensive tactics at greater distances. The handgun is a most important tool in the performance of professional protection work and there is no tolerance for amateur or careless handling of weapons.

There are some personal protection teams that seldom carry weapons due to the problems of licensing, permits, liability, lack of proper qualification/practice resources and low threat level. When there is a perceived need for armed protection they employ licensed private protection personnel or off duty police officers. On the other hand there are also many teams that due to the threat assessment level, location of operations and travel are more heavily armed. They may choose appropriate shoulder weapons such as short barrel shotguns, carbines and sub-guns to be carried in follow or tail cars. This trend is generally not common presently in the United States except for protection of public officials or visiting dignitaries by public officers. It is common however in many other nations of the world. Additional weaponry including rifles and various shoulder weapons are normally available on remote estates, farms and ranches for protection of the principal.

The use of non-lethal weaponry such as stun-guns, chemical sprays or striking instruments have not been popular with personal protection personnel. Primarily their responsibilities are totally defensive and concerned with covering their principals and evacuating in the event of a threat or attack. Their duties restrict them in most instances to rely upon their hands or possibly a small defensive weapon such as a persuader, kubotan or small expandable baton in the event of an immediate attack upon themselves or their principals.

Conclusion

What I have learned over the years in personal protection is that a common myth abounds "that, **anyone** can protect anyone else." Perhaps this may be true, but I offer that a dynamic difference exists between "day labor" protectors and skilled performers. Many men and women seek to enter the personal protection field with an attitude that their background and limited experience are adequate to offer their services. In reality most candidates with this attitude fail the basic principles: "If **you can not** be where you are supposed to be, at the time you are supposed to be there, properly dressed with the equipment and supplies necessary to do your work, then **how can you** expect to protect and escort someone to where they are supposed to be, at the time they are supposed to be there with what they need to have to perform, have a meeting, give a speech or attend a social or business function."

Men and women may bring many useful and desirable traits to the personal protection career field. Experience dictates that once you have learned to have yourself under control the more important traits of adaptability, flexibility and discipline should follow easily. We can go on to list dozens of desirable traits, suffice to say proper training received in the proper manner will cause successful personal protection candidates to become sensitive to their needs for improvement of personal traits. For example: communication means much more than written or verbal dialogue. It also means always call when you say you will call someone by telephone and always do what you say you will do without excuses for why you did not do it.

Protective actions must be instinctive and reflexive if they are to be successful. And they often must be performed following periods of routine and what are perceived to be mundane or boring, protective measures. The mental reflection necessary to be always prepared should concentrate upon two points:

What If—Some Specific Activity Should Happen

So What—Am I Prepared To Do About It

You are not the protectee nor related to the principal whom you are protecting. You are not and will never be "part of the party" if you are doing your work well. Your personal and professional satisfaction should be in the completion of a successful protective assignment each day. This will not occur through bullets, brakes or bully tactics, but, through pre-planned, thought-out avoidance of unnecessary exposure blended with control and based upon superior continuous advance work. A concentration upon the essentials of **How** to think rather than **What** to think. An attempt to become a subtle professional **Master of Control** over: Crowds, Ego, Environment, Hardware, Relationships, "Stalkers" and Travel.

My sincere appreciation for your time and attention in reading through our offerings. Personal protection is a demanding but fascinating dynamic service oriented professional career field. If you are interested in pursuing your knowledge and I can be of assistance, please call me at any time.

—Dr. Richard W. Kobetz

Dr. Richard W. Kobetz

DR. KOBETZ HAS BEEN AND CONTINUES to be a pioneer in the training of personnel engaged in protective services. With a background of service from police patrolman to Chief of Police and Security Officer to Director of Security, he joined the staff of the International Association of Chiefs of Police in Washington, D.C. in 1968 on a leave of absence as a commanding officer in the Chicago Police Department.

For the I.A.C.P. he created the first world-wide series of week-long training programs made available to law enforcement, military and security officers which were conducted on a tuition basis. His presentations became the influence for program offerings to this day by educational and non-profit institutions, corporations and trainers. With selected instructors he presented the first tuition programs beginning in 1972 on Hostage Tactics and Negotiation Techniques, Counter-Terrorism and VIP/Dignitary Protection, featuring the most realistic actual training scenarios ever offered to attendees at any program.

While at the I.A.C.P. he traveled throughout the world on training programs and as a liaison to INTERPOL. He served on several national commissions involved in the development of doctrine and response standards for law enforcement and criminal justice personnel, authored seven (7) books and contributed numerous articles for professional magazines and journals. His major projects include: Directing the U.S. Attorney General's International Conferences on Narcotics, Smuggling Intelligence and Crime Prevention for over a decade; Developer of the U.S. Coast Guard Law Enforcement Manual (Maritime); Director of the D.E.A. Narcotics Investigators Manual (Enforcement); and Program Director for National Crime Prevention Program for senior citizens.

After departure as an Assistant Director from the staff of I.A.C.P. in 1979, he formed Richard W. Kobetz and Associates, Ltd., and opened North Mountain Pines Training Center and the Executive Protection Institute. His training programs continue to be offered on an international basis with on-site training for corporations, universities, military personnel, and law enforcement academies. His concept of providing executive protection has become the standard of the personal protection career field.

Over the past two decades the professional contributions made by Dr. Kobetz in the field of private and public protective services have been and continue to be original, in-depth and thought provoking. He is regarded as the "Trainer's-Trainer" and received the first designation of Certified Security Trainer (C.S.T.) and is a Fellow of the prestigious Academy of Security Educators and Trainers (A.S.E.T.). He has served on committees of the American Society for Industrial Security (A.S.I.S.), is on the Board of Directors and Vice President for Certification for A.S.E.T. and is the Executive Secretary of the Nine Lives Associates (N.L.A.) a fraternal organization of dedicated professionals in the field of personal protection.

APPENDIX

Sample Guidelines

HOTELS

1. Date of Survey: _____ 2. Time of Survey: _____

3. Dates for visit: _____

4. Names of principals/guests/staff to stay at hotel: _____

5. Reservations under the name of: _____

6. Written confirmation: _____

7. Name of Hotel to be visited: _____
   Address: _____
   Phone: _____
   Fax: _____
   Telex: _____

8. Meet with manager to discuss the following:
   - ☐ Location of rooms, ensure that room is not overtop or next to a lounge, banquet facilities, elevator, ice machine, (noise factor).
   - ☐ Arrange for payment of bill.
   - ☐ Check in time/check out time.
   - ☐ How to handle incoming phone calls to principals room.
   - ☐ Any other VIPs in hotel at time of visit.
   - ☐ Special events at time of visit.
   - ☐ Special requests.
   - ☐ Obtain the following hotel employees names & phone extensions.
   - ☐ General Manager.
   - ☐ Manager.
   - ☐ Assistant Manager.
   - ☐ Reservation Manager.
   - ☐ Guest Services, Concierge.
   - ☐ Bell Captain.
   - ☐ Director of Security.

9. Services offered by hotel.
   Laundry _____ Valet _____ Secretarial Services _____
   Limousine Serv. _____ Rec. Activities _____ Health/Fitness Club _____
   Newsstand/Lobby Shop (Newspapers/Merchandise) _____
   Safety deposit boxes _____
   Fur vault _____ Beauty parlor _____ Barber Shop _____
   Room service, hours _____
   Doctor on call _____ Dentist on call _____
   Others _____

10. Restaurant survey at hotel: (For each dining facility)
    Name _____ Location _____
    Hours _____ Maitre d/Manager _____
    Sample of menu _____ Wine list _____
    Dress code _____ Floor plan attached _____
    Nearest telephone _____ Nearest restroom _____
    Nearest fire exit _____ Seating capacity _____

11. Meet with Director of Security to discuss the following:
    ☐ Problems encountered in the past, i.e., room thefts, bomb threats, car thefts, fire alarm problems, etc.
    ☐ Any problems forseen during visit, i.e., special events, construction, demonstrations, etc.
    ☐ Number of security officers on duty.
    ☐ Radio dispatched _____
      Pager system _____ Armed/Unarmed _____
    ☐ Police jurisdiction _____
    ☐ Closest hospital with trauma unit _____
    ☐ Ambulance response time _____
    ☐ Obtain floor plans for hotel _____
    ☐ Does hotel have back up generator _____

12. Security overview:
    ☐ Entrances and exits to hotel _____ Emergency lighting _____
    ☐ Emergency staircases entrances and exits_____
    ☐ Do emergency staircase doors lock behind you _____
    ☐ Fire extinguishers, date last charged, type _____
    ☐ Fire hoses _____ Smoke detection system _____
    ☐ Elevators, inspection, capacity _____ Restrooms _____
    ☐ Telephones _____ Parking _____

13. a. Room survey:
    Room number _____ Nearest emergency exit _____
    Door locks and type _____ Window locks and types _____
    Smoke detectors _____ Sprinkler system _____
    Telephones _____ Television _____ Radio _____
    Lights _____ Heat/AC _____
    Mini bar _____ Hazardous objects _____
    Adjoining door(s) _____
    b. Problems encountered, list on back of form.

14. General comments, list on back of form.
    Survey conducted by: _____
    Date/Time _____

PRIVATE AIRCRAFT

1. Owner of Aircraft _____
2. Year and make of aircraft _____ Tail #_____
3. Total hours of flight time _____
4. Number of hours to next maintenance _____
5. Fuel range _____
6. Seating capabilities _____
7. Luggage capacity _____
8. Interior layout: couch _____ bed _____ bathroom _____
            kitchen _____ phone _____ VCR _____
            other _____
9. Flight attendant on aircraft _____
10. Number of pilots required to fly aircraft _____
11. Pilots name, work, and home phone number _____
12. Co-Pilots name, work, and home phone number _____
13. Are both pilots rated to fly from left seat _____
14. Aircraft based at _____

DEPARTURE INFORMATION

1. Departure site _____ 2. Departure time _____
3. Pilots at aircraft at what time _____
4. Check weather, departure and arrival site as well as enroute _____
5. Catering _____ 6. Plane side drop _____
7. Flight time _____ 8. Arrival site _____
9. Alternate arrival site in the event of bad weather _____
10. Have pilots radio arrival site 15 minutes before touchdown _____
11. If pilots are overnighting at a hotel contact numbers _____

PRIVATE AVIATION FACILITIES

1. Date of survey _____ 2. Time of survey _____
3. Airport facility is located at _____
4. Name, address and phone number for aviation facility _____
_____

5. Contact for facility, direct phone number and home phone number
_____

6. Hours of facility _____ 7. Night landings _____
8. Noise restrictions _____
9. Restrictions on aircraft _____
10. Length of runway _____
11. Customs clearance possible _____
12. Mechanics, fuel _____
13. Catering services _____
14. Restrooms, phones _____
15. Restaurant _____
16. Meeting facilities _____
17. Parking overnight, hangers _____
18. Airport security _____

19. Emergency response crews at airport _____
20. Deicing capabilities _____
21. Snow removal equipment _____
22. Clearance for plane side pick-up _____
23. Police jurisdiction _____
24. Nearest hospital with trauma unit _____
25. Ambulance response time _____
26. Problems encountered, list on back of form _____
27. Additional comments, list on back of form _____

Survey conducted by: _____
Date/Time _____

AIRPORT SURVEY

Date of survey _____
Name of airport, airport code, phone number _____
Location of airport _____
Daily passengers ranking _____
Time Zone _____
Distance from city centre _____
Location of the following areas:
   ☐ Airline terminal and ticket counters, to be used _____
   ☐ Airline administrative offices _____
   ☐ Airline baggage area _____
   ☐ Airline lost baggage office, phone number _____
   ☐ Airline gates _____
   ☐ Airline clubs _____
   ☐ Police station and phone number _____
   ☐ Medical, first aid trauma, phone number _____
   ☐ Lost and found, phone number _____
   ☐ FAA phone number _____
   ☐ Airport authority number _____
   ☐ Customs office, and phone number _____
   ☐ Customs area _____
   ☐ Information office _____
   ☐ Foreign currency exchange _____
   ☐ Telephones _____
   ☐ Restrooms _____
   ☐ Gift shop, items available _____
   ☐ Barber shop _____
   ☐ Meeting facilities, business center _____
   ☐ Taxi stand, buses, limos _____
   ☐ Car rentals, names and phone numbers _____
   ☐ Observation deck _____
   ☐ Closest hotel _____

☐ Overall condition of airport, construction, etc. _____

_____

☐ Time to be allowed for check in _____
☐ Time to be allowed for luggage retrieval _____
☐ Time to allow to clear customs _____
☐ Airport map attached _____
☐ General comments _____

Survey conducted by: _____
Date/Time _____

COMMERCIAL AIRLINE SURVEY

Airline and flight information _____
Duty manager, name and phone number _____
Passenger Service Manager, name and phone number _____
Airline club, location, phone number _____
Confirm flight information _____
Reconfirm seat assignments _____
Type of aircraft _____
Aircraft originates where _____
Aircraft arrives airport, what time _____
Phone on board aircraft _____
Proposed gate, gate supervisor _____
Special arrangements luggage (last on, first off) _____
Special arrangements, carry on luggage _____
Boarding arrangements, first or last _____
Special menu requests _____
Special request, medical, oxygen, wheel chair, etc. _____
Any VIPs aboard the flight _____
Have rep telex ahead with details of VIP arrival, request to be met plane side by airline rep
upon arrival _____

Anticipated delays, check weather _____

Back up flight information in the event of cancellation. In the event you have a connection to
make, it is best to have a back up flight for your connecting flight as well _____

In dealing with coast to coast flights or international flights, keep in mind that it is possible to
arrive at the final destination much earlier than scheduled _____

When booking flights, be aware that airline seats vary in dimension as well as leg room, this
is especially true of foreign airlines _____

Survey conducted by: _____
Date/Time _____

ROUTE SURVEY

1. Consideration in choosing routes:
   - What is the date and time route to be used
   - Holidays, different traffic flow
   - Weekends, different traffic flow
   - If near factories, government buildings, major enterainment facilities. What are the shift changes or when crowds released.
   - Train tracks
   - Bridges, tunnels
   - Overpasses, underpasses
   - School zones
   - Construction in area
   - Special events, parades, demonstrations, sporting events
   - Parks, wooded areas
   - How many intersections, stop lights, stop signs
   - Number of buildings, windows
   - Storage areas, mail boxes, sidewalk obstructions
   - Pedestrian traffic
   - Hospitals, police stations, fire houses, medical facilities, etc.
2. Detailed routes should be completed with accompanying map
3. Alternate routes in detail with accompanying map
4. Note: Conditions along the routes you plan on taking may vary by the hour, so always plan ahead and remain flexible.

Survey conducted by: _____

Date/Time _____

LIMOUSINES

1. Company name _____
2. Owner/Manager name _____
3. Years in business _____ Number of vehicles in fleet _____
4. References _____
5. Vehicles used:
   Stretch Limos _____ Limos _____ Sedans _____ Luggage _____
6. Charges for Limos _____ Sedans _____
   Luggage _____
7. Arrange for billing _____
8. How long to get back up vehicle _____
9. What type of equipment is in vehicles _____
   - Reading lights _____ Telephones with long distance capacity _____ Maps _____
   - Two way radio _____ Jumper cables _____ Flash lights _____
   - Fire extinguisher _____ First aid kit _____ FAX _____
10. Request 2 sets of keys for each vehicle _____

11. The following information on the driver should be obtained 2 days prior to your arrival:
Name, address and home phone number_____
Pager number_____ Years with company _____
12. Driver should be briefed of his responsibilities prior to the arrival of the principal:
- Security person will conduct sweep of vehicle prior to use
- Maps in vehicle for areas to be visited
- Second set of keys to security person
- Ignition key separate from trunk key
- Go over emergency signal in the event of trouble
- Obey all traffic laws
- On multi lane road, use right lane
- Do not blow horn unless it is an emergency
- Vehicle not to go below one half a tank of fuel
- No smoking or eating while driving
- Do not play radio unless requested
- Conversation with principal only when initiated by principal
- Do not use cellular phone in car for personal use
- Vehicle to be at comfortable temperature prior to principal entering
- Driver to stay behind wheel, security person will open door
- Lock doors after principal enters
- Driver will stay with vehicle unless otherwise advised

Security conducted by _____
Date/Time _____

RESTAURANT SURVEY

1. Date/Time of survey _____
2. Name/address/phone of restaurant _____
_____
3. Manager name _____
4. Maitre d name _____
5. Hours of operation _____
6. Menu, wine list _____
7. Lounge in restaurant _____
8. Non-smoking restaurant areas _____
9. Dress code _____
10. Lighting in restaurant, back up generator _____
11. Floor plan, arrange for specific seating for security reasons _____
12. Seating capacity _____
13. Time to be allowed for dinner _____
14. Special needs _____
15. Arrange for billing _____
16. Restrooms, phones _____

17. Private rooms _____
18. Special events the date of visit _____
19. Entrances/exits/fire equipment _____
20. Police jurisdiction _____
21. Nearest hospital with trauma unit _____
22. Additional comments _____

Survey conducted by _____
Date/Time: _____

DETAILED AUTOMOBILE SEARCH CHECKLIST

Auto Make _____   Model _____   Doors _____   Year _____   Body _____
License _____   County _____   State _____   Safety Sticker _____
Location of security check _____
Date/Day/Time search _____

Note: Searcher will place initials in appropriate blanks, you are to use proper equipment to perform checks.

I. Exterior scan of vehicle:

HANDS OFF ONLY

1. _____ Signs of forced entry
2. _____ Signs of tampering (palm or fingerprints, fluids on the ground, exposed or hanging wires.
3. _____ Area around and under each tire
4. _____ Inspect telltale tape for breakage

II. Inspect undercarriage of vehicle:

5. _____ Left front engine compartment & suspension
6. _____ Right front engine compartment & suspension
7. _____ Left rear engine compartment
8. _____ Right rear engine compartment
9. _____ Transmission
10. _____ Drive shaft
11. _____ Emission control system
12. _____ Muffler, resonator, tail pipe
13. _____ Differential
14. _____ Rear axle and suspension

ANYTHING UNUSUAL—ISOLATE THE VEHICLE—DO NOT TOUCH—CALL FOR HELP

III. Search the interior—physical check
REAR

15. _____ Doors
16. _____ Door panels
17. _____ Floor mats
18. _____ Rear seat & arm rest
19. _____ Rear deck

20. _____ Headliner
21. _____ Dome light/switch
22. _____ Under front seat
23. _____ Back of front seat

FRONT

24. _____ Doors
25. _____ Door panels
26. _____ Floor mats/pedals
27. _____ Fuse Box
28. _____ Front seats
29. _____ Dashboard areas
vents/controls

30. _____ Radio/Speaker/
Lighter/Ash tray
31. _____ Glove box
32. _____ Sun visors
33. _____ Dome light/switch
34. _____ Headrests, both

IV. Search the trunk area—physical check

35. _____ Floor mats
36. _____ Spare tire
37. _____ Back of rear seats
38. _____ Tool compartment

39. _____ Electrical wiring
40. _____ Underside of rear deck
41. _____ Inspect gas tank
(make sure cap is locked)

VI. Search the engine compartment

42. _____ Check at safety catch level
43. _____ Check entire compartment

VII. Start the engine

_____ Operate horn, lights, turn signals, flashers, brakes, air conditioning, heater,
power seats, power mirrors, radio, electric trunk.

VIII. Check fuel tank level, battery charge, oil pressure.

Survey conducted by: _____

Date/Time _____

Selected Bibliography

Adams, Brian. *The Medical Implication of Karate Blows*. New York: A.S. Barnes, 1969.

Air Traveler's Handbook: *The Complete Guide to Air Travel, Airplanes and Airports*. New York: St. Martin's Press, 1990.

American Red Cross. *Expect the Unexpected*. Washington, D.C.: American Red Cross, 1986.

Baldrige, Letitia. *Amy Vanderbilt's Everyday Etiquette*. New York: Bantam Books, 1980.

Barbare, Richard and Hafendorfer, Linda. *Traveler's Guide to Major U.S. Airports*. Atlanta: Peachtree Publishers, Ltd., 1989.

Barber, Don C. *Official Airport Hotel Guide Book*. Omaha: Don C. Barber, 1989.

Barnard, Robert L. *Intrusion Detection Systems, 2nd Edition*. Stoneham, Massachusetts: Butterworth-Heinemann, 1988.

Blanchard, Robert G. *The Mechanics of Judo*. Rudland, Vermont: Tuttle, 1961.

Bolz, Frank A. *How to be a Hostage and Live*. Secaucus, New Jersey: Lyle Stuart, Inc., 1987.

Bottom, Norman R. Jr. and Kostanoski, John I. *Introduction to Security and Loss Control*. Englewood Cliffs, New Jersey: Prentice-Hall, 1990.

Bremer, Arthur H. *An Assassin's Diary*. New York: Harper's Magazine Press, 1973.

Broder, James F. *Risk Analysis and the Security Survey*. Stoneham, Massachusetts: Butterworth-Heinemann, 1984.

Camellion, Richard. *Assassination Theory and Practice*. Boulder, Colorado: Paladin Press, 1977.

Chapman, Robert D. and Chapman, Marian L. *The Crimson Web of Terror*. Boulder, Colorado: Paladin Press, 1980.

Clarke, Chris M., Gittes, Fred T. and Keller, Paul D. *American Shorin-Ryu Karate Association, A Manual for Students and Instructors*. Fort Washington, Maryland: ASKA Press, 1989.

Clarke, James. *American Assassins. Princeton, New Jersey: University Press, 1982*.

Clede, Bill. *Police Handgun Manual*. Harrisburg, Pennsylvania: Stackpole Books, 1985.

Clede, Bill. *Police Shotgun Manual*. Harrisburg, Pennsylvania: Stackpole Books, 1986.

Clede, Bill. *Police Nonlethal Force Manual*. Harrisburg, Pennsylvania: Stackpole Books, 1987.

Clutterbuck, Richard. *Kidnap, Hijack and Extortion*. London: Macmillan, 1987.

Collins, Patrick. *Living in Troubled Lands*. Boulder, Colorado: Paladin Press, 1981.

Cooper, H.H.A. *On Assassination*. Boulder, Colorado: Paladin Press, 1984.

Cooper, H.H.A. and Redlinger, Lawrence J. *Making Spies*. Boulder, Colorado: Paladin Press, 1986.

Cooper, H.H.A. and Redlinger, Lawrence J. *Catching Spies*. New York: Bantam Books, 1990.

Corcoran, John and Farkas, Emil. *Martial Arts: Traditions, History, People*. New York: Gallery Books, 1983.

Cunningham, William C., Strauchs, John J. and Van Meter, Clifford W. *Private Security Trends: 1970-2000 aka The Hallcrest Report II*. Stoneham, Massachusetts: Butterworth-Heinemann, 1990.

Danto, Bruce L., M.D. *Identification and Control of Dangerous and Mentally Disordered Offenders.* Laguna Hills, California: Eagle Books, 1985.

Danto, Bruce L., M.D. *Prime Target: Security Measures for the Executive at Home and Abroad.* Philadelphia: The Charles Press, 1990.

Demaret, Pierre and Plume, Christian. *Target De Gaulle.* New York: Dial Press, 1975.

Dinges, John and Landau, Saul. *Assassination on Embassy Row.* New York: Pantheon Books, 1980.

Draeger, Donn F. and Smith, Robert W. *Asian Fighting Arts.* New York: Berkley Publishing Co., 1969.

Fast, Julius. *Body Language.* New York: Pocket Books, 1975.

Forsyth, Frederick. *The Day of the Jackal.* New York: Viking Press, 1971.

Hacker, Frederick J. *Crusaders, Criminals, Crazies: Terror and Terrorism in our Time.* New York: W.N. Norton, 1976.

Haines, Bruce A. *Karate's History and Traditions.* Rutland, Vermont: Charles E. Tuttle, 1968.

Hoffman, Peter. *Hitler's Personal Security.* Cambridge, Massachusetts: M.I.T. Press, 1979.

Jackson, Geoffrey Sir. *Surviving the Long Night: An Autobiographical Account of a Political Kidnapping.* New York: Vanguard Press, 1973.

Jenkins, Brian. *Terrorism and Personal Protection.* Stoneham, Massachusetts: Butterworth-Heinemann, 1985.

Kidner, John. *Crimaldi: Contract Killer.* Washington D.C.: Acropolis Books, 1976.

Kim, Richard. *The Weaponless Warriors.* Los Angelos: Ohara, 1975.

Kirkham, J.F. and Levy, S. *Assassination and Political Violence.* National Commission on the Causes and Prevention of Violence. Washington D.C.: U.S. Government Printing Office, 1969.

Knowles, Graham. *Bomb Security Guide.* Stoneham, Massachusetts: Butterworth-Heinemann, 1976.

Kobetz, Richard W. and Cooper, H.H.A. *Target Terrorism: Providing Protective Services.* Gaithersburg, Maryland: I.A.C.P., 1978.

Koehler, William R. *The Koehler Method of Guard Dog Training.* New York: Howell Book House Inc., 1967.

Kubota, Takayuki. *Kubotan Keychain.* Thousand Oaks, California: Dragon Books, 1985.

Leek, Sybil and Sugar, Bert R. *The Assassination Chain.* New York: Corwin Books, 1976.

Levine, Isaac Don. *The Mind of an Assassin.* New York: Farrar, Straus and Cudahy, 1959.

Levitt, Mortimer. *Class: What It Is and How to Acquire It.* Fairfield, Pennsylvania: Fairfield Graphics, 1984.

Levitt, Mortimer. *The Executive Look, How to Get It-How to Keep It.* New York: Atheneum, 1985.

Livingstone, Neil C. *The Complete Security Guide for Executives.* Lexington, Massachusetts: Lexington Books, 1989.

Livingstone, Neil C. *The Cult of Counter Terrorism.* Lexington Massachusetts: Lexington Books, 1990.

Long, David E. *The Anatomy of Terrorism,* New York: The Free Press, 1990.

Man-ch'ing, Cheng and Smith, Robert W. *T'ai-chi.* Rutland, Vermont: Charles E. Tuttle, 1967.

Martin, Judith. *Miss Manners Guide for the Turn of the Millennium.* New York: Pharos Books, 1989.

McConnell, Brian. *The History of Assassination.* Nashville, Tennessee: Aurora Publishers, 1970.

Monahan, John. *Predicting Violent Behavior.* Beverly Hills, California: Sage Publications, 1981.

Mundis, Jerrold J. *The Guard Dog: Maximum Protection for You, Your Home and Your Business.* New York: David McKay Co., Inc., 1970.

National Research Council, Study Committee (National Academies of Science and Engineering). *Computers at Risk: Safe Computing in the Information Age.* Washington, D.C.: National Academy Press, 1990.

Nudell, Mayer and Antokol, Norman. *The Handbook for Effective Emergency and Crisis Management.* Lexington, Massachusetts: Lexington Books, 1988.

Paine, Lauren. *The Assassin's World.* New York: Taplinger, 1975.

Parker Pen Company. Do's and Taboos Around the World: A Guide to International Behavior. Elmsford, New York: The Benjamin Co., Inc., 1985.

Post, Elizabeth L. *Emily Post's Etiquette— 14th Edition.* New York: Harper and Row Publishers, Inc., 1984.

Rapoport, David C. *Assassination and Terrorism.* Toronto: Canadian Broadcasting Company, 1971.

Roberts, Wess. *Leadership Secrets of Attila the Hun.* New York: Warner Books, Inc., 1989.

Rush, George. *Confessions of an Ex-Secret Service Agent.* New York: Donald I. Fine, Inc., 1988.

Savage, Peter. *The Safe Travel Book: A Guide for the International Traveler.* Lexington, Massachusetts: Lexington Books, 1988.

Schultz, Donald O. *Principles of Physical Security.* Houston, Texas: Gulf Publishing Co., 1978.

Scotti, Anthony J. *Executive Safety and International Terrorism.* Englewood Cliffs, New Jersey: Prentice-Hall, 1986.

Scotti, Anthony J. *Police Driving Techniques.* Englewood Cliffs, New Jersey: Prentice-Hall, 1988.

Shackley, Theodore G., Oatman, Robert L., and Finney, Richard A. *You're the Target, Coping with Terror and Crime.* McLean, Virginia: New World Publishing, 1989.

Shioda, Gozo. *Dynamic Aikido.* Tokyo: Kodansha, 1968.

Todd, Ian. *Ghosts of the Assassins.* New York: Seemann, 1976.

Turkus, Burton B. and Sid Feder. *Murder, Inc.* New York: Bantam Books, 1972.

Underwood, Grahame. *The Security of Buildings.* Stoneham, Massachusetts: Butterworth-Heinemann, 1984.

U.S. Department of State. *Key Officers of Foreign Service Posts: Guide for Business Representatives.* Washington, D.C.: U.S. Government Printing Office, 1989.

Wathen, Thomas W. *Security Subjects: A Primer for Protection Officers.* Van Nuys, California: Guardian Security Publications, 1989.

Weber, Thad L. *Alarm Systems and Theft Prevention.* Stoneham, Massachusetts: Butterworth-Heinemann, 1985.

Professional Resource Information

THE ACADEMY OF CRIMINAL JUSTICE SCIENCES (A.C.J.S.) publishes *A.C.J.S.: Today* and *Justice Quarterly*. Write to: Academy of Criminal Justice Sciences, Northern Kentucky University, 402 Nunn Hall, Highland Heights, KY 41076-1088 (606) 622-1178.

THE ACADEMY OF SECURITY EDUCATORS AND TRAINERS (A.S.E.T.) publishes *The Educator* and conducts the Certified Security Trainer (C.S.T.) Program. Write to A.S.E.T., Route 2, Box 3644, Berryville, VA 22611. (703) 955-1129.

AMERICANS FOR EFFECTIVE LAW ENFORCEMENT, INC. (.A.E.L.E.) publishes the *Liability Reporter*. Write to: A.E.L.E., 5519 N. Cumberland Avenue, #1008, Chicago, IL 60656-1498. (312) 763-2800.

AMERICAN SOCIETY FOR INDUSTRIAL SECURITY, (A.S.I.S.) publishes *Security Management,* Write to: A.S.I.S., 1655 North Fort Myer Drive, Suite 1200, Arlington, VA 22209. (703) 522-5800.

AMERICAN SOCIETY OF LAW ENFORCEMENT TRAINERS (A.S.L.E.T.) publishes *The A.S.L.E.T. Journal.* Write to: A.S.L.E.T., 9611 400th Avenue, P.O. Box 1003, Twin Lakes, WI 53181-1003. (414) 279-5700.

ASSOCIATION OF FEDERAL INVESTIGATORS (A.F.I.) publishes *The Investigator Journal.* Write to: A.F.I., 1612 K Street, NW, Suite 202, Washington, DC 20006. (202) 466-7288.

ASSOCIATION OF FORMER INTELLIGENCE OFFICERS (A.F.I.O.) publishes *Periscope.* Write to: A.F.I.O., McLean Office Building , 6723 Whittier Avenue, Suite 303A, McLean, VA 22101. (703) 790-0320.

BRIEFING: TERRORISM & LOW INTENSITY CONFLICT, P.O. Box 120008, 750 3rd Avenue, Chula Vista, CA 92012. (619) 476-0390.

CANADIAN SECURITY published by Security Publishing Limited, P.O. Box 430, Station "O", Toronto, Ontario, Canada M4A 2P1. (416) 755-4343.

CENTER FOR RESEARCH IN LAW AND JUSTICE publishes *Criminal Justice International.* Write to Center for Research in Law and Justice, University of Illinois at Chicago. 1333 S. Wabash, Box 55, Chicago, IL 60605. (312) 996-3200.

COLLEGE SECURITY REPORT published by Rusting Publications, 403 Main St., Port Washington, NY 11050. (516) 883-1140.

CRIME CONTROL CORPORATION publishes *Security Law Newsletter.* Write to: Crime Control Corporation, 2125 Bancroft Place, NW, Washington, DC 20008. (202) 797-7410.

CRIMINAL JUSTICE NEWSLETTER published by Pace Publications, 443 Park Avenue, S., New York, NY 10016. (212) 685-5450.

EXECUTIVE PROTECTION INSTITUTE publishes the *Nine Lives Associates Network.* Write the Executive Protection Institute, Arcadia Manor, Route 2, Box 3645, Berryville, VA 22611 (703) 955-1128.

HOTEL/MOTEL SECURITY AND SAFETY MANAGEMENT NEWSLETTER, PARKING SECURITY REPORT and *HOSPITAL SECURITY AND SAFETY MANAGEMENT NEWSLETTER* all published by Rusting Publications, P.O. Box 190, Port Washington, NY 11050. (516) 883-1140.

INFORMATION SYSTEMS SECURITY ASSOCIATION (I.S.S.A.) publishes *The Access.* Write to: P.O. Box 9457, Newport Beach, CA 92658.(714)854-5500.

INTERNATIONAL LOSS CONTROL INSTITUTE publishes *International Risk Control Review.* Write to: International Loss Control Institute, P.O. Box 345, Loganville, GA 30249. (404) 466-2208.

INTERNATIONAL ASSOCIATION OF BOMB TECHNICIANS AND INVESTIGATORS (I.A.B.T.I.) publishes *The Detonator.* Write to: I.A.B.T.I., P.O. Box 6609, Colorado Springs, CO 80934. (719) 636-2596.

INTERNATIONAL ASSOCIATION OF CHIEFS OF POLICE (I.A.C.P.) publishes *Police Chief.* Write to: I.A.C.P., 1110 North Glebe Road, Suite 200, Arlington, VA 22201. (703) 243-6500.

INTERNATIONAL ASSOCIATION OF LAW ENFORCEMENT FIREARMS INSTRUCTORS, INC. (I.A.L.E.F.I.) publishes *I.A.L.E.F.I. Newsletter.* Write to: I.A.L.E.F.I., RFD 3, Box 57N, Laconia, NH 03246. (603) 279-8869.

INTERNATIONAL ASSOCIATION OF LAW ENCFORCEMENT INTELLIGENCE ANALYSIS (I.A.L.E.I.A.) publishes *Intelscope.* Write to: I.A.L.E.I.A., P.O. Box 876, Washington, DC 20044.

INTERNATIONAL NARCOTIC ENFORCEMENT OFFICERS ASSOCIATION, INC. (I.N.E.O.A.) publishes *NarcOfficer.* Write to: I.N.E.O.A., 112 State Streeet, Albany, NY 12207. (518) 463-6232.

INTERNATIONAL POLITICAL SCIENCE ASSOCIATION publishes *International Political Science Abstracts.* Write to: International Political Science Association, 27 Rue Saint Guillaume, 75341, Paris, Cedex 07, France.

INTERNATIONAL SECURITY published by FMJ International Publications, Ltd., Queensway House, 2 Queensway, Redhill, Surrey RH1 1QS, England, Telephone (0737) 768611.

JOHN JAY COLLEGE OF CRIMINAL JUSTICE publishes *Law Enforcement News.* Write to John Jay College of Criminal Justice, 899 10th Avenue, New York, NY 10019. (212) 237-8442.

LAW & ORDER published by Hendon, Inc., 1000 Skokie Blvd., Wilmette, IL 60091. (312) 256-8555.

LAW ENFORCEMENT TECHNOLOGY published by PTN Publishing Co., 210 Crossways Park Drive, Woodbury, NY 11797. (516) 496-8000.

NATIONAL CRIME PREVENTION INSTITUTE (N.C.P.I.) publishes *N.C.P.I. Hotline.* Write to: N.C.P.I., School of Justice Administration, College of Urban and Public Affairs, University of Louisville, Louisville, KY 40292. (502) 588-5987.

NATIONAL FRATERNAL ORDER OF POLICE (F.O.P.) publishes *The F.O.P. Journal.* Write to: 2100 Gardiner Lane, Louisville, KY 40205-2962. 1-800-451-2711.

NATIONAL INSTITUTE OF JUSTICE (N.I.J.) publishes *NIJ REPORTS.* Write to National Institute of Justice/NCJRS User Services, Box 6000, Rockville, MD 20850. 1-800-851-3420.

NATIONAL POLICE CHIEFS & SHERIFF'S INFORMATION BUREAU publishes *The National Directory of Law Administrators, Correctional Institutions and Related Government Agencies.* Write to: National Police Chiefs 7 Sheriff's Information Bureau, P.O. Box 92007, Milwaukee, WI 53202. (414) 272-3853.

NATIONAL RIFLE ASSOCIATION (N.R.A.) publishes *American Rifleman,* 1600 Rhode Island Avenue, N.W., Washington, D.C. 20036. (202) 828-6000.

NATIONAL SHERIFF'S ASSOCIATION publishes the *National Sheriff.* Write to: The National Sheriff's Association, 1450 Duke Street, Alexandria, VA 22314. (703) 836-7827.

POLICE published by Hare Publications. Write to: Police, P.O. Box 847, Carlsbad, CA 92008-0151. 1-800-624-6377.

POLICE COLLECTORS NEWS published by Mike Bondarenko. Write to: PC News, 2392 U.S. Highway 12, Baldwin, WI 54002. (715) 684-2216.

POLICE MARKSMAN ASSOCIATION (P.M.A.) publishes *Police Marksman.* Write to: P.M.A., 6000 E. Shirley Lane, Montgomery, AL 36117. 1-800-223-7869.

*POLICE TECHNOLOGY AND MANAGE-
MENT* published by Hare Publications.
Write to: Police Technology and
Management, P.O. Box 846, Carlsbad,
CA 92008-0151. 1-800-624-6377.

*PRIVATE SECURITY CASE LAW
REPORTER* published by Strafford
Publications, 1375 Peachtree Street, NE,
Suite 235, Atlanta, GA 30367. (404)
881-1141.

PUBLIC AFFAIRS INFORMATION
SERVICE, INC. (P.A.I.S.) publishes the
P.A.I.S. Bulletin. Write to: P.A.I.S., 521
W 43rd Street, 5th Floor, New York,
NY 10036-4396. (212) 736-6629.

PUBLIC SAFETY PERSONNEL
RESEARCH INSTITUTE, INC.
publishes *Fire And Police Personnel
Reporter.* Write to Public Safety
Personnel Research Institute, Inc., 5519
N. Cumberland Avenue, Suite 1008,
Chicago, IL 60656. (312) 763-2800.

RETAIL SECURITY MANAGEMENT
published by Strafford Publications,
1375 Peachtree Street, NE, Suite 260,
Atlanta, GA 30367. (404) 881-1141.

SECURITY JOURNAL published by
Butterworth's, 80 Monvale Avenue,
Stoneham, MA 02180. (617) 438-8464.

SECURITY MAGAZINE published by
Cahners Publishing Co., 44 Cork
Street, Denver, CO 80206. (303)
388-4511.

*SMITH & WESSON ACADEMY
TRAINING NEWSLETTER,* 2100
Roosevelt Avenue, Springfield, MA
01101. (413) 781-8300.

TACTICAL RESPONSE ASSOCIATION
(T.R.A.) publishes Tactical Response.
Write to: T.R.A. International, 7130
Village Drive, Prairie Village, KS 66208.
(913) 432-5856.

TERRORISM FILE published by UMI
Research Collections Information
Service, 300 North Zeeb Road, Ann
Arbor, MI 48106. 1-800-423-6108.

*TERRORISM VIOLENCE AND
INSURGENCY (T.V.I.) REPORT*
published by Brian Michael Jenkins.
Write to: T.V.I., P.O. Box 1055, Beverly
Hills, CA 90213.

UNITED STATES DEPARTMENT OF
STATE, Private Sector Liaison Staff,
3rd Floor SA-10, U.S. Department of
State, Washington, DC 20520. (202)
633-0025.

WASHINGTON CRIME NEWS
SERVICES publishes *Training Aids
Digest, Corporate Security Digest,
Juvenile Justice Digest, Crime Control
Digest, Corrections Digest, Narcotics
Control Digest, Criminal Justice Digest,
Organized Crime Digest.* Write to:
Washington Crime News Services, 3918
Prosperity Avenue, Suite 318, Fairfax,
VA 22031. (703) 573-1600.

WOMEN & GUNS published by Little
River Press, 201 Paradise Point, Hot
Springs, AK 71913. (501) 767-3160.

Index